Bigamy and Christian Identity in Late Medieval Champagne

THE MIDDLE AGES SERIES

Ruth Mazo Karras, Series Editor
Edward Peters, Founding Editor

A complete list of books in the series
is available from the publisher.

Bigamy and Christian Identity in Late Medieval Champagne

Sara McDougall

PENN

UNIVERSITY OF PENNSYLVANIA PRESS

PHILADELPHIA

Published by
University of Pennsylvania Press
Philadelphia, Pennsylvania 19104–4112
www.upenn.edu/pennpress

Printed in the United States of America on acid-free paper
10 9 8 7 6 5 4 3 2 1

Library of Congress Cataloging-in-Publication Data
McDougall, Sara.
Bigamy and Christian identity in late medieval Champagne / Sara McDougall. — 1st ed.
p. cm. — (The Middle Ages series)
Includes bibliographical references and index.
ISBN 978-0-8122-4398-7 (alk. paper)
1. Bigamy—France—Champagne-Ardenne—History—To 1500. 2. Bigamy (Canon law)—History—To 1500. 3. Marriage—France—Champagne-Ardenne—History—To 1500. 4. Marriage (Canon law)—History—To 1500. I. Title. II. Series: Middle Ages series.
HQ980.5.F8M33 2012
306.84'1094431—dc23

2011043926

CONTENTS

Introduction 1

Chapter 1. Marriage and Remarriage in the Later Middle Ages: Law, Theology, and Culture 9

Chapter 2. Bigamous Husbands 49

Chapter 3. Abandoned Wives 71

Chapter 4. Why Commit Bigamy? 95

Chapter 5. Why Prosecute Bigamy? 113

Conclusion: Christian Identity at the End of the Middle Ages 135

Appendix: Selected Transcriptions from a Register of the Officiality of Troyes 143

Notes 153

Bibliography 189

Index 211

Acknowledgments 215

Introduction

In the course of the final three centuries of the thousand-year period known as the European Middle Ages, between the Fourth Lateran Council (1215) and the early decades of the sixteenth century, the Christian institution of marriage became at the same time an object of veneration and a source of deep concern. On the one hand, marriage became widely and intensely valued. Men and women at all levels of the social hierarchy married, and these marriages were treated as entrance into a respectable and pious stratum of society, sometimes referred to as the "order of matrimony," or the order of married persons. This "order" was considered comparable, if not equivalent, to the holy orders of monks and nuns.[1]

At the same time, as varied contemporary and especially sixteenth-century reports claim, the Christian institution of marriage underwent a considerable crisis at the end of the Middle Ages. The nature of that crisis, as found in northeastern France, is the subject of this book. Mine is far from the first modern book to discuss this crisis of marriage. Steven Ozment, to offer one example, describes the fifteenth century as a time in which the institutions of marriage and the family suffered greatly, largely because of the ways in which the Catholic Church handled marriage.[2] This book is premised, however, on the argument that Ozment and other scholars have misunderstood the nature of this crisis, at least as it emerged in northern France.

What indeed was this crisis of Christian marriage in the later Middle Ages? Ozment attributed the blame largely to the Catholic Church and its policies, which praised celibacy at the expense of marriage and the family and also espoused laws and legal practices that made marriage an unstable and disgraced business. Other scholars have different perceptions. In particular, most accounts have focused on the problem of "clandestine marriage." From the time of Pope Alexander III (1159–81), Western Christians—as opposed to Byzantine—could marry on the basis of nothing more than an exchange of consent between a would-be husband and his wife. This meant that a couple, even a very young couple,[3] could validly and indissolubly marry not only without the permission of their parents but also without any publicity or priestly participation. Simply making the declaration "I marry you" sufficed to create a lifelong marital bond, based upon the consent of the two spouses. The result of this "consensualist" marriage law, many scholars believe, was a crisis of parental and ecclesiastical control over marriage formation. If young Christians could enter into valid marriages by such exchanges of promises, this could only have greatest dangers for the authority of both families and the Church. Ozment argues that the writings of Protestant and Catholic reformers alike demonstrate the depth of the resulting crisis.

This book also considers this problem of clandestine marriage. However, as I shall argue, in fifteenth-century northern France, clandestine marriage was not the problem that caused a crisis, nor was it such a grave problem at all. The "crisis of marriage" in late medieval northern France was not in fact an outbreak of young Romeos and Juliets engaging in illicit romances. The fifteenth-century court records studied in this book do not reveal a widespread practice of runaway youths engaging in secret marriages. They do not reveal an ecclesiastical court overwhelmed by concern over clandestine marriage practices, nor do they reveal the malcontent of parents whose children married against their wishes.

Instead, those records document a different problem. They document the practice and prosecution of men and women who, already married to living spouses, attempt to marry again. Moreover, many of these marriages took place in public and with a priest's blessing. Clandestine marriage was simply not at issue in the prosecution of matrimonial offenses that mattered most to church court officials in Troyes, the diocese that is the primary focus of this book. The crisis of marriage at the end of the Middle Ages, at least as found in northern France, was not a conflict over parental control—though it was, in a sense, a battle over ecclesiastical control. It was, at core, a crisis about the legal requirement that marriage must be a monogamous and indissoluble bond, about the high and holy status accorded monogamy. This crisis emerged as a conflict between laity, on the one hand, who valued marriage so much that they wanted to marry even if already married to a no-longer desired spouse, and, on the other hand, ecclesiastical officials, who valued marriage as a sacrament and considered illegal remarriage an intolerable abuse of this sacrament.

To understand the depth of this crisis, we must begin by understanding the strength of the Christian commitment to marriage as a holy monogamy. Both indissolubility and monogamy were central to the problems of Christian marriage law as applied in much of medieval Europe. Christian doctrine prized monogamy above all, insisting that a Christian marriage could not involve more than two spouses. According to this doctrine, no Christian could be married to more than one living spouse at once. Additionally, divorce was forbidden. Christian marriage, once made, could only end with the death of a spouse.

Indeed, Christian custom disdained even remarriage following the death of a spouse. Widows and widowers could remarry, but these marriages, while tolerated, were frowned upon. Even these lawful remarriages were thought to deviate from the ideal of marriage as a unique commitment made between one man and one woman. Further, beginning in the late twelfth century, canon law considerably restricted the numbers of those men and women who might technically claim widowed status. New laws proclaimed that no man or woman married to an absent spouse could be considered free to remarry unless they could prove in court that this absent spouse had died. By the later Middle Ages these laws were enforced in at least some dioceses.

By the later Middle Ages, however, Christian society had made so much of marriage that many previously married people were determined to marry a new partner even if they broke the law in so doing. They wished to partake of the wide range of spiritual and social benefits marriage bestowed upon a wedded couple. However, they could not legally marry because they were already married to a living—if absent or otherwise undesirable—spouse. That these men and women could not legally marry, however, does not mean that they did not marry.

The consequence of this conflict between social practice and the law was an epidemic of illegal marriages in northern France. In marrying despite being already married, men and women of the later Middle Ages committed a crime I will somewhat anachronistically refer to as bigamy, for reasons explained in the next chapter.[4] As a result of this widespread behavior, I argue, bigamy became a matter of grave concern.

Earliest evidence is found in the fifteenth century, in northern France and in Burgundian lands, and this book will focus on these earliest surviving sources. In the dioceses of Paris, Rouen, Cambrai, Châlons-en-Champagne, and most notably Troyes, local ecclesiastical officials made determined efforts to prevent and punish these illegal remarriages. Based on the current scholarship on ecclesiastical proceedings in other regions of medieval Europe, it appears that northern France stands out as exceptional in this regard. In England, Italy, southern France, southern Germany, and Spain, scholars have so far identified no such efforts at regulating marriage in the fifteenth century, and certainly not to the same degree or with the same emphasis on punishment as found in Troyes.[5]

This apparent exceptionalism of northern France does need to be qualified, though, and for reasons that will be explored further below.[6] Even if we retain the assumption that Troyes was unusual, however, that does not mean that it is unimportant for an understanding of the development of Christian marriage law and practice or undeserving of study. This is true for two reasons. First, if the law as applied in practice in northern France was different, the law on the books was not. The courts in northern France—and that of Troyes in particular—were enforcing the rules established in canon law that all these places had in common, even if most courts did not implement them. By studying Troyes, we can learn something of real importance about what it means to put law into practice. Second, and perhaps more significant, what was possibly or even probably exceptional in the fifteenth century unquestionably became the rule in the sixteenth century, at least in Catholic lands.

Indeed, the issue of how to reconcile popular marriage practice with ecclesiastical requirements for Christian marriage and especially remarriage did not die with the end of the Middle Ages. Some of the most striking evidence for the character of the late medieval crisis of marriage emerges from sixteenth-century sources. The matter seemed so pressing to the Church hierarchy as a whole that they took it up at the Council of Trent (1545–64). At that fundamental council, Church officials decided to alter the laws of marriage radically, and for the explicit reason of preventing bigamy. Previously, couples could lawfully and indissolubly marry by the exchange of consent, with no need for publicity, parental consent, or the blessing of a priest. The Decree Tametsi of the Council of Trent (1563) finally abolished clandestine marriages, proclaiming that no Christian could legitimately marry without the participation of a priest and with banns announced beforehand.[7] Any marriage made without these precautions was invalid and nonbinding.

The Catholic officials of the Counter Reformation did not make this decision, as previous scholarship has suggested, because of a concern over couples like Romeo and Juliet, who had so disastrously married in secret. Catholic leaders made their decision, as explained in the text of the decree, because of the great problem of bigamy, a problem found not only in northern France. Too many men and women, the text decreed, despite being already married to a living spouse, were taking additional spouses. Such behavior was too grave a threat to Christian society to be tolerated. Throughout the sixteenth century and beyond, prosecutions of bigamy took a prominent role in judicial proceedings across Catholic Europe and in the New World.[8]

The purpose of this book is to take that declaration from the Decree Tametsi at face value. Scholars have paid too little attention to the stated reason for the prevention of bigamy given in this decree. As a result, they have first not recognized that bigamy was perceived as a problem in medieval society, and second they have misunderstood the reasons why bigamy was the subject of widespread prosecutions in subsequent centuries. By studying the beginnings of this practice and prosecution as found in northern France, I thus call for a broad reconsideration of the history of Christian marriage as Europe emerged from the Middle Ages.

This reading of the meaning of bigamy also aims to force a reconsideration of the idea of identity and its relationship to criminal prosecution in the sixteenth century. Over the last forty years, scholars of early modern Europe have focused on the role of identity in pre-modern culture. Natalie Davis has made the widely embraced argument that the problem with a crime such as bigamy, or passing as the husband of another man's wife—as in the case of *The Return of Martin Guerre*—was a problem of identity, of imposture and fraud.[9] An attempt to so distort identity grievously offended a world as preoccupied with status and honor as early modern Europe. Davis's *Return of Martin Guerre* is undoubtedly the most famous book related to the problem of bigamy known to most modern readers, and it may seem natural to apply Davis's interpretive approach to the cases of bigamy found in my study.

It is my contention, however, that identity in the sense in which scholars influenced by Davis use the term was not what the crime of bigamy was about, at least not in the fifteenth century and probably not in the sixteenth century either. The problem with the crime of bigamy was different, at least at that time. Bigamy was viewed with such horror for reasons that had to do with theology, with *Christian* identity rather than identity alone. As a contemporary editor of Voltaire's encyclopedia remarked in expanding on the entry "polygamy," bigamy and polygamy were viewed with horror in Christian society "because of the sacrament [of marriage]."[10] The Catholic tradition insisted that marriage, as a sacramental sign of the exclusive and indissoluble union of Christ with the Church, had to be monogamous and binding. Bigamy was not a violation of norms of early modern identity but a violation of Christian identity, an unchristian act. In this book I address these issues by seeking out an understanding of the meaning and function of marriage in late medieval Christian theology, law, culture, society, and legal practice. I aim in particular to understand the role of bigamy in these developments, treating bigamy as the negation of the monogamy inherent in a Christian understanding of what marriage should be.

This book begins with an exploration of the place of bigamy in medieval law, theology, and culture. It turns next to court action in the late medieval diocese of Troyes, examining over a hundred investigations of alleged bigamy, focusing on first male and second female behavior, in two separate chapters. I treat the bigamy committed by men and by women separately for an important reason. Modern scholars generally assume that few people committed bigamy in the Middle Ages, but that those few would have almost all been male. This supposition requires some correction. Certainly most convicted bigamists were male. One of my discoveries described in my dissertation, however, was that both men and women committed bigamy in late medieval France. The ecclesiastical courts and their communities responded to the two acts of remarriage in different ways, depending on the gender of the bigamist.[11] As I have argued elsewhere,[12] for a woman to commit bigamy had different social, cultural, and economic consequences than those found with male bigamy. If her husband disappeared and she was left in precarious social and financial straits, even her husband's own family might wish to see her remarried and provided for.[13] These two chapters seek to explain both these differences in behavior and the different response male and female bigamy found in society and in the courtroom.

Two subsequent chapters address first, why people—men *and* women—committed bigamy, and second, why ecclesiastical officials in Troyes came to prosecute bigamy. As I argue, men and women living in fifteenth-century northern France committed bigamy for a number of reasons, emotional and economic. The chief reason, however, was not that they had been insufficiently Christianized, as some scholars have argued. The contrary is the case. In fact, these men and women had been quite successfully convinced of the various blessings and benefits that Christian, sacramental marriage conferred on a couple. This conviction, however, did not always arrive accompanied by a notion that the canon law of marriage need in all things be respected. These men and women who remarried despite being already married to a living spouse made a significant choice in remarrying. With a first spouse distant or undesirable, they had found someone else whom they wished to live with and have children with, and wanted to marry. Or they wished to marry, when economic need or social status required it. In any case, they wished to marry, not because they were insufficiently Christianized and as a result thought so little of marriage, but because they had accepted the Christian ideal of marriage and thought a great deal of it. Marriage had become an extremely important institution in late medieval society. Quite a few people were willing to break the law to marry, legally or not. This shows not a lack of Christianization but rather what might be described as too much or too successful Christianization. Ecclesiastical officials, however, were not always willing to tolerate this abuse of marriage law. At least the judicial officers of the bishop's court of Troyes acted to prevent and prosecute bigamy throughout the fifteenth century. The activities of those ecclesiastical officials in Troyes are the topic of the final chapter.

Beginning in the second decade of the fifteenth century, in the wake of the Hundred Years' War, we find traces of a massive effort to police marriage practice in the dioceses of northern France. Ecclesiastical officials made an astonishing effort to regulate both marriage formation and intact marriages in a time and place of upheaval and confusion; a time and place in which married life and marital status were often uncertain. Who, indeed, amid outbreaks of plague or the Hundred Years' War, was clearly a widow or widower? Nevertheless, the court in Troyes summoned hundreds of men and women before it, ordering them to put an end to irregular or suspect unions and return to their spouses, if they could be found.

The chief reason for this is that marriage mattered a great deal, to ecclesiastical officials and to their parishioners alike. Men who had left their wives behind or had been themselves abandoned wanted new wives, new families. Abandoned wives wanted husbands and risked violating the law to remarry, for better or worse. In peace and in war, marriage was an institution in which these men and women were eager to partake. However, these desires came into conflict with an ecclesiastical drive to restrict married Christians to one living spouse. The essential role of monogamy in Christian identity thus served as a site of conflict and as a defining feature of Christian marriage as formed in the Middle Ages.

CHAPTER 1

Marriage and Remarriage in the Later Middle Ages

Law, Theology, and Culture

The fifteenth-century registers of the Bishop of Troyes's judicial court tell a strange story.[1] Amid the destruction and chaos of the Hundred Years' War, in the Champagne region of northeastern France people were marrying more often than the law permitted. More curious still, in the course of concerted efforts to restore order in the diocese, the bishop's judicial court investigated and prosecuted many of these oft-married men and women, detaining them in the bishop's prison in the course of an investigation and fining the largest number of offenders. Those found to have willfully violated the law in their mode of marrying (almost all men) the court subjected to public punishment and lengthy imprisonment.

That such prosecutions took place at all, let alone with such vigor, will surprise many historians of medieval and early modern France. Historians have not recognized how interventionist northern French church courts could be in matters of remarriage. To be sure, scholars who study the records of local church courts, called officialities, have begun to recognize that northern France served as host to unusually proactive and regulatory ecclesiastical courts.[2] But we have not understood two central factors of this regulatory behavior: we have recognized neither the importance of remarriage in this context nor how energetically these courts, and the diocesan court of Troyes in particular, acted to prevent and prosecute bigamy.

My purpose in this chapter is to situate the reader in the legal, theological, cultural, and social context of marriage and remarriage at the end of the Middle Ages, as background to the court action that took place in fifteenth-century Troyes. Beginning with some of the major historiographical trends, I then turn to the theological and legal rules for marriage and marriage symbolism in particular, studying the impact of these rules in late medieval law, court practice, and society. I close with a description of the surviving court records of the officiality of Troyes, the principal sources for this book, and an initial analysis of the bigamy cases found in the these records.

We have known for some time that marriage arrived at something of a crisis point at the end of the Middle Ages. We have known this not least because postmedieval sources say so with such vehemence. For somehow the sixteenth century bursts forth with complaints, criticisms, and the most radical solutions to seemingly all-consuming problems with marriage—problems not only with the canon law of marriage itself and the ecclesiastical courts charged with implementing these rules but also with the behavior of ordinary Christians who married in ways that offended ecclesiastics, theologians, jurists, and reformers of all stripes on both sides of a growing confessional divide.[3]

What was this crisis about? If the rules governing Christian marriage were to blame, scholarship on medieval law and the family has suggested two possibilities: incest prohibitions and clandestine marriage. This book will offer a third: remarriage.

To begin with incest prohibitions, it might seem natural to suppose that the medieval Church's infamously expansive prohibitions on marriage between those related by blood, marriage, or spiritual bonds were the principal source of the crisis. In fact, there was a time when many scholars described these incest prohibitions as one of the most burning issues of medieval marriage litigation. Out of all of these rules and regulations that emerged in the Christian Middle Ages, those concerning consanguinity, or blood ties, were long considered the most important aspect of medieval marriage formation and dissolution.[4] In particular, the prominent and influential scholars Jack Goody and Georges Duby occupied themselves greatly with explaining and emphasizing medieval concerns over incestuous marriage.[5] One can certainly understand why these scholars focused on consanguinity prohibitions and their role in western European marriage practices. Medieval canon law and theological writings offer a wealth of discussion on forbidden, incestuous marriages, accompanied by genealogical trees depicting kinship and expressions of horror over the monstrous children incestuous unions might produce. If we measure the importance of a topic by the sheer volume of treatment in known medieval canonical and theological sources, there is hardly any doubt that the rules on prohibited relationships were of fundamental importance.

Moreover, the forbidden degrees of relationship are also natural subjects for litigation and of considerable importance for two other reasons. First, the western Church's definition of forbidden degrees poses a major social mystery. Medieval canon law, especially before 1215, included among the prohibited relationships for a marriage so many different types of blood, marital, sexual, or spiritual relationships that the rules, if applied, would have made legitimate marriage a rather difficult feat in most parts of Europe.[6] Even after 1215, for a legally binding marriage a man still had to avoid marrying not only blood kin extended as far as four degrees but also close relatives of a prior spouse or relations of those who had married his own close blood kin, close relatives of former sexual partners, close relatives of his godparents, close relations by adoption, and also close relations of someone he had previously promised to marry. This necessarily meant that he found himself excluded from marrying many of the people at all close to him. With incest prohibitions drawn so broadly, we might expect to see a good deal of litigation, and indeed we do see some. This litigation arose in two main different ways. It might involve seeking a papal dispensation to stay married in spite of an impediment of this kind; or, to move to our second example, a party might initiate litigation to prove the existence of an impediment so as to render a marriage null and void.

It would be a mistake, however, to think that all of that litigation ran counter to the wishes of those whose marriages were dissolved. In fact, the Church's incest prohibitions played an extremely important role in permitting at least some medieval Christians to avoid the harsher consequences of a rule that is central to this book: the Christian ban on divorce with a right to remarry. Duby recognized that medieval nobles and royalty exploited the prohibition on consanguine marriages as a de facto tool for divorce.[7] Faced with evidence of an existing consanguine marriage, popes of the eleventh and twelfth centuries preferred to dissolve a marriage rather than allow an incestuous couple to remain together. Far from representing a purely harsh imposition of Christian values on a reluctant faithful, this papal practice actually served to relieve much of the pressure caused by the ban on divorce. Heirless or otherwise unhappily married kings and nobles often took advantage of these ecclesiastical laws and priorities, demanding the nullification of unwanted marriages on questionable (and sometimes not so questionable) grounds of consanguinity.[8]

One might also assume that similar patterns of behavior could be found among ordinary men and women of the fifteenth century, the medieval Christians who serve as the main subjects of this book. Would not these nonnobles similarly exploit marriage law to allow for an escape from unwanted marriages and the freedom to remarry legally? If making supplication to the papal curia proved too expensive a venture (and one that more often served as a source for dispensations to stay married despite an impediment rather than annulments of marriages on the grounds of an impediment), bishops had the power to dissolve incestuous or indeed otherwise invalid marriages. If the incest prohibitions affected ordinary lives as they affected noble and royal lives, we could expect some evidence of this behavior to survive in officiality records. Indeed, the great historian of the common law F. W. Maitland offered an argument much like that of Georges Duby, speculating that medieval officialities provided litigants with an easy nullification on the grounds of consanguinity.[9]

All this might lead us to expect that the marriage litigation found in fifteenth-century officiality registers would have largely concerned questions of incest. However, legal and social historians specializing in the study of the officialities have proven Maitland wrong.[10] Not only, they have concluded, did officialities not serve as a convenient site for the dissolution of an unwanted marriage, but the complicated rules of incest played a small role at best in any of the surviving records of the officialities under consideration.[11]

Whatever place consanguinity had in the pondering of canonists or theologians, it seems to have played a surprisingly limited role in the social practice of the lower orders of society. In fact, no scholars working with officiality records have found any significant number of cases involving the complicated laws of prohibited relationships, not in England, France, the Low Countries, Italy, or Germany.[12] This finding is of considerable interest. Did most people then really avoid marrying within forbidden degrees, even including the strictures on marrying those related by marriage ties or by godparentage? Even including the ban on marrying a close relative of a prior sexual partner? If so, it shows remarkable, indeed almost impossibly fastidious compliance with the canonical rules of marriage formation, or at least a strikingly strong incest taboo.

It seems more likely that many people did marry within forbidden degrees but for some reason did not litigate over it. Moreover, courts did not bother and perhaps even preferred not to prosecute it. We need a better understanding of the absence of incest in these court records to be sure. Nevertheless, it is striking that incest prosecutions are scarcely to be found in surviving officiality records. This is especially true because, as we shall see, court officials and married couples certainly found occasion to litigate over marriage formation, to contest the grounds of Christian identity and authority in practice and in the courtroom. However, our evidence reflects concerns other than incest.

If incest prohibitions did not serve as an important topic of nonnoble fifteenth-century marriage litigation, what did? Having for the most part dispensed with the idea that incest rules played a role in the crisis of marriage at the level of diocesan courts, scholars have taken up another problem of some renown, that of clandestine or informal marriage.[13] In medieval western Europe, based upon rules formulated by Pope Alexander III in the late twelfth century, Christian doctrine declared that marriage could be indissolubly made by an exchange of promises. Saying "I marry you" (words of the present tense) or saying "I will marry you" followed by intercourse (a marriage made in the future tense) created a valid marriage regardless of the venue, the presence or absence of a priest or witnesses, with or without a contract, banns, or any other means of publicity or solemnity, such as the blessing of a priest at the doors of a church. Men and women could thus validly and indissolubly marry in secret, with no witnesses to later confirm that a marriage had in fact taken place.

This allowed, of course, for a wide range of fraud, deceit, and considerable confusion. The availability of clandestine marriage posed, in theory, more than one possible danger. People who entered into a clandestine marriage might knowingly or not violate some incest prohibition, as they had married without public announcement of their intentions and without giving any party the opportunity to object or to investigate their genealogy or their marital or sexual history. Young people might clandestinely marry without parental consent. A dishonest or inconstant spouse might later abandon the match when it no longer suited them, perhaps leaving a pregnant woman in a difficult position, or conversely leaving a man deprived of the woman he considered his lawful wife. So Martin Luther would later complain, and he was far from alone.[14] Finally, the availability of clandestine marriage might make it easier for people who were already married to enter into a second, bigamous union. If the first marriage had been made in secret, how to prove it so as to prevent the second? If the second marriage was made in secret, who would be there to object?

In all these respects, clandestine marriage seemed to invite trouble. Even as medieval Church officials continued to insist on the primacy of free consent for Christian marriage, they expressed considerable concern over the opportunities for abuse that clandestine marriage allowed. Indeed, at the seminal Fourth Lateran Council in 1215, Pope Innocent III forbade all marriages made without publicity and investigation where deemed necessary and without the prior and repeated announcement of banns made in the churches of the home parishes of aspiring spouses.[15] To forbid, however, was not to invalidate marriages made by more informal promises. While Innocent III prohibited marriages based purely on consent, these marriages still remained valid and binding unions. The distinction between forbidden and invalid may seem forced, but it meant a great deal in that these clandestine marriages, while illegal acts, still resulted in valid unions that nevertheless bound a couple for life.

Local legislation on clandestine marriage often included more strict rules than the legislation issued by the papacy, sometimes extending even to engagements.[16] Nevertheless, local legislation did not invalidate these marriages either. The synodal statutes issued in Rouen, Cambrai, Paris, and Troyes offer some of the more striking examples of strict legislation on marriage formation, all demanding a great deal of aspiring spouses if they wished to marry without incurring excommunication or other sanctions.[17] For example, Paris statutes, issued in the late twelfth century, not only required banns and publicity for marriages contracted in the diocese but also punished by automatic excommunication any couples who violated this rule.[18] Statutes issued in Rouen in 1230 threatened excommunication and a fine for any present-tense marriage made elsewhere than at the doors of the church.[19] In Troyes, by the fourteenth century and probably well before, we find much the same rules.[20]

As ever, both the practices and the rules for marriage formation differed considerably across Europe. We know best, of course, the sorts of marriages that later served as subjects of litigation. Marriage practice in medieval Europe, as many scholars have urged, is best understood as a process, a process that may have begun either in a haystack or with a meeting between parents and a notary and might involve several stages that sometimes involved the local church and sometimes did not. In London, couples often married in the home of the bride's parents or in another home, in a tavern or in a public hall, and ideally but by no means necessarily in public, with witnesses.[21] Marrying couples and their families in London seem to have often skipped a visit to church but nevertheless married with ritual, publicity, and in stages.[22] Across England couples often promised to marry in the present tense—that is, saying "I marry you" and sometimes, if they followed through on the marriage, reiterating these promises at the church door.[23] In Italy—if one dare generalize about so diverse a place—couples often married in private homes and with a marriage contract drawn up by a notary.[24] Marriage in Spain at least sometimes included a blessing in or near a church, at least more often than in Italy, if not perhaps as often as ecclesiastical officials preferred.[25] In Sweden, marriage might take place at the church door, but canonical insistence on the free consent of the bride came into conflict with older, secular traditions that required the consent of the bride's "marriage guardian," usually her father or closest living adult male relative. A priest who married a couple without the marriage guardian's consent could face a considerable fine.[26] Before the Council of Trent, or before the various Protestant churches changed the rules for marriage formation (or, in the case of England, did not), for the most part officialities became involved only when a party or parties initiated a marriage dispute in court.[27]

Meanwhile, records from fifteenth-century northern France and Burgundian lands reveal a difference in marriage practice and in marriage regulation. The broadly similar patterns of marriage practice and litigation found in northern France and the Burgundian lands offer many contrasts to marriage practice and litigation found in England, Italy, Spain, Switzerland, and Germany: many contrasts in the rules, in the regulatory attitude of courts, and in social practice. As alluded to already, synodal statutes detailed strikingly high requirements for entrance into marriage without risk of legal penalties, requiring not only publicity and a priest's blessing but also documentation proving that an aspiring spouse was free of prior marriage bonds.[28] Such requirements could, of course, be avoided by means of a clandestine marriage, but those who married without banns, a priest, and some paperwork might face fines and investigation into the validity of the marriage. Even so, many more couples seem to have made use of the church door and the blessing of a priest in northern France than elsewhere, for engagements as well as for marriages.[29]

Engagements took place in a variety of ways, described in different terms in the court registers. Common practice included an exchange of promises in the future tense made in any number of more or less formal or intimate venues, but the church door and a priest's blessing seems to have been the intended destination for most marriages.[30] *Creantare*, a Latinate rendering of the French word *creanter*, was used, at least in Champagne—and in Switzerland and the Savoy region, if evidently nowhere else—to mean a sort of engagement that took place in a home, often over a meal and with family and neighbors present, or in private. A typical informal contract of this type might involve promises to marry toasted with a drink or sealed with a gift such as a flower or a coin.[31] These informal promises to marry were technically illegal but were valid and binding forms of engagement nonetheless. The Troyes officiality collected a fair number of fines from couples who had exchanged vows in this way.

Other forms of engagements were made with more formality and publicity. These engagements and marriage often involved Church participation in some form, either full *in facie ecclesie* vows with the announcement of banns and at a parish church or less public espousals made in a chapel or with the participation of an ordained cleric. Canon law and court registers made use of different terminology for these more formal forms of engagement and marriage, though these differences are difficult to understand. Carole Avignon has argued that the terms "affidationes" and "sponsalia" should have been used for future and present-tense engagements respectively. "Desponsatio" and "sponsalia" in late medieval practice developed different meanings. "Desponsatio" came to mean a marriage, while "sponsalia" still referred to an engagement, consistent with older, Roman usage.[32] In any case, the court in Troyes does not seem to have managed always to uphold these distinctions.[33]

All this reveals considerable local variety. When it comes to the rules and practices of marriage formation, when it comes to the distance between law and court practice and the actual behavior of couples who married, we find with late medieval marriage a complex state of affairs indeed. Depending on when and where a Christian lived, the rules and the social norms differed considerably. Nevertheless, despite all this great variation in local practice, the canon law of marriage did not vary on the validity of clandestine marriage. Canon law, seemingly despite itself, required only an exchange of promises for a marriage to be valid, and so a great number of people who had promised one thing or another were technically married, if they liked it or not, and some people had good reason not to be sure of their marital status.

So was clandestine marriage the dominant factor in marital litigation that thrust the institution of marriage into crisis? And if so, how? It is clear that the availability of clandestine marriage created some problems. But where precisely did these problems with clandestine marriage lie? There is, after all, more than one possibility. Martin Luther and John Calvin both, along with many staunch Catholics, believed that the canon law of marriage posed a major challenge to parental authority. Many scholars have concurred, reading the later Middle Ages largely through Luther's eyes. Yet careful modern studies of the late medieval sources have provided little support for this belief. Nor do the late medieval sources reveal any widespread problems with the exploitation of clandestine marriage as practiced to conceal a violation of one of the many incest prohibitions. Here again, recent research does not bear out the hypothesis that clandestine marriage—because of incest prohibitions—was the burning issue.

In point of fact, it was not clandestine marriage but remarriage, as this book will demonstrate, that was the great and burning problem that led to crisis. Inevitably, the canon law of marriage created immense difficulties for abandoned or confused spouses scattered throughout western Europe. In such circumstances, it could be difficult indeed to prove that an absent or reluctant spouse was indeed your spouse. Moreover, remarriage compounded the problem, as many of those men and women entered into new unions, doing so both clandestinely and also publicly. As Church officials themselves recognized, Christians married all too often, binding themselves first to one and then to another spouse and sometimes even yet another, marrying more times than legally possible.

Clandestine marriage certainly played a part. The Church's own rules on marriage formation contrasted sharply with the rules that virtually prohibited both dissolving any valid marriage and supplementing another spouse while a first lived. The disparity between the ease with which people could marry and the absolute refusal to allow any person, once married, to take another spouse while the first spouse lived set up a stark conflict. It meant in principle that people could easily enter into marriages they might later want to escape, and also that they could easily enter into second marriages despite being already committed elsewhere. This was precisely the objection to clandestine marriage that we find in the mid-sixteenth century at the Council of Trent, which finally declared clandestine marriage invalid. Despite the belief that consent alone made a marriage, man's bad behavior, "man's disobedience," required the Church to change its policies. Clandestine marriage could no longer be allowed because of "those parties who live on in a state of damnation, when, having left their former wife, with whom they had contracted marriage secretly, they publicly marry another, and with her live in perpetual adultery."[34]

Out of all of the objections to the canon law of marriage voiced in the sixteenth century, this decree comes closest to describing what the fifteenth-century problem with marriage actually was. Even this ban on clandestine marriage—a ban established because informality could conceal an act of bigamy—does not precisely describe the fundamental cause of the crisis of marriage found in fifteenth-century sources. In northern France, at least, the problem was not so much that people were marrying in secret but that they were marrying and remarrying in public, with the Church's blessing. They also married and remarried in secret, but the problem was the remarriage itself much more than how publicly or privately the remarriage was made.

This book traces the developing crisis over remarriage as found in fifteenth-century northeastern France, with some reference to the rest of northern France and Burgundian territories. Focusing on this region rather than making a broader geographical study may seem an artificial means to discuss a much larger and more diverse situation of marriage at the end of the Middle Ages. But one of the most important aspects of this crisis of marriage is that it only manifested as crisis, only existed, only mattered, in such places and times as the law on indissolubility and the ban on bigamous marriages was implemented.

Looking to the surviving ecclesiastical court records of northern France, we find evidence of considerable efforts on the part of diocesan officials to prevent marriages made otherwise than with banns and the public blessing of the match by a priest. We also find a large number of cases in which men and women made public and blessed marriages but in which the courts subsequently dissolved or cast into a sort of legal limbo the legitimacy of these marriages. These courts took this drastic step because one or the other spouse had failed to prove their freedom from prior marriage bonds. Finally, the registers of the officiality of Troyes reveal a remarkable number of cases in which men and women found to have willfully married despite being already married faced harsh public punishment and imprisonment for this act of double marriage, a crime we would call bigamy.

It must be emphasized once more that nothing like this crackdown on bigamy is known to have taken place elsewhere in Christian lands before the sixteenth century. Certainly we find the threat of such punishments in ecclesiastical and secular legislation as early as the thirteenth century. It is, however, one thing to threaten people with such punishments, but quite another thing to actually impose it.

In fifteenth-century Troyes, such punishments were actually imposed. Whatever problems clandestine marriage may have caused in fifteenth-century Troyes, bigamy was considered a far more grave problem. As Beatrice Gottlieb, the first scholar to make a full-scale study of marriage litigation in fifteenth-century Troyes and neighboring Châlons-en-Champagne, wrote: "[Bigamy] was unquestionably the worst of all the offenses related to marriage and sex, as can be seen from the penalty . . . Clandestine marriage, no matter what form it took [in a chapel, at a tavern, using words of the present or future tense] was regarded as less reprehensible."[35]

Having identified as the central cause of crisis this conflict over remarriage, which in the diocese of Troyes resulted in the prosecution of bigamy, we must also ask why. Why did northern French courts make such efforts to regulate marriage? Why did northern French couples marry and remarry so often in the first place? Why did marriage matter so much, to the ecclesiastical officials and to the men and women who married and remarried?

We cannot understand this behavior without extensive recourse to law and to theology extending far back before the fifteenth century. Actual records of prosecution emerge only from the surviving sources of the later Middle Ages, but laws against bigamy date back to antiquity. We must also immerse ourselves not only in what is sometimes referred to as the legal culture of a court and community but also in the culture of the community more broadly. We must understand what marriage meant in late medieval Troyes, as found in its laws, its theological traditions, and its culture, high and low. We must, in short, understand the place of bigamy within the Christian tradition. The role of bigamy and of the laws prohibiting it in the Middle Ages has received little scholarly attention. It is, however, of fundamental importance, both for an understanding of marriage in the later Middle Ages and for the history of marriage in the West.

The exaltation of monogamy and the ban on bigamy proved central tenets of Christian identity at the end of the Middle Ages, but their origins trace back far earlier. Bigamy was important above all because monogamy was so important to Christian marriage and to Christian identity, identity as defined by the Church Fathers in late antiquity and their Western successors. It is important to emphasize that the ideal of monogamy, central to the Christian definition of marriage, had a tremendous impact not only on married couples but also on clergy. The symbolic power of the ideal of monogamy played a role in all manner of vows and obligations. Many different status and societal relationships were symbolically understood as marriages, and all marriages had to emulate the model, monogamous marriages of Adam and Eve and Christ and the Church, about which a great deal more follows.

Recent scholarship, most notably that of David d'Avray, has shown the importance of marriage symbolism in medieval law and theology and its dissemination in medieval society.[36] As I argue, this marriage symbolism also played a central role in the practice and prosecution of those Christians who married while already married to a living spouse. Indeed, such double marriages shook this symbolism at its core. The ecclesiastical court and perhaps even the community understood few other actions taken by a married person as such a challenge to the fundamentals of Christian marriage, its core values of monogamy and indissolubility.

In the Christian tradition, remarriage in any form was a problematic act. Christians were, in principle, supposed to marry only once. This rule applied both to laity and to clergy, and to all forms of remarriage: successive, concurrent, and figurative. Marriage was always ideally a singular and exclusive event. We gain a great deal in recognizing the ways in which the symbolic nature of all of these forms of marriage derived from the same roots.

The Christian tradition set forth two models for what Christian marriage should be, one from the Old Testament and one from the New. First, marriage had to resemble the union of Adam and Eve in the Garden of Eden. As recounted in the Book of Genesis, God created Eve from one of Adam's ribs and joined the couple together, in a phrase constantly repeated throughout the Middle Ages, as "two in one flesh."[37] This first model marriage, instituted in paradise by God and blessed with the injunction "increase and multiply," implied that Christians, if they could not live a life of sworn celibacy, should marry, one man to one woman, chastely united as two in one flesh, as closely and inseparably joined as in the model marriage of Adam and Eve.

Christian marriage was to resemble not only the Old Testament model of Adam and Eve but also the New Testament model of the union of Christ and the Church. Here the key text was the fifth chapter of Ephesians, which instructed Christians to imitate God.[38] In particular, Ephesians compared marriage between a man and a woman to the symbolic "marriage" of Christ and the Church. Both marriages, earthly and spiritual, required love and submission, with husbands the head of their wives just as Christ was the head of the Church. All those who married should follow the model of Christ and Church. As the Church married only Christ and no other gods, so too should Christians take only one spouse.

In late antiquity the Church Fathers drew upon both these models in forming a definition of marriage as an exclusive, monogamous bond, one that could not be divided and one that should not be repeated.[39] Just as priests and monastics were to consecrate themselves to the Church in an indissoluble bond, so laypeople ought to consecrate themselves once, if at all, but only once, to a marriage. To quote Saint Jerome:

> The creation of the first man should teach us to reject more marriages than one. There was but one Adam and but one Eve; in fact the woman was fashioned from a rib of Adam. Thus divided they were subsequently joined together in marriage; in the words of scripture "the twain shall be one flesh," not two or three. "Therefore shall a man leave his father and his mother, and shall cleave unto his wife." Certainly it is not said "to his wives." Paul in explaining the passage refers it to Christ and the church; making the first Adam a monogamist in the flesh and the second [that is; Christ] a monogamist in the spirit.[40]

Jerome was not alone in this view. The orthodox view shared among the Church Fathers, even as they expressed more or less extreme views on the subject, was clearly that Christian marriage ought to be this singular and indivisible bond. In insisting on this definition of marriage, they confronted a problem that was not precisely the same as that of late medieval bigamy: the problem of polygamy, which manifestly violated their definition of marriage. In particular, the polygamy of the Old Testament patriarchs seemed to pose a challenge to the Christian insistence on monogamy. Indeed, the patriarch Jacob had two wives and two concubines, and King Solomon had hundreds of each. As the Church Fathers claimed, however, the polygamy of the patriarchs was not to be understood as an example to follow but rather as a sign. Jacob's marriages to Leah and Rachel, for example, prefigured Christ's marriage to the Old and New Testaments. Weak-eyed Leah stood in for the blind Jews (who failed to recognize Christ's divinity), while Jacob's beloved Rachel was the spouse who signified the Church.[41] These theological conclusions would also apply to the bigamous Christians of northern France who did not actually keep their multiple spouses with them but were married to more than one at a time.

In the Western Church, most clearly from the ninth century onward, an absolute ban on both bigamy and divorce with any right to remarry held firm throughout the Middle Ages.[42] To give one example, in the thirteenth century Innocent III completely rejected the idea that the polygamy allowed to the patriarchs might also be permitted Christians:

> We have read that the patriarchs and other just men before the law and after the law had many wives in common. . . . But this seems incompatible and contrary to Christian Faith, where from the beginning one rib was turned into one woman, and it was testified in divine Scripture that because of this a man shall leave his father and mother, and cleave to his wife, and they shall be two in one flesh. It did not say, "three or more" but "two" nor did it say "shall cleave to wives," but "to wife." . . . And so that truth may prevail over falsehood, without any hesitation we state: that it was never in any way lawful for anyone to have several wives at once, unless it was conceded by divine revelation. . . ."[43]

In short, Christians who married were told to follow not the example of the patriarchs but the example of Adam and Eve.

In this context, what did canonists and theologians say about the real possibility that Christians might nevertheless, in defiance of the law, marry themselves to more than one living spouse? Here an important terminological question presents itself. To marry while already married to a living spouse was an offense that, in the Christian Middle Ages, had no name. In the modern world we describe such a marriage as "bigamous" and the twice-married person as a bigamist. However, in the Middle Ages, bigamy was a term used to describe any manner of remarriage, both those marriages made following the death of a spouse and also marriages contracted while a first spouse lived. The great thirteenth-century canonist Hostiensis made some effort at resolving this ambiguity by distinguishing between "true" bigamy (two at once) and "interpretive" bigamy (remarriage after death or annulment),[44] but on the whole those called "bigamists" were spouses who had married more than once in succession, especially clergy.

Indeed, medieval canon law and theological texts emphasized most clearly the considerable importance of bigamy in determining clerical status.[45] Under the rubric of "bigamy," medieval canonists and theologians most often discussed the status of clerics who had either married more than one wife in succession or who had married a widow. In marrying in these ways, clerics transformed themselves into bigamists. This meant that they could never become priests and never rise in the ecclesiastical hierarchy above the rank of subdeacon. They also could not seek the milder justice of ecclesiastical courts if threatened by secular authorities.[46]

As this shows, to become a bigamist was to make an irrevocable change in one's status. While even a priest guilty of fornication or some other crime might be allowed to continue as a priest after penance, a man married to more than one wife in succession could not ever become a priest. Drawing on Genesis and Ephesians and upon centuries of tradition, Innocent IV gave his reasons for this rule, reasons that we have seen before. Why did the priesthood exclude bigamists?[47]

> I reply it is because the words: "os, caro, carne, uxori" "bone, flesh, from flesh, to wife" are in the singular. And also because of the final word of the phrase "they are two in one flesh" . . . marriage between two only is the sign of the one Church of which Christ is the one Husband.

But what about concurrent remarriages? As for those Christians already married to a living spouse who concurrently remarried, as another great thirteenth-century canonist, Raymond of Peñafort, insisted, it was improper to call those who had two wives at the same time "bigamists," because it was not possible to be legitimately married to two women at once.[48] If canonists debated over what to call the offender, the offense of marrying while already married at least had a name, if a rather imprecise one in that it could easily seem to describe successive remarriage as well as concurrent: "binae nuptiae" or "bina matrimonia."[49]

The main topic of this book is not the bigamy that prevented clerics from advancing in holy orders but the crime of bigamy. Having just admitted that many weighty authorities said that one should not call a person who was married to more than one spouse at once a bigamist, such a statement may seem anachronistic or just wrong. In light of this traditional use of the term bigamy to describe clerical status rather than a criminal remarriage, the use of the word "bigamy" may seem inappropriate to describe a medieval act of concurrent remarriage. Indeed, David d'Avray included the text of Innocent IV quoted above in his discussion of bigamy in his book *Medieval Marriage*[50] and drew from it and other passages the plausible conclusion that for the Church, concern over bigamy was concern over clerics who could not become priests, not Christians who married while already married to a living spouse. For d'Avray, the marriage symbolism found in this passage is related only to the prior marital status of a cleric who wished to become a priest or to the remarriage of a widow or widower following the death of a spouse.

D'Avray is clearly right insofar as prosecution records against men and women who married concurrently almost never use the word bigamy. Nevertheless, while there are risks any time a scholar chooses to use arguably anachronistic terminology, I think there are good reasons to use the term as I use it in this book. My reasons have to do precisely with d'Avray's analysis of the importance of a monogamous bond as a symbol. In fact, unless we permit ourselves the modern use of the term "bigamy," we will not grasp the full significance of the marriage symbolism that d'Avray has so powerfully described. The theological concern over bigamy so central to marriage symbolism extended well beyond the status of clergy; to concurrent marriages, to criminal bigamy.

We must not allow fidelity to medieval terminology to prevent us from recognizing the medieval links between all sorts of remarriage and the real theological significance of concurrent remarriage. We must not exclude these ideas from our understanding of the criminal bigamy a layperson might commit. Even as they did not use the same words, medieval popes, canonists, and theologians clearly saw the two as connected. The quotation I reproduced earlier from Innocent III, as well as that of Innocent IV, makes this connection clear. In medieval canon law, the symbol or sacrament that barred a bigamist from becoming a priest similarly barred any person married to a still-living spouse from remarriage, and for the same reason: all Christian marriages—between two Christians and between a priest and his parish—had to be monogamous and indissoluble, like those of Adam and Eve and of Christ and the Church. Those who acted as if it were possible to lawfully marry while already married to another violated the same symbolic requirement as twice-married men who subsequently sought to become priests.

Accordingly, for two hopefully persuasive reasons, I will use the term bigamy. First, as I am writing for a modern audience and not for medieval canonists, I want to use the term because the behavior I wish to describe most closely resembles the crime of bigamy as we understand it today. Second, linking the legal and illegal forms of remarriage in using the term makes an important point: while these two methods of marrying were two very different things with two very different consequences, they were at the core inherently linked.

There is another reason why we should not limit ourselves to a narrow understanding of bigamy, for the hostility toward remarriage affected more Christians than those clergy who wished to advance in orders and those men and women who wished to remarry despite being already married to a living spouse. It also affected a third category of persons: Christian widows and widowers were also tainted by the brush of bigamy when they remarried, even though their remarriages did not violate canon law.

The attitudes of medieval people toward widows have received a good deal of attention from scholars whose findings reveal manifold pressures on widows not to remarry.[51] Katherine Clark has argued that making marriage one of the sacraments of the Church and the concern over helping souls out of purgatory as formed in the High Middle Ages had real impact on widows in particular, and above all in the later Middle Ages. These theological ideas, she argues, provided an incentive to push women toward maintaining a chaste widowhood on the death of their husbands. If widows refrained from remarriage, they might instead focus their energies on a "spiritual housekeeping" that would propel their late husbands all the faster into heaven.[52] Clark gives the example of a fourteenth-century poetic tale entitled "The Gast of Gy." This story recounts the experiences of a widow haunted by the ghost of her husband, who was suffering in purgatory because of an undisclosed sexual sin they had committed together. Tormented, he begged her to intercede for him. The wife consulted a Dominican friar, who convinced the deceased husband to stop haunting his wife if she promised to remain unmarried and pay for three hundred masses to save his soul.[53] Widows, Clark concludes, were encouraged to remain faithful to their deceased spouses. Doing so not only upheld the principles of indissoluble marriage but also might concentrate and improve on a widow's efforts to hurry a deceased spouse out of purgatory.

Other scholars have concurred with Clark that hostile attitudes toward widows who sought to remarry had hardened by the High and especially late Middle Ages. In places such as Italy, England, and the Low Countries, social and economic disincentives for widows who remarried increased.[54] Scholars point in particular to legislation on property rights and inheritance. They argue, for example, that marital property regimes in some places were specifically designed to discourage remarriage.[55] Widows who remarried might lose guardianship of their children or some or all of their inheritance from their deceased husband.[56]

Moreover, widows who remarried might face social derision in addition to economic losses. Scorn for those who remarried was often expressed in a popular ritual such as charivari.[57] In these carnivalesque events, the wedding night of a couple was disturbed by a procession of rowdy singers and hecklers.[58] It is important to recognize how prominently scorn for remarriage by widows as well as widowers figured in the culture of charivari. Charivaris have generally been understood by modern scholars as popular expressions of unrest by young unmarried men who were reacting to the marriage of an older man to a young woman they themselves might have liked to marry.[59] Natalie Davis has offered a refined version of this interpretation. As Davis argues, charivari took place because of a need to placate the dead spouse and as a sort of expression of consideration for the children from the first marriage. Most important for Davis, the rites took place as expression of communal resentment when an old widow or widower took a young, eligible spouse, thus depriving village youths of a spouse their own age and the village itself of the greatest possible number of offspring.[60]

These popular rites are also susceptible to a quite different interpretation.[61] As Claude Gauvard observed, these rites did in fact typically involve the remarriage of a widow or widower. If viewed in the larger cultural context of medieval marriage symbolism, it seems probable that the charivari was enacted against second marriages because of a distaste for second marriages that developed more from theological quibbles than societal. Theologians and canonists had offered much by way of derision and exclusion for second marriages, depriving these unions of the nuptial blessing, a ritual reserved to first marriages only,[62] and even debating if such marriages were sacramental, if ultimately deciding they were. Charivaris too robbed second marriages of their honor.

Second marriages may well have provoked charivari simply as second marriages, different and less holy than first unions, and therefore to be treated differently both by the priest who refused to perform the nuptial blessing and by the rowdy enforcers of public morality. Certainly the Church legislation suggests as much. Church officials in northern France perceived these rituals as a response to second marriages. Synodal statutes from late medieval dioceses across France include prohibitions of charivari deriding second marriages in particular:[63]

> As it is damnable to condemn or vituperate first or second marriages, as the sacred canons declare, and as is documented in the New and Old Testaments, therefore it is a shameful or noxious game, contrary to good mores, and especially going against the sayings of the Apostle, for any marriages especially the second to be in any small way disparaged. Marriage (which our Lord Jesus Christ honored and found honorable) is overthrown in derision by those games vulgarly called charivari, games effected through horrible and blasphemous shouting and obscene sayings, under the base transfiguration of insulting devils, with insult and clamor deriding second marriages. We reprove equally libelous or slanderous songs, and we prohibit them entirely in the city and diocese of Troyes, instructing all priests and rectors of parish churches that these things be published in their churches, so that none can pretend ignorance of this prohibition, and that such games are forbidden from the part of the Reverend Father on penalty of excommunication and ten *livres*, to be applied in pious uses, as against the actors in these games, and as against those who help, advise, and assist them.[64]

Seeking to put an end to these public disturbances, Church officials throughout France, in Troyes and in other dioceses, threatened offenders with excommunication and fines if they mounted charivaris against second marriages.[65] Registers of the officiality of Troyes record fines levied, for example, against those who organized a charivari for the marriage of a widow.[66] In all of these sources, the perception of the charivari is the same: it is a rite enacted in mockery of second marriages. What we have with charivari is thus a popular ritual enacted to shame those who married more than once.

There is a paradox in the efforts of the Church to prevent these disturbances. The Church sought to prevent charivari but was in some sense hampered by its own doctrinal practice, for it was confronting a form of social disorder that had emerged in response to its own teachings. To be sure, the Church had traditionally insisted that all marriages, even second marriages, be performed with solemnity.[67] However, second marriages were hardly treated as equal to first marriages in theology and liturgy. The charivaris were thus related to the mixed message sent by the Church's own doctrines, by which second marriages were declared to be at once licit and reprehensible.

Further, second marriages clearly stood out in that they were denied the nuptial blessing reserved for first marriages.[68] Pope Alexander III and subsequent popes forbade priests officiating at second marriages to give the nuptial blessing. As Urban III wrote, "A man or a woman, going over into bigamy [in this case, entering into a successive marriage], should not be blessed by a priest, since, having been blessed on another [previous] occasion, their blessing ought not to be repeated."[69] Alexander III ordered that a chaplain who celebrated the nuptial blessing for a second marriage be suspended from his office and benefice until absolved by the apostolic see.[70]

What was this blessing? Gratian described the nuptial blessing as one that we have had cause to study before in this chapter: God's blessing of Adam and Eve in Genesis 1:28, the injunction "be fruitful and multiply."[71] As Philip Reynolds has argued, use of this blessing by a priest evoked the doctrine that no man should separate what God had joined.[72] This distinction, if employed by dutiful priests, offered the lay public a clear demarcation between the two kinds of marriage, as well as a sort of invitation to recognize this difference and to shame their neighbors when they married in less holy circumstances than provided by first marriages.

We also have further evidence that the presence—or absence—of the nuptial blessing mattered. As James Brundage explains, parishioners often asked priests to give them the nuptial blessing regardless of their status. Priests had to decide how to handle couples entering into second marriages who sought the nuptial blessing despite the prohibition. Apparently, these priests often granted their parishioners' requests and presumably were often well paid for their willingness to grant their parishioners' wishes. This happened so often, in fact, that the commissions given papal legates and nuncios regularly included the power to dispense clerics from the irregularity they fell into by giving the nuptial blessing at second marriages.[73] The work of Jean-Baptiste Molin and Protais Mutembe on marriage rituals in France offers further evidence of the importance of the nuptial blessing. In northern France, priests seeking to avoid incurring irregularity and to appease their parishioners conferred different blessings to replace the forbidden one and recited the new benediction at a different point in the ritual.[74]

Deprived or granted some form of the nuptial blessing, in northern France, widows and widowers who remarried also faced considerable legal difficulties. Certainly canon law in no way prohibited the remarriage of widows or widowers, despite the great importance attributed to the ideal of monogamous marriage. Nevertheless, beginning in the late twelfth century, papal letters placed heavy and indeed—if implemented fully—potentially insurmountable obstacles in the path of those men and women who wished to enter into remarriages. To be sure, according to Church doctrine, a widow could remarry without fear of ecclesiastical prosecution. But in defining who was a widow, canonists settled on a lawyerly requirement. According to the canon law of the late twelfth century and thereafter, a widow was a woman who could provide proof that her husband had died. Without such proof, however, those already married to a living spouse, a spouse not proven to be dead, could not enter into any other marriages. The bonds of matrimony could only be dissolved by proven death. To understand the impact of these rules on widows and widowers—illegitimate or legitimate—we must review the medieval canon law of marriage and remarriage in more detail.

The central texts on marriage from the "classical" period of canon law are found in two main collections of medieval canon law: several chapters from the compilation of canons known as *Gratian's Decretum* (now believed to have been compiled in two recensions, probably by two different men, both known to posterity as Gratian) and book 4 of the five supplemental books known collectively as the *Liber Extra*, a collection of decretals prepared by Raymond of Peñafort (d. 1275) and published by Pope Gregory IX in 1234. As we will see, the handling of remarriage underwent a considerable shift.[75]

On the subject of absent and missing spouses, Gratian offered papal letters that allowed remarriage on the grounds of belief, of good faith. If the spouse left behind believed her husband had died and remarried on that basis, she was without fault as long as she left the second husband and returned to the first as soon as she learned he still lived. Gratian's selected texts urged forgiveness for a wife who had remarried on the presumption that her absent and missing husband had died. As long as she left her second husband and returned to the first, she could not be prosecuted as an adulteress.[76] This forgiving rule, however, left unresolved how long an abandoned wife ought to wait before remarriage and what might constitute an acceptable reason to assume that her spouse had died.

That gap provided ample space for subsequent interpretations of the laws.[77] At the close of the twelfth century, amid preparations for the Third Crusade, Pope Lucius III (1181–85), writing ostensibly "to all Christians held in captivity by Saracens" but answering the requests of wives left behind, argued that "a wife should not remarry without knowing for certain of her spouse's death, and indeed nor should a husband."[78] The letter of Lucius III originally allowed remarriage only if the abandoned spouse had "complete certainty" about the death of the missing spouse. However, Raymond excluded this certain knowledge, an improbably ambitious state of mind in these matters, from the text he included in the collection of decretals.[79] The successor to Lucius III, Pope Clement III (1187–91), required something more than certainty of mind. Responding to the petitions of women who had waited more than seven years for their absent husbands' return, Clement ordered these women to wait until they had "certain news" of death, however long it may take.[80] Now, instead of belief, there is a requirement of "certain news." Instead of "complete certainty" we have a requirement of external evidence. This, then, was how the marital designs of men and women with absent spouses ought to be handled henceforth. "Certain news" meant full proof, which was obtained, for example, with the sworn testimony of two witnesses to a death or documentary evidence.

Raymond of Peñafort provided further commentary on the subject of remarriage in his "Summa" on marriage. As Raymond explained, a wife could not remarry without proof of death, without having "good reason" to think her husband had died. "Regardless of her youth," if her husband had gone to fight the Saracens or in another faraway place, she could not remarry unless she was certain he had died. This certainty required, for Raymond, the oath of the missing man's commander or of his friends who knew that he had died.[81] Raymond thus placed an imposing obstacle in the path of those married to absent spouses who wished to remarry.

Thirteenth-century secular law offers a mixed record in upholding these rules. In Spain, with evident disregard for the Church's position on remarriage, the *Siete Partidas* allowed for the presumption of death after ten years of absence.[82] In northern France, meanwhile, the *Coutumes de Beauvaisis* of Philippe de Beaumanoir (1250–96) offered strict allegiance to the canon law discussed above. As de Beaumanoir wrote, it used to be said that wives whose husbands had left the country could remarry after seven years. But "because of the dangers that resulted," the Church ordered that no married woman could remarry without certain news of her husband's death, no matter how long he stayed away. Wives who nevertheless remarried by means of false testimony or some other manner were concubines and their children bastards.[83]

To return to canon law and to commentary, canonists commenting on the decretals offered a range of views on remarriage, but they generally agreed that full proof posed too heavy a burden for spouses with absent partners and allowed remarriage on a presumption, ideally one adjudicated in court and with a judge's assessment of the likelihood of life or death. According to these commentators and as found in the most important commentary, the *Glossa ordinaria*, a reasonable presumption of death was all that was necessary to allow for remarriage. Hostiensis, perhaps the most celebrated canonist of the thirteenth century (c. 1200–1271) and a most "humane" scholar,[84] offered a practical, flexible, and compassionate interpretation of the laws in his *Summa aurea*, arguing that a reasonable presumption of the death of a first husband was all that should be required for a second marriage, which arrived when it was generally believed that the first husband had perished.[85] Hostiensis recognized that not everyone agreed with this view but maintained that he was more nearly correct than they. Nevertheless, in the *Lectura*, written later in life (1270–71), Hostiensis warned strongly against remarriage without sufficient cause to presume an absent spouse had died.[86]

In the fifteenth century we find a voice of dissent. Nicolao de Tedeschi (1386–1445), bishop of Naples and an extremely influential canonist known as Panormitanus, required evidence for remarriage in the strictest of terms. In calling for a "certificate of death," Panormitanus insisted that canon law should not ever presume that a missing person has died. Instead, the law should presume that a person will live a hundred years.[87] Perhaps once a missing spouse's hundredth birthday had passed, any surviving spouse might then remarry. If something of an outlier among the commentators, the strict requirement offered by Panormitanus had its advocates in the realm of local law and legal practice.

Let us turn now to local law. However important these works of legal commentary such as the *Glossa ordinaria* or the work of Hostiensis might be to the minds of canonists, their efforts at mitigating the strict rules for remarriage were either unknown or discounted in the making of synodal statutes in much of northern France and in Burgundian lands. As found beginning in the thirteenth century, the diocesan legislation of northern France handled the question of remarriage with far more severity than that proposed in much of the classical, central canon law texts, and certainly with much more severity than found in much of the commentary written on these laws.

Thus the statutes of Rouen, Paris, Cambrai, and Troyes required documentation attesting to the marital status of anyone who had previously lived in a different parish or diocese from the one in which they wished to marry.[88] The fourteenth-century statutes of the diocese of Troyes prohibited remarriage without first providing proof of death, which required a great deal more than a "reasonable presumption of death.[89] In both places, men and women found to have violated these rules regularly faced fines.[90]

In the records from local courts in other parts of Europe, further evidence of such a firm line on remarriage does not emerge with any consistency. One fifteenth-century court exhibits if anything the reverse attitude to that found in Troyes. In southern Germany, in the diocese of Regensburg, not only did the officiality not subject bigamists to public punishment or imprisonment, but men and women who approached the court seeking permission to remarry—or even to stay married despite being already married to an absent spouse—received explicit permission from the official to do so.[91] In England

and Italy, while courts did not go so far as to grant permission to remarry without proof, the courts seemed on the whole to handle remarriage with a policy of "don't ask don't tell," a policy that often continued well into the sixteenth century.[92] Those married to an absent spouse simply—and not necessarily quietly—remarried, and the court asked no questions unless a suit was brought to challenge the legitimacy of the marriage because of a prior bond. Emlyn Eisenach has found remarkably overt abuse of the canon law governing remarriage in Verona, practices that ended in the 1520s, when regulation of remarriage and prosecution of bigamy began at the instigation of a reforming bishop.[93] These differences in both practice and court proceedings concerning remarriage in the fifteenth century, with Regensburg and Troyes at opposite extremes in legal practice, offer some indication of the range of ways in which ecclesiastical courts in fifteenth-century Europe implemented marriage law. At the same time, the evidence of different social attitudes toward remarriage at some, usually lower, levels of society in Verona and Venice may well be indicative of much broader social practice in other parts of Europe.

Even within northern France and Burgundian lands, courts did not see fit always and everywhere to require proof of death before allowing a remarriage. Emmanuël Falzone found one case from Cambrai in which a married woman approached the court seeking permission to remarry.[94] On 22 September 1452 Renaude Coppine, the wife of Pierre, had not seen Pierre in two years and wished to remarry. Pierre had left on pilgrimage to Rome but had not returned. In order to prove that Renaude could claim the status of a widow, the official ordered the announcement of banns, designed to seek out any evidence that Pierre lived. If no objections were made, Renaude could be permitted to remarry.

We find a similar practice in one case from Rouen, examined in Carole Avignon's dissertation. In 1520, two wives who claimed their husbands had abandoned them wished to remarry and approached the official. The official ordered that the parish priests of each man should issue summons during mass for three successive Sundays, calling for the missing husbands to present themselves. If the men themselves or some news of their status did not emerge, the two women could remarry.[95]

Such a handling of remarriage may have had deep roots in France. A comparable practice is found in Gautier d'Arras's twelfth-century story "Ille et Galeron,"[96] a tale dedicated to a second wife, Beatrix, the wife of Frederick Barbarossa. In that tale the pope wishes the valiant Ille to marry the emperor's daughter in Rome, but Ille demurs on the grounds that he is already married to the absent (but really not at all far off) Galeron. The pope then orders that a summons seeking Galeron be issued in Galeron's home diocese. No trace of Galeron is found, Ille agrees to remarry, and the marriage is only prevented (temporarily) by the arrival of Galeron at the door of St. Peter's on the wedding day.

If Gautier d'Arras, and much more to the point, Hostiensis—along with most canon law commentators—and the officials of Cambrai and Rouen all found such a procedure satisfactory, however, the official in Troyes did not, and this "new" attitude found in Troyes would slowly come to prevail in the Catholic countries of the sixteenth century. A similar attitude can be found in the records of the Paris officiality, in at least one case. In 1500, one Marguerite came before the court seeking permission to remarry. She claimed to be the wife of a long-absent husband who had left her, gone to London, married another woman and had children with her, and died. In this case, Marguerite produced two witnesses to her husband's death in hopes that she could receive permission to remarry.[97] The scholarship of Charles Donahue, Ruth Karras, and Léon Pommeray on Paris reveals similar cases, as well as the prosecution of those who failed to find proof before remarriage.[98]

This strict regulation of remarriage also extended to include harsh punishment, or at least the threat of it. The real seriousness with which some courts, at least, viewed bigamy is demonstrated by the prescribed treatment of those found to have seriously violated the law. In some statute collections we find specified punishments for those who willfully married despite being already married. Deemed "infamous" in Roman legal tradition,[99] their infamy, their status as infamous, was to be displayed to the public by exposing them upon the ladder of the scaffold. A crime committed against the public, as the underlying logic explained, required public punishment, public acknowledgment, and expiation of the wrongdoing.

To offer two examples, the thirteenth-century synodal statutes of the diocese of Tours and the statutes of the neighboring northwestern diocese, Château-Gontier, threatened those guilty of double marriages or engagements with public punishment, enacted on the "scala."[100] As explained in Ducange's glossary of medieval Latin[101] and as illustrated in images such as those identified by Barbara Morel,[102] this tool of punishment was the ladder leading up to the scaffold. Such public display on the ladder was used to punish those found guilty of bigamy, of false testimony, of blasphemy, or public scandal of some kind.

So at least the statutes declared. We can and should distinguish between laws that mention this type of punishment and actual evidence of its use. In fact, we know of no bigamists actually placed on the ladder of the scaffold in

Tours or Château-Gontier. Indeed, we know of no case in which such punishments were carried out for such an offense in any part of Europe before the fifteenth century. The court records of the fifteenth century are often the earliest surviving sources. As a result, when exactly enforcement of these rules began remains a question we cannot satisfactorily answer.

Nonetheless, we do find scattered evidence of use beginning in the fourteenth century. Bigamists were punished on the ladder in fifteenth- and sixteenth-century Troyes and, if evidently less often, in Paris, Senlis, Rouen, Malines, Pamiers,[103] and in the fourteenth century in Marseilles.[104] In the south, this punishment came at the hands of secular rather than ecclesiastical officials. Returning north, we can also point to similar proceedings against bigamists that resulted in different punishments, such as penitential processions, pilgrimage, or imprisonment, from Châlons, Cambrai, Bourges, Paris, and Brussels.[105] Secular court records from Dijon include fines levied against bigamists in the fourteenth century, possibly if not necessarily part of a process that also included ecclesiastical prosecution and punishment,[106] and in 1520 the *prévôt* of Sens, a secular official, sentenced a bigamist to be whipped before sending him on to the official of Sens, presumably for annulment of the second marriage and for some form of ecclesiastical punishment.[107] The surviving synodal statutes from Paris, Rouen, and Troyes, unlike Tours and Château-Gontier, do not specify the use of the punishment of the ladder for bigamy, or indeed any other punishment. Nevertheless, these courts certainly made use of both the ladder of the scaffold and the bishop's prison as instruments of punishment for bigamy throughout the fifteenth century. As we will see in the final chapter, the officiality in Troyes used these punishments for a variety of offenses in Troyes, and bigamy ranked among them. In fact, the laity of the diocese met punishment on the ladder for no other crime so often as bigamy.

Indeed, between 1426 and 1468 we have remarkably consistent evidence of use, in Troyes, of the ladder and the prison to punish bigamy. The combination of exposure on the ladder and imprisonment was used against those seen to have most grossly violated the norms of the community: bigamists and clerics who became brigands, clerics who not only bore arms but fought battles and attacked noncombatants, stole, pillaged, killed, and raped. Also of great importance is the contemporary context of these prosecutions. In the fifteenth century, we find evidence of such handling of bigamy in northern France and Burgundian territories. We find scattered cases from throughout these dioceses in which bigamists met with harsh punishment. The punishments are always the harshest handed down for any matrimonial offense. The largest number of cases has so far been found in records from Troyes.

It seems, therefore, that Troyes stood alone among local courts in its handling of bigamy. Harsh punishments aside, only one other venue, by no means local, has been shown by current scholarship to have adhered to the same standards for preventing potentially bigamous remarriage as found in Troyes and throughout northern France and Burgundian lands. As Ludwig Schmugge has shown, the papal penitentiary seemed to be in agreement with the standards of proof before remarriage required most notably by the officiality of Troyes, found seemingly nowhere else in Christian Europe in the fifteenth century.

At the level of the papal penitentiary, which considered petitions for annulments and dispensations, granted with the pope's delegated jurisdiction, Schmugge has found a number of petitions related to bigamy.[108] Schmugge identifies, first, cases of missing persons and, second, cases of marriages contracted bigamously. These cases demonstrate that the laws governing remarriage were consistently upheld. In these cases, the penitentiary did not allow spouses of a missing husband or wife to remarry without proof, no matter how long they had waited. Those who had contracted a bigamous marriage found that second marriage dissolved by the penitentiary. Interestingly, if this first spouse subsequently died, the bigamists were often successful in their petitions to remarry the spouse they had previously married bigamously. This was the only concession the penitentiary allowed those who had contracted concurrent marriages.[109] If Troyes was in fact the only fifteenth-century court to punish bigamists so frequently, the court's efforts at preventing and dissolving bigamous marriages, more broadly present in northern France and Burgundian lands, were in accord with the actions of the papal penitentiary.

Our current scholarship thus suggests that northern France and the papal penitentiary stood alone in their strict attitude toward potentially bigamous remarriages and that Troyes stood completely alone in consistently inflicting harsh punishment on certain male bigamists. Perhaps that is the case. The matter, however, is not quite so clear, for there are too many silences and lacunae in our current understanding of the surviving sources. All this raises once more the question of the evident exceptionality of the handling of bigamy in fifteenth-century Troyes.

How exceptional was the prosecution of bigamy found in Troyes? Modern scholarship on fifteenth-century officiality records seems to show that bigamy was of slight concern elsewhere in Europe. Scholarship on England, Germany, Spain, and Italy particularly encourages this perception. To be sure, in all of these places many people seem to have married more often, or at least more confusedly, than they should have. Their ecclesiastical courts, however, do not seem to have been interested in punishing bigamous offenders beyond a fine or the requirement that any prior bond be recognized as the valid marriage.[110] That the officiality of Troyes prosecuted and punished bigamists stands out as exceptional. However, this evident exceptionality requires some qualification and may require some revision.

On the surface, it seems to be the case for England, Italy, Germany, and Spain that ecclesiastical courts did not subject bigamists to criminal prosecution or punishment. Instead, as Martine Charageat explains for Saragossa, in the fifteenth century bigamy was treated more as a civil matter, as a violation of a contract, than as a crime against the sacrament of marriage.[111] Beginning in the last decades of the fifteenth century in Spain and in the first decades of the sixteenth century in Italy, bigamy began to be prosecuted as a crime against the sacrament.[112] Only in fifteenth-century Troyes can we find the sort of criminal prosecution and punishment of bigamy that is otherwise a feature of the sixteenth or seventeenth century in Catholic lands. We must recognize, however, that we currently have at best an incomplete knowledge of ecclesiastical court criminal proceedings in Spain, Italy, and Germany, and our knowledge even of the extensively studied English criminal cases is limited with respect to bigamy.

To begin with Italy and Spain, scholars have located and studied Italian medieval officiality records only from Lucca, Venice, and Pisa; and only Saragossa and Barcelona for Spain.[113] With the exception of Barcelona—and it is a limited exception—criminal cases do not form a part of these studies. Even the scholarship on Barcelona cannot tell us much, since only a handful of fifteenth-century criminal records from the ecclesiastical court have survived. The criminal cases of Saragossa, meanwhile, remain sealed. The cases in Lucca have only just been made available to scholars. For Venice, criminal records from the fifteenth century have not survived. The Pisan records date to the thirteenth century and are not concerned with criminal matters.[114] All this certainly implies that bigamists could have been punished by officialities in Italy or Spain; secular courts may well also have done some punishing. This should not be taken to mean, however, that ecclesiastical courts would have fully ceded jurisdiction. Even in the sixteenth century in Spain, some bigamy cases made their way to ecclesiastical courts rather than to the Inquisition (and sometimes in addition to the Inquisition).[115]

The case of Spain is particularly important, because of the evidence we have for both ecclesiastical and secular sanctions for bigamy, as well as evidence for harsh sanctions on the part of the secular courts. Additionally, if only beginning at the very close of the fifteenth century, it is in Spain that we find the earliest evidence of the enforcement of these punishments for bigamists by secular courts. In Aragon, convicted bigamists typically faced imprisonment.[116] In Castile, bigamists met a punishment derived from Roman law, banishment to an island, and sometimes also the punishment of branding on the face with a *q* (or maybe not a *q* but a *b* or a cross, or two parallel lines, or a *10*).[117] For this, too, we have evidence of enforcement, but not before the final decades of the fifteenth century.[118]

German officialities, meanwhile, appear on the other end of a spectrum from the criminal prosecutions found in Troyes. These courts may well not have punished bigamy largely because they, if Augsburg is any example, lacked jurisdiction over all criminal matters.[119] As explained above, it is also from Germany, from the court in Regensburg, that we have evidence of the most open attitude toward potentially bigamous marriage found in any surviving ecclesiastical court records.[120] German courts, then, might be assumed to have had the least interest in punishing bigamy as a crime, either because they could not, as with Augsburg, or because they did not think of bigamy as a crime, as, perhaps, with Regensburg.

It seems most likely, then, based on the current state of research, to assume that bigamy prosecutions and punishments in ecclesiastical courts at least possibly happened in Spain and Italy and that they were far less likely to have taken place in German courts.

English courts, best-known of all medieval officialities, offer a more complicated story. Scholarship on medieval marriage litigation in England, particularly that of Charles Donahue, has on the whole presented ecclesiastical courts as user-friendly and rather gentle in their handling of the matrimonial projects of the laity, especially as compared to their counterparts in northern France or Cambrai and Brussels. There is certainly something to this comparison—indeed, a great deal to it.[121] However, it is important to recognize that scholars have focused on different kinds of cases and brought different concerns to the study of officialities in England and in France. This has perhaps exaggerated the differences between the courts of the two countries. Even as most of the scholarship on marriage litigation presents a friendly picture of the English ecclesiastical courts, many of these courts assigned penalties of fines or other penances, including a not inconsiderable amount of corporal punishment, largely for sexual offenses. This sort of punitive behavior does not appear to have so often directly involved marriage cases as found in northern France or Cambrai, but it did take place and was certainly sometimes attached to marriage suits. There is therefore some cause for caution in maintaining the description of English and northern French litigation as so very different, especially if we broaden our view to include sexual offenses alongside the marriage litigation so skillfully analyzed by Donahue. Civil suits involving marriage certainly came before English courts at the behest of parties who did not seem to suffer for it as much or as often as they would have in northern France, but there is nevertheless more to this English story, including some strong hints of a much more punitive side to English ecclesiastical justice, certainly more focused on sexual offenses but nevertheless also touching on marriage.

The work of a handful of scholars, including L. R. Poos and Richard Wunderli, offers discussion of much more regulatory and intrusive English ecclesiastical court action, with much of that action aimed at the marital as well as the sexual practices of the laity.[122] Scholarship that focuses more exclusively on marriage litigation also makes at least occasional references to punishment for marital or sexual offenses.[123] As Helmholz explains, some marriage litigation involved couples accused of fornication, who risked "humiliating public penance" if they did not marry or at least promise to be automatically married if they ever slept together again.[124] In the thirteenth century, church courts punished adultery and fornication with a whipping around the parish church or market, or both, practices that persisted into the fourteenth century in the diocese of Rochester.[125] In the fifteenth century, in Canterbury and Rochester, we find instead the use of public procession on a Sunday or Sundays, barefoot and in sackcloth, carrying a burning candle. This punishment does not seem to have been universal in late medieval England: whipping for sexual offenses appears in records from York and Hereford in the late fifteenth century, and we see the use of fines as well, at least for adultery.[126] Fines seem to have been made use of most prominently in London: Shannon McSheffrey and Richard Wunderli show the widespread use of fines as punishment for a range of marital and sexual infractions.[127]

Drawing on records from across England spanning the fourteenth through sixteenth centuries, Poos points to attempts on the part of various local courts—sometimes clearly working in tandem with visitation records—to regulate marriage, suspect cohabitation, and adultery or fornication. Much as in northern France, couples were ordered to separate until they could prove that an absent spouse had died or otherwise prove their marriage was valid.[128] For marital and sexual infractions, Poos identifies penance and excommunication as punishment. Sheehan also offers an example of the punishments of excommunication and penance in Ely (and that it was performed, whatever it was).[129] In London, according to Wunderli, the commissary court normally punished offenders with public or pecuniary penance. Here, as in fifteenth-century Canterbury and Rochester, public meant a public procession leading to the church, with the penitent in sackcloth and carrying a lighted candle. Public punishment was often commuted to fines, which ranged at a judge's discretion depending on the wealth of the individual and the severity of the crime.[130]

As alluded to already, the fourteenth-century court of Bishop Hamo of Rochester punished offenders with beatings or whippings around the church and/or around the market. These punishments are extremely difficult to parse, but for what it is worth it seems on the whole that the court punished "simple" fornication as well as fornication related to clandestine marriage with whippings around the church (only), while adultery and some other marital offenses, meanwhile, often included whippings around both the church and the market. Johnson posits that poor and low-status persons faced beatings, while higher-status persons were punished instead by fines and pilgrimages.[131] We can add to that distinction that the court also punished clergy found guilty of sexual offenses with fines and pilgrimages rather than public physical punishment. Lindsay Bryan made use of Bishop Hamo's register to study 124 cases involving marriage and sexual morals, including a number of ex-officio cases, cases brought ostensibly on accusation, rumor, or as a result of an episcopal visitation.[132] Fornication was punished by a fine or by a public beating three times around the church. Adultery was punished by two or three beatings around the market and the church. Sorcery met with six beatings around the church and the market, usury three around the church and one around the market.[133] Looking to late medieval Durham, we find once again an emphasis on the prosecution of sexual rather than marital offenses and the use of the archdeacon's court. In Durham, the prior's archdeaconal court seems to have done the sentencing and whipping for sexual delicts, delicts that often had ties to marriage and more than a whiff of bigamy about them. To be sure, bigamy is not the focus of the investigation or the explicit reason for punishment in the bulk or even mass of cases studied thus far.[134]

All this makes England look something more like northern France in its general character and handling of the laity. One difference lies in the English use of whipping or beating, which may well have happened in northern France but is not mentioned in the northern French court records.[135] There is additionally a difference in focus, with English courts seemingly more preoccupied with the punishment of sexual offenses, while northern France regulated and punished both illegal marriages and sexual offenses. There are potentially real differences in the numbers, but that is difficult to access. As for public punishment, what Helmholz and Wunderli describe as public penance, the penitent processing to church with a candle, resembles what we sometimes see in Cambrai and Rouen.

All this took place alongside the cases studied by Donahue, civil cases that dissolved bigamous unions and made no discernible mention of prosecuting or punishing the guilty bigamist. It is as if we have visited two parallel worlds, one in which the English punished marital and sexual offenses and one in which they did not. There are many reasons for this. Donahue, for example, could not discuss punishment in any detail for the cases from York, because the sentences did not usually survive. Donahue found only a few references to sentences, but not what any punishment was, and some mention of penance for perjury related to a marriage case.[136] The court in Ely studied by Donahue kept a separate register of fines, so some offenders in Ely were presumably fined, or at least could have been fined, but those fines do not play a role in Donahue's analysis of marriage litigation at Ely, and so we cannot bring them into this discussion. Donahue's description of court activity does give a vague sense that in Ely the archdeacon did the punishing (or at least warning) when couples lived together and should not (or lived apart and should not), but that the bishop of Ely claimed jurisdiction over defining a marriage as legitimate or not.[137] Perhaps even in those latter cases further punishment beyond any fines recorded in the bishop's register of fines was also handled by the archdeaconal courts. The bishop sentenced to penance a chaplain involved in an illegal solemnization of a marriage (illegal because of a known prior bond).[138] According to Donahue, the Ely court imposed a penance for no office cases involving informal marriage. The court did impose penance for a confession of fornication, but "the court did not think that its job was to punish people for having contracted informally." As Donahue adds, however, there must at the very least have been fees, as all medieval courts, except evidently in Sweden, charged fees.[139]

All this said, where did bigamy—as found in both marital litigation and adultery prosecution—fit in between these brighter and darker sides of English ecclesiastical justice? We know from Bishop Hamo's register that a bigamist, like an adulterer, might face the punishment of whipping. Bishop Hamo's register also includes a handful of precontract cases that do not seem to have resulted in any penances.[140] These were usually cases in which the banns of a marriage were interrupted with a claim of a prior bond that the court would subsequently investigate and rule on. There are a few other cases, however, that look something more like punishment for bigamy, though they could easily fall into the broader category of punishment for fornication or adultery, or—if perhaps less frequently—a consummated clandestine marriage. For example, Alice, who had contracted marriage with John and consummated it, later contracted marriage and consummated it with Ralf. The court ordered Alice and John to solemnize their marriage on penalty of excommunication and stipulated that Alice have no communication with Ralf. The court punished

John and Alice with three whippings.[141] Another example of a bigamy case that resulted in punishment begins with the excommunication of one John, who had failed to perform the required penance for adultery. The court also investigated his "marital projects" with three different women. He admitted that the first marriage was clandestine and that he had also married the next two women in some fashion. John was ordered to solemnize his first marriage and to be whipped three times around the market and the church.[142]

In short, apart from these few examples, punishment for bigamy is difficult to find in records from medieval England. Moreover, it is, in fact, difficult to say if these punishments noted above did not have more to do with fornication or adultery than bigamy. It is even more difficult to find descriptions of punishment, as well as explicit statements that punishment was absent, in scholarship on bigamy in medieval England. Even scholars who worked expressly on bigamy in England do not offer us a great deal of guidance in this matter. Philippa Maddern, writing on bigamous marriages, analyzed records from London, York, Canterbury, Norwich, Rochester, and Wisbech, ranging from 1350 to 1500. She found 75 cases in which litigants sued for divorce on the grounds of an existing prior marriage, 53 additional cases involving bigamy or adultery brought to court, and 91 ex-officio accusations of bigamy. At least sixteen confessed. Some people, seeking to avoid detection, traveled considerable distances from the place they were known to be married, even to the Continent.[143] However, one matter that Maddern does not address is how, if at all, the courts punished those bigamists found to be guilty.[144]

Sara Butler, writing on husband desertion, found that in her 121 selected cases a number of wives remarried. For example, five out of seventeen wives brought before the court of Canterbury were accused of bigamous remarriage. We do not know if or how the court punished them. Butler does explain that deserting wives faced the threat of excommunication and imprisonment and also risked exposing anyone who aided them to accusations of ravishment or abduction. Wives who agreed to return home often did so on penalty of a fine and beatings around the marketplace.[145] Butler describes these judgments as "typical." All this leaves us, then, with the idea that bigamy took place rather often in England. Courts may well have regularly punished bigamous offenders, even those detected in the course of civil marriage litigation, but we simply do not know at present. We can assert that some punishment for some bigamous marriages is at least a real possibility, at the very least as a kind of adultery and possibly as a more serious violation of the sacrament of marriage. We do not know, however, if or how the courts punished bigamists, but I would argue that we have some reason to suspect that they, like the officiality in Rochester, well might have done so. Nevertheless, scholarship on English officialities taken as a whole does not encourage the view that bigamy mattered a great deal to church court officials in late medieval England. Courts seem to have been much more intent on punishing sexual offenses, and the few bigamists we see punished appear to have been punished more for their adultery than for their multiple marriages.

At present, therefore, we can assert that bigamy seemed to matter in Troyes as it mattered nowhere else in the fifteenth century. We must, however, remember that the sources from Spain, Italy, and perhaps also Germany and England may yet have a good deal more to say on the matter; they await future scholarship. Nevertheless, at least for the present, scholarship on other local courts does not tell anything like the tale about bigamy found in Troyes. In other parts of late medieval Europe bigamy does seem, to return to Charageat's useful distinction, more a matter of contract violation than a crime against the sacrament of marriage.

That does not mean that bigamy did not matter at all in these other parts of Western Christendom. Punishment is not the only issue. Prevention offers further evidence of concern over bigamy, and evidence for prevention is far more widespread. In northern France and arguably in other parts of Europe, we find assiduous efforts to prevent bigamous marriage. Indeed, the prevention of bigamy was one of the main reasons church officials acted to punish—if not invalidate—clandestine marriage. Certainly it was one of the reasons the northern French dioceses studied by Carole Avignon made such assiduous efforts to require letters proving freedom to marry from all strangers to the diocese or parish. An outsider to a community was far more likely to be a potential bigamist than a distant relative of a prospective spouse.

Having attempted to assess the evident lack of bigamy prosecutions elsewhere, we must also return to Troyes itself and seek out the limits of what the surviving sources permit us to know about the prosecution of bigamy there. To continue, then, on to another issue that lies at the margins of what we can learn about bigamy prosecutions, we have the thorny question of when the prosecution of bigamy actually began in Troyes. Chronology is a major concern in attempting to describe how bigamy came to be perceived as a crime that called for prosecution and punishment in an ecclesiastical court in northern France. Evidence for the subjection of bigamists to public punishment of some kind emerges only in the fifteenth century with any consistency. In particular, records detailing an ecclesiastical court's use of the ladder of the scaffold and of prison to punish bigamists appear only beginning in the fifteenth century. That evidence of this handling of bigamy emerges only from fifteenth-century records, however, does not mean that bigamy was not already so prosecuted in earlier centuries. As explained above, the punishment of exposure on the ladder of the scaffold for bigamy dates to the thirteenth century in some northern French synodal statutes. Even as the description of a punishment must always be kept apart from any assumption that it may have been applied, the possibility of application nevertheless exists from the thirteenth century. We also have no clear date to mark as the beginnings of the officiality of Troyes's proactive regulation of the sex, marriage, and violence of their laity and clergy. Court records on this subject, evidence of court action, again date to the fifteenth century. In the fourteenth century, however, we already have some suggestions of a court that at least competing jurisdictions and some unhappy members of the laity considered to be overactive and overly punitive in its handling of the laity.

Sources that date to the five years in which Jean Braque served as bishop of Troyes (1370–75) offer both evidence that suggests an active—and perhaps even reforming—bishop and also evidence of an active officiality. During those five years, Braque issued synodal statutes and either went on parish visits in the diocese or required others to do so, two possible signs of a resident and active bishop, one interested in reforming morals in his diocese.[146] Secular jurisdiction in Troyes at that time included at the highest level the Grands Jours de Troyes, a deputation of the Paris Parlement. In 1371 this body reproached Jean Braque for "l'immixion de son official dans les affaires purement temporelles et seculieres," an accusation that has a good deal of resemblance to the conflict between officials of the king and those of the bishop between 1458 and 1462.[147]

That Braque was reprimanded by the Grands Jours de Troyes certainly suggests that the Troyes officiality may at least have had moments of regulation of lay morals prior to the fifteenth century. Théophile Boutiot, a nineteenth-century archivist and historian of Champagne and its institutions, goes so far as to describe Braque as continuing the traditions of his predecessors in pushing his jurisdiction into matters that secular officials claimed as fully secular. This description, however, Boutiot does not support with any examples.

To be sure, the activity of Jean Braque and his official may have had more in common with the court activity of fifteenth-century Rouen or Paris concerning marriage and morals, which is to say, they might have been more inclined to collect fines than to subject an offender to public punishment or imprisonment. Nonetheless, we have another example that suggests that the officiality of Troyes made use of its prison to punish laity, if for reasons unknown to us, prior to the fifteenth century. In 1391 the Grands Jours considered a defamation suit brought by Pierre d'Arcis, then bishop of Troyes, and his official. The bishop accused the bailiff of Rameru and two women, the widow and the mother of a man who had died in the official's prison, of calumny against the bishop and his official. They had allegedly said that the bishop and his official had left the man, one Jean Hubert, to die in their prison.[148] The bishop and the official won their case, but for our purposes, we know at least that the bishop made use of his prison and that the prisoners included at least one member of the laity. All this, of course, is only suggestive, but it is at the very least just that, and so prior prosecution of bigamy in Troyes should certainly remain in the realm of the possible, if not quite the probable.

If we can suspend any remaining disbelief until further research addresses these questions, if we focus instead on working with the scholarship and sources as they stand, certainly northern France remains unique in its efforts to regulate marriage in the fifteenth century. These efforts focused particularly on the prevention and prosecution of bigamous marriage. Among the ecclesiastical courts of Western Christendom, Troyes stands apart above all in the repeated subjection of male bigamists to public punishment and imprisonment, a special combination of ecclesiastical punishments usually reserved for male clergy who had most seriously violated their religious obligations, notably the ban on shedding blood.

With this background in law, theology, and custom in hand, having stretched also to the limits that the surviving sources and current scholarship allow, we can now turn, for the remainder of this chapter and the chapters that follow, to a detailed study of the crisis of marriage in late medieval Troyes. As we have seen, men and women who sought confirmation of their remarriages at the papal penitentiary were not permitted to remain married to a second spouse; those who asked permission from the pope were refused. However, sometimes spouses in southern Germany found more sympathetic officials, and even in northern France and Cambrai exceptions were made for women married to long-absent spouses. Most often, people probably remarried much more quietly, without asking a judicial officer to interfere. A crisis emerged only when officials not only refused to tolerate more quiet acts of bigamy but also dissolved or suspended any suspect marriages and made spectacular examples of some of the male offenders found to be bigamous. Crises only emerged when and where the laws were upheld in their strictest sense. Such a crisis is found in fifteenth-century Troyes.

The sources that lie at the heart of this inquiry belong to the Archives Départmentales de l'Aube, in the city of Troyes, ancient capital of the Champagne region. These fifteenth-century registers are among the earliest surviving records of the bishop of Troyes' judicial court, known as an officiality in honor of its judge, the official, who held the delegated judicial powers of the bishop. In northern France, ecclesiastical court procedure made use of a figure much less present elsewhere, the promotor, a sort of public prosecutor acting on behalf of the court.[149] A promotor could bring cases before the court at the court's own initiative, ex officio, without any outside accusation. The active use of these promotors to bring "office" cases against alleged offenders gave northern French and Burgundian officialities a distinctly different character than the relatively more litigant friendly courts of fourteenth- and fifteenth-century England or Italy, and probably Spanish and German courts as well.[150]

The surviving records of the medieval officiality of Troyes can be divided into four main categories. First we have registers involving testaments, goods, and legal separations. Only one such register survives, covering the period of the last decade of the fourteenth century. For the fifteenth century we have two registers of sentences, warnings, and agreements called *assecurationes* (*asseurements* in French). We also have fifteen registers covering the daily business of the court, called "cause registers." These cause registers begin in 1455 and continue with few interruptions into the sixteenth century, for which many more registers survive. We also have several registers describing fines collected by the officiality, from the early decades of the fifteenth century and again from midcentury. Most of these entries offer only the name of an individual and the sum paid, but some of the earliest registers also describe the offense individuals were accused of having committed. This book is based largely upon extensive analysis of four of the earliest surviving registers: the two registers of sentences and other matters, G4171 (1423–76) and G4172 (1426–47), and the two earliest cause registers, G4173 (1455) and G4174 (1456). I also draw upon the registers of fines, a number of additional cause registers, and various other records kept by the officiality and by the bishop of Troyes.

Reading the register of sentences, one is overwhelmed first by the scrawled handwriting, seemingly indecipherable—and perhaps intentionally so—and then by the sheer number of cases instigated by this court. Hundreds of men and women suspected of illegal relationships are ordered to quit each other's company, to avoid causing further scandal. In some cases, they are fined for illegal cohabitation, for fornication, for adultery, or for concubinage. In the course of the century couples faced warnings, orders, fines, detention in prison, and even excommunication and terms of imprisonment if they did not separate. The officiality made a considerable effort, it seems, to summon and fine anyone in the diocese suspected of partaking in a nonmarital male-female relationship that caused scandal.

In some cases, those accused of adulterous relationships faced additional orders to return to their spouses and resume married life, on penalty of excommunication, imprisonment, and heavy fines. These orders, however, were issued rarely, in perhaps only a dozen cases over the course of the century. The implications of the difference in numbers between the few thousands of men, women, and couples ordered to abandon an illicit relationship and the very few ordered to resume married life merit further study. It seems at least possible that informal separation was tolerated in Troyes, as it seems to have been in so many other places in Christian Europe, as long as neither husband nor wife went on to engage in an extramarital relationship, which did, by contrast, seem to draw the attention and energy of the court.

In addition to policing sex and marriage, the court often served as a venue for redress of violence or for dispute resolution. We find case after case of alleged violent attack, men fighting men and women, women fighting women and men, laymen and women fighting with clergy, and clergy fighting with all manner of persons. Additionally, hundreds of men and some women came before the court to swear oaths to not harm others. All this suggests an environment of feud, an impression that builds as we find additionally several investigations of defamation or insults that often led to violence, violence that often involved members of the clergy and sometimes took place on sacred ground, in the church or at the cemetery.

We find as well a hundred or so cases that stand out. They draw our attention first of all because they are written relatively carefully and well, even attractively. This extra effort on the part of these notaries suggests that these cases were important, that the notaries thought they might be read in the future. Second, these cases stand out because of their relative length. The typical entry found in these registers is a few lines or so, but these hundred-odd cases take up one or even several sides of the folios, if unfortunately—for our purposes—never more than that. Third, and most important, these entries document the spectacular punishments of the crimes considered most serious by the court: heresy, brigandage, perjury, false testimony, clerical brigandage, sacrilege, . . . and bigamy.

The prominence of bigamy in these records is noted first of all in the extensive and even sensationalist inventories prepared by the historian, philologist, and archivist Marie Henri d'Arbois de Jubainville.[151] Beatrice Gottlieb also noticed the importance of these cases.[152] Gottlieb went to the archives in Champagne intending to determine whether Luther's complaints about clandestine marriage and ecclesiastical courts had any resemblance to what the surviving court records describe. Instead, she found little evidence that bore out the main complaints voiced in the sixteenth century. Gottlieb argued, and probably quite rightly, that many of these sixteenth-century objections had more to do with political concerns than with widespread social practice.[153] While she observed that bigamy met with harsh punishment, she did not understand the full significance of that punishment, nor did she notice that the court made a practice of dissolving any bigamous engagements or marriages that it found. Well over a hundred investigations of bigamy emerge from analysis of the few registers described above. Most cases were resolved with the annulment or suspension of any suspicious engagement or marriage, an order to separate on penalty of excommunication, and the payment of a fine. Twenty cases we know to have resulted in harsh punishment. The chapters that follow in this book present the practice and prosecution of bigamy in Troyes in detail. Here, to begin, is an example:

In 1423, in the diocese of Troyes, in northeastern France, a man called Étienne "Languedoc" was condemned to public exposure on the ladder of the scaffold in front of the cathedral, where he would be attached to the rungs of the ladder by his wrists, standing there for one Sunday or feast day, a day when the largest number of people might come to hear mass and to see who had been set out to be punished on the scaffold. After his ordeal, Étienne was to spend six months in the bishop's prison, on bread and water and in chains.[154]

As explained in the sentence passed against him, Étienne was not native to Troyes. Despite his nickname of "Languedoc" he came from the neighboring diocese of Langres, in Burgundy, where some fourteen years before he had married a woman named Isabelle. They had married with the blessing of the parish priest at the doors of the parish church in a village of that diocese. About nine years later, Étienne sought to marry again, this time in the diocese of Troyes. As a stranger to the diocese, Étienne was asked about his marital status before he was allowed to contract a marriage. The synodal statutes of Troyes required as much, and Étienne's new parish priest seems to have fulfilled this duty. Étienne duly went to the bishop's court and claimed that his wife, Isabelle, had died. Accepted as a widower, Étienne was given permission to marry in the diocese and married one Marguerite, herself a widow. However, it seems that Étienne's first wife was still alive, still living back in the diocese of Langres where Étienne had abandoned her. Moreover, Étienne had known that she was probably alive at the time he married, or in any event had made no effort to find out for certain. He had nonetheless sworn that he was a widower and free to marry Marguerite. All this was revealed in the course of Étienne's prosecution at the hands of the bishop's delegated judicial official, three years after his marriage to Marguerite. In consequence of his acts he met one of the harsher punishments handed down by this court.

Étienne's case was one of many. From 1423 to 1468 the bishop's court in

Troyes so prosecuted nineteen men and one woman for knowingly contracting two concurrent marriages. These men and one woman came from various dioceses across northern France. They had, on the whole, left a spouse behind in another diocese and come to Troyes, where they married again. Others were native to Troyes and had left wives behind there before moving on to remarry. Still others married twice without leaving Troyes at all. Some men had been abandoned first by their wives, rather than the other way around. Regardless, all were punished for bigamy.

The activities of this court in so prosecuting bigamous offenders are incomprehensible without knowledge of the theological and legal traditions of bigamy found in Christian marriage law and traced in this chapter. The language of the judgments found in these records makes this clear. The ecclesiastical judges in Troyes perceived in the crime of bigamy not only perjury, deception, and fraud but also an attack on the very nature of sacramental marriage. For example, here are the terms in which Étienne was condemned. The court accused Étienne of having "vilified the state of marriage," a thing created, as the court reminded Étienne, "in the terrestrial paradise, instituted by Jesus Christ."[155] Étienne's fraudulent marriage defied the model marriages of Adam and Eve and Christ and the Church. Further, "he had shown contempt for the people of the holy church militant, above all his deceived second wife." That is to say, Étienne's act was not a private violation but a public action, an attack on the Christian community. These crimes had been committed publicly and against the body public and thus, implicitly, deserved public punishment. And so, Étienne was sentenced to exposure on the ladder and after that to prison. As with Étienne, so with the other convicted bigamists. Such was the punishment for these violations of the obligations of what the court records refer to as the "order of matrimony."

To conclude, the insistence upon marriage as monogamous had ancient roots in Christianity. Looking to the eleventh century, it is not going too far to link Christian insistence on indissoluble monogamy to the requirement for priestly celibacy.[156] Married to the Church, fully ordained clergy could have no other spouse. As for the laity, they married each other, but this bond too had to mirror the bond of Adam and Eve or Christ and Church. These ideas had important consequences for how all Christians were meant to conduct their lives at the end of the Middle Ages, and we see the earliest signs of this in fifteenth-century northern France and Burgundian lands.

All of this was not just theological theorizing; in Troyes it became part of an active judicial court practice. By investigating bigamy as prosecuted in the diocese of Troyes we learn about the role of theology and law in prosecution, about the priorities and attitudes of ecclesiastical judges in late medieval northeastern France. Moreover, in studying the prosecution of bigamy, we learn not only about the role of law and theology in court practice but also about the behavior of ordinary Christians. We learn that we are in a world that attributed great importance to getting married. The people prosecuted in Troyes knew they ran tremendous risks in committing bigamy, in this sort of imposture, which was a threat to salvation and to the legitimacy of their marriages, a threat to family property and inheritance, to social status, to honor in their communities. Nevertheless, they remarried.

We can only understand their motives if we understand the broader religious and cultural world in which they lived. Marriage removed much of the sin from a sexual relationship; it accorded legitimacy to any children. Marriage provided legal protections and benefits. It provided social standing and participation in a holy sacrament. Only married women were allowed to partake in certain blessings such as reentry into a church after the birth of a child. Only married women could have children without fear of prosecution for adultery. Only married men could be sure that their children would have the full benefits of whatever inheritance or position in the world their fathers might confer.

To be sure, those who remarried bigamously only seemingly gained these advantages: their marriages had no real legitimacy and their sexual relationship was a sin for whichever spouse knew the marriage was bigamous. Nevertheless, even bigamous marriages had advantages. The children of bigamous marriages were recognized as legitimate as a rule, on the presumption that at least one spouse believed the marriage legitimate. Also, even a bigamous marriage offered at the very least the semblance of a legitimate, sacramental marriage, especially if celebrated with a priest's blessing.[157]

All of this incited ordinary people to commit what I call "bigamy." In the Middle Ages, there were many kinds of bigamy. "True bigamy," "bina matrimonia" when willfully contracted, stood apart as a crime, and a crime that was understood as an attack on the fundamental nature of the sacrament of marriage. Christian marriage required strict adherence to the model marriages of Adam and Eve and Christ and the Church. By the later Middle Ages, in northern France, those who married despite being already married to a living spouse thus faced prosecution and punishment for an unchristian act, an act that violated Christian identity: the crime of bigamy.

CHAPTER 2

Bigamous Husbands

Between 1423 and 1468, the officiality of Troyes convicted twenty men including one Franciscan friar for the crime of willfully marrying "de facto, cum de jure non posset"; in fact only, as not legally permissible. Who were these men, and why did the court in Troyes prosecute them? The second half of that question is a more appropriate topic for Chapter 5, "Why Prosecute Bigamy?" In this chapter we will seek out what information we can gather about who these men were, what common identity, if any, they shared, and what about them as a group led to their denunciation, prosecution, and conviction. Learning as much as we can about the men prosecuted and convicted for bigamy will thus further inform our reading, in the final chapter, of why the court chose to prosecute these men in particular.

Almost all of the information we have about these men is drawn from the sentences passed against them by the court. Indeed, the court's record of the sentence is usually the only opportunity we have to encounter these men in the sources; almost no other surviving records offer any information about them. As with the sentence passed against Étienne "Languedoc" described at the close of the previous chapter, these sentences gave the date, listed the court officials present at the sentencing, and then proceeded to describe the convicted bigamist and some details of the first and second marriages. These sentences declared that two marriages had taken place during the lifetime of a first spouse and that the bigamist either did not seek out proof of death or else provided fraudulent proof before remarrying. Such, it seems, was sufficient to define a crime.

We have, then, usually, at least that much information to work with. Some of the sentences offer more details than others. A few sentences provide information about where the first wife resided at the time of prosecution; others mention children born to the first or second marriages, or both. All of this contributes to a rough understanding of who these men were and how they came to marry twice. These records can offer important clues about these men, how they set about marrying and remarrying, and the deeper questions of why they acted as they had, and why the court responded as it did.

To begin with a caveat, accepting the information provided in these sentences as true or factual requires something of a leap of faith. It is quite possible that these men lied to the court. They may have lied about where they were from, about their names, and also about the details of their prior marital histories. After all, these men had almost all attempted to pass themselves off as widowers, or in any case as men free to marry, while in reality they had a living wife, occasionally children, and other familial and social ties that they had concealed. They are patently not a class of inherently trustworthy witnesses to their own activities. How to correct for further potential falsehoods in their "confessions" of bigamy? In point of fact, it is hard to say what scholars might do to extract "truth" from these records.

In dealing with this problem, which makes it difficult to study either testimony or litigation, we must follow the example of John Arnold in his critical reading of the sorts of stories told to inquisitorial judges.[1] We must read these legal depositions more as a source of narrative, of carefully constructed narrative, than fact. A man might claim he had married seven years before in Chartres and have in fact married ten years before in Paris. We must do our best with what information we have. If that information is not a true rendering of events, it does at least show the sorts of narratives that the men being punished by the officiality told about themselves or that the court had garnered in interrogating witnesses and collecting depositions. We can additionally read these records on the presumption that the information contained therein is at least plausible, if not the whole truth. These men probably did not venture too far afield from what would have made for a plausible life history in late medieval Champagne.

That said, let us begin our analysis and categorization of the twenty men convicted of "de facto" marriages. We can set one man apart from the beginning. Nineteen of the men were still married to living wives at the time of their second marriages. One man, a friar and deacon, had abandoned his religious habit and the religious life in favor of matrimony,[2] an act that canon law treated as a symbolic doubling of marriage vows. Married to the Church, he could not abandon his Spouse and marry a woman.[3] For this crime he faced a year's imprisonment. His punishment, notably, differed from the nineteen other men's but matched that applied to the only woman convicted of bigamy, whose sentence is analyzed in the following chapter on abandoned wives. All the other convicted bigamists, all male, minor clergy and laity alike, faced both public punishment on the ladder of the scaffold and imprisonment. The friar's case, which had very different motivations and issues than these other cases, we will exclude from the rest of the chapter and focus instead on the nineteen men who married twice.

Setting aside our friar, the other nineteen men also share something else in common. They seem to have limited their excessive marriage to bigamy rather than trigamy or more. While we have no cases of men who married more than two wives in succession from the officiality of Troyes, court records from other dioceses, such as those of Senlis and Paris, yield investigations of men alleged to have married three wives in succession.[4] As for the bigamists in Troyes, in addition to the fact of bigamy, their most obvious shared characteristic was their gender.

What should we make of this clear predominance of men in the prosecution—and especially punishment—of bigamy? In a way it is not surprising that these men bore the brunt of the punishment, as men generally were the focus of late medieval justice.[5] This does not mean, however, that we should not try for a deeper or more nuanced understanding of why men served as the main targets of this form of prosecution. After all, not all crimes were necessarily associated with male behavior. Some crimes had associations with female behavior, such as infanticide or witchcraft. Other crimes seemed to involve the regulation of both male and female activity.

In addition to recognizing a gender distinction in prosecution, we can also ask why these men in particular faced prosecution. Beyond being male, was it anything (else) about these men that contributed to their denunciation, prosecution, and punishment? Did any of these commonalities seem to contribute to their identification as bigamous and subsequent prosecution for the crime? What characteristics, if any, did they share? Where did they come from? What professions, if any, did they claim? At the date of prosecution, were they relatively old men or were they young? How did they go about remarrying?

To begin, who were these men? We learn very little about their background or social status from the records, usually only their name and place of origin, but even those scraps of information offer a useful starting place. All these men had surnames and often nicknames in addition. The records do not include any titles indicating noble status. In total their names—Anthony, Barthélémy, Bertrand, Casin, Étienne, Guillaume, Hugh (2), Jean (5), Pierre (3), Mathieu, Renard, and Simon—suggest mainly northern French and possibly some Italian origins, as do the surnames: Bonnart, Richon, Freppier, Chenalier, Pomier, Ferrand, Lugnet, and so on.

We learn more in examining where these men came from. Most of them hailed from neighboring dioceses rather than Troyes itself. Five men did come from Troyes, but most of the others arrived in Troyes from Langres (5), Autun (2), Châlons-en-Champagne (2), Soissons, Auxerre, and Besançon. Some of the men came from more distant parts of northern France, such as Chartres, Toul, or Laon. Burgundian origins dominate, which seems appropriate as in and out of wartime, Burgundy and Burgundians played a large role in the world of neighboring Troyes and the Champagne region. Interestingly, no English soldiers have roles in this prosecution, despite their considerable presence in the Champagne region during and for many years after the Hundred Years' War.[6] Indeed, none of the men are described as soldiers or as involved in any of the fighting. The Hundred Years' War must have a role in this story, but it is one that we trace with the greatest difficulty and scant results.

To return to the largely extradiocesan origins of the majority of the bigamists, can we make something of the fact that most of these men were not native to the diocese of Troyes? That all but five of the men came from nearby dioceses instead of Troyes itself may be significant. Can we go so far as to assume a distrust of "foreigners"? Perhaps. On the one hand, the predominance of non-Troyen bigamists seems to suggest that men not native to Troyes might be more likely targets of bigamy prosecution. Certainly, some of the synodal statutes raised explicit concern that men who came into the diocese might have left wives behind, and so these men might have been required to produce letters from their home parishes that explained their marital status.[7]

On the other hand, as we will see, the majority of these men, while born elsewhere, had been living in Troyes for several years before their prosecution for bigamy. They managed, despite their status as outsiders, to establish these marriages and to persist in them for several years before prosecution. Also, we could only arrive at any conclusions about potential discrimination with difficulty, since we cannot compare these numbers to any general picture of the population, native to Troyes or otherwise. We have no way to know how many men born outside of the diocese faced any greater or lesser trouble in their matrimonial projects than those men native to the diocese.

To be sure, five of the men prosecuted for bigamy did come from Troyes. That said, none of these men made both of their marriages in Troyes. Of these five, two of the men took first wives in Troyes but went elsewhere to make their second marriages. Three others, while native to Troyes, had made their first marriages while away from home and returned to Troyes to remarry. One of these three, Pierre de Louay, married his first wife, Colette, in a nearby diocese and took her to live with him in Troyes. She left him after a few months, and he remarried in Troyes on the false claim that she had died. She seems to have heard rumors of his plans and returned home to ask him not to remarry, but he remarried nevertheless and only faced prosecution seven years later.[8]

I would suggest that we should not necessarily assume that prejudice against outsiders was at work. Instead, I think we have more clear evidence that in Troyes, and perhaps also in neighboring dioceses, those who wished to remarry despite being already married to a living spouse did not linger close to that first spouse. More precisely, these men tended to distance themselves from both the first wife and the site of the previous marriage before they remarried. We can perhaps assume that a man remarried with difficulty unless he put some distance between himself and his first wife and the site of their marriage and married life.

Having made what we can of these men's names, places of origin, and movements, what can we learn of their social standing? As to their economic status, we do not know if they were rich or poor. Three men had clerical status. One of these clerics was a barber, as was one of the laymen. Other men of the laity claimed cooper (barrelmaker) and farmer as professions, and two men were linen weavers. We do not know if these tradesmen were apprentices, journeymen, or masters, nor if the farmer had much or any land of his own to his name.

To treat each of the men whose professions we know something of in more detail, we can begin with Renaud des Maraulx, married cleric and barber.[9] Barber-surgeons trained as apprentices, and their skills were supposed to include shaving, drawing teeth, "minor" surgeries, cauterization, and especially bloodletting.[10] Members of the minor clerical orders, such as Renaud, often worked as barbers or as notaries. Canon law sought to exclude clergy, even minor clergy, from a number of professions considered "inhonesta" or "vilia officia," such as jongleur or actor or any trade that involved usury or animal carcasses.[11] The Fourth Lateran Council of 1215 forbade only clergy above the rank of subdeacon the practice of surgery.[12] Lower-ranking clerical barbers could thus both shed blood and serve as members of the clergy.

Returning to the question of Renaud's status beyond his membership in the clergy, he seems neither noble nor altogether ordinary. Whatever the "des" implied about his status, "maraulx" could mean vagabond. In this context, especially as Renaud is further described as the son of Thomas des Maraulx, of Moselme, we can probably assume that the name did not mean that he or his father were vagabonds, at least, even as we should hesitate to go so far as to attribute noble status. Nevertheless, Renaud is certainly the only bigamist and one of very few men in these records whose father is named, which suggests at the very least the importance or at least significance of his parentage, if not necessarily nobility.

The account of Renaud's first marriage implies neither noble nor vagabond status. In 1450 or so he had married a woman of Mussy l'Evêque in the diocese of Langres and lived with her there, presumably exercising his trade as a barber and raising four children, three boys and a girl. Then he left (we are not told why) and went to the village of Courtisot in the diocese of Châlons-en-Champagne. Once there he claimed his name was Jean Juignet and married Marie, the daughter of the deceased Colin Coulon, at the Church of the Blessed Mary of the Thorns in Courtisot. That Renaud felt it was necessary to change his name certainly suggests that he had some concern that even in Courtisot he might have had to conceal his identity to successfully remarry. He was not, however, successful for long. A year later, Renaud faced arrest and prosecution in Troyes.

Did he continue in his trade as barber or in his status as a cleric for the short time he spent in Courtisot with Marie? Could he, in fact, practice his trade or even claim his clerical status under a false name and in a new diocese? If we could answer these questions we might press closer toward an understanding of how these men could or could not fully create new and successful lives for themselves after leaving their wives and their identities behind. Unfortunately, our sources do not help us here.

We learn nothing further on the subject of the profession of barbers as practiced in Troyes, nor of any possible relationship to the crime of bigamy, by looking to the case of the other barber turned bigamist, the layman Mathieu Rucin.[13] Mathieu hailed from the locale furthest from Troyes of any of the bigamists, Vendôme, in the diocese of Chartres. In the early 1440s Mathieu had come to live in Sézanne in the diocese of Troyes with his wife, Jeanette, and stayed with her for three years. If he was practicing his trade or not, we do not know. Then, Mathieu attempted a remarriage in Sens, where his first wife surprised him in the act. He next attempted to flee the first wife and keep the second, traveling to Orléans, Paris, and Verdun, and was ultimately arrested. This account gives us nothing by way of information about his status, wealth, or attachment to the practice of his trade.

What of the two linen weavers, Pierre Chenalier and Jean Freppier? We know that their profession did not have the highest artisanal status and ranked lower, for example, than that of wool weaver.[14] We know also that the profession of linen weaving often included women among its ranks.[15] As for these two men, we do not know how well established either man was, or if they were masters or journeymen. Both may have apprenticed in the neighboring diocese of Toul, birthplace of Jeanne d'Arc and a part of the Holy Roman Empire until 1552. Apprentices in Toul or not, both men certainly made their first marriages there. Pierre came from the city of Troyes originally, and Jean from Dammartin, in the diocese of Toul.

We do not know when Pierre Chenalier first arrived in the diocese of Toul.[16] Perhaps he had apprenticed himself there to a linen weaver or had already received his training before he left Troyes and came to Toul in search of a new position. We do know that in 1452 or so, Pierre had married Isabelle, the daughter of Jean le Maulvaix, of Chemin in the diocese of Toul, in Graffigny, a town a few miles from Chemin. As stated above, linen weaving was far from an exclusively masculine profession. Did Isabelle herself weave? Or her father? We do not know that, but we know that Isabelle and Pierre had a son and a daughter. Then, in 1457, Pierre returned to his home diocese of Troyes, where in the town of Fontvannes he married Jacquette, the daughter of the deceased Jehan Jehanart. In traveling to Fontvannes Pierre placed some hundred miles between himself and his first family. Could Jacquette have been a weaver or perhaps the daughter of a master weaver, and would the remarriage have helped Pierre pursue his profession in Fontvannes? This scenario is certainly possible, but we cannot assume so far with what little information we have.

As for the weaver Jean, he was born in Dommartin[17] in the diocese of Toul.[18] In 1440, Jean first married Marguerite, the daughter of Jean Gigny. The couple lived together in Doulevant-le-Château, a town near the "border" of the diocese of Troyes whose chateau served as host to the marauding raiders who had provoked Jeanne d'Arc to visions.[19] Between 1440 and 1462 Jean and Marguerite had ten children, of whom six still lived in 1463. In 1462, however, Jean left his wife and their children and married a new wife, a widow, in Preize, a town just north of Troyes and roughly twenty miles from Doulevant-le-Château. Once more, could the widow Jeanne have been a linen weaver or the widow of a master weaver? Unfortunately for our purposes here, it was the crime of bigamy and not the professional exploits of these men that interested the official in Troyes.

As for that bigamy, once more we are left wondering how and why this remarriage happened. When Pierre Chenalier left his wife in Toul and returned to Troyes, did he know that he could find and marry a second wife? Had Jean known either the widow or the town of Preize before he went there and married her? The sentence describes Jean as "continually" residing with Marguerite, his first wife, up to 1462, when he left her and married the widow Jeanne in Preize. If he had not known Jeanne before, however, he seems to have managed to find, woo, and win her in a short period of time, as his arrest and sentencing took place less than a year after his departure from Marguerite and their children.

What of the farmer, the "agricole" Simon Lugnet? Could he have had land of his own or was he a more itinerant farm laborer? He certainly may have owned land, or at least had land that he had worked on and might have invested in and had some attachment to. If so, he did manage to leave it, once his wife had left him.

Simon was from Rumilly-les-Vaudes, in the diocese of Troyes.[20] In 1444 he married one Agnès, the daughter of Jean Marrey, of Neuville-sur-Seine, in the city of Dijon in the diocese of Langres. The couple settled in Bar-sur-Aube, also in Langres, and lived together there for seven years, giving birth to a daughter. Agnès then left Simon and ran away to Metz with a tailor called Paset Galon. We never hear from Agnès again. Some time after her departure, Simon also left Bar-sur-Aube. Crossing into the neighboring diocese of Troyes, he spent seven years in Rumilly, where presumably some work was to be had. After that, he moved on to Vauds, also in the same diocese, where he contracted marriage with Margot, a widow of Vauds. Simon and Margot had four children before his arrest on suspicion of bigamy. On the whole, we have too little information, it seems, to offer any generalizations about these men's social or professional status. Some had education, skills, and a trade; some, perhaps, did not. Our ability to assess the impact of any of this upon their bigamous behavior and prosecution is tenuous.

One matter on which we have considerably more information is the two marriages themselves, the heart of the matter. In every case at least something is said as to where and how each of the marriages took place. The first marriages almost all seem to have been celebrated at the doors of a church and in the presence of a parish priest. So too were many of the second marriages. This solemnity and publicity certainly facilitated the court's efforts in establishing that a marriage had taken place and roughly when it had taken place. That so many of these marriages happened in at least outward compliance with the synodal statutes that demanded publicity, banns, and the participation of a priest has a good deal of significance in its own right. The details of these marriages, the degree of ecclesiastical involvement and publicity of these marriages, is explored in more detail in Chapter 4, "Why Commit Bigamy?"

If the bigamists almost all married with some solemnity and publicity, we find fewer common trends in the number of years they spent with a first wife before finding a second. The first marriages almost all took place several years before remarriage and prosecution. Seven of the first marriages had happened fifteen to twenty-seven years prior to prosecution, and eight marriages took place ten to fourteen years before prosecution. The remaining five first marriages occurred between three and six years before prosecution.

These first marriages quite often lasted many years before one spouse or the other left the marriage. We find, however, no evidence for a "seven-year itch" or any other such "typical" year for the ending of the first marriages. The range of years is broad and sparse, with no more than two or three marriages lasting the same number of years. Three marriages fell apart after eight months or less. One marriage lasted about two years, and four marriages lasted four or five years. Two marriages lasted seven years. One marriage lasted eight years; another lasted nine years, one lasted ten, another lasted twelve, one fourteen, one twenty, and one more than twenty years. The weaver Jean Freppier, out of all the bigamists, seems to have stayed longest with his first wife. He married her before 1440 and stayed with her until 1462. During that time they had ten children, of whom six still lived in 1463. In 1462, however, Jean had left his wife and their children.

As for the second marriages, their duration seems to have been largely determined by the date of prosecution, as all of the marriages, or cohabitation and adultery, as the court usually described it, seem to have continued up to the time of arrest. The time spent in a second marriage ranges from 11 years to 4 months, with no discernible trends save that over time the court seems to have detected bigamous relationships with more speed than previously, which must say more about changes in the court than about these marriages.

The claimed duration of these marriages offers some puzzles but also an interesting result concerning the group identity of the men. It must be said, however, that calculating the time each husband spent with each of his two wives, and the length of time in between the two marriages, is an imperfect art at best. We have only the information provided to the court, and the court seems to have been satisfied with whatever numbers were offered to them, however occasionally improbable. There does not seem to have been any effort to straighten out chronologies that did not add up. To offer one of the more puzzling examples, we can look to the case of Jean "le Gros" Jehan and his first wife, Perrette, who seem to have parted by mutual consent and then each remarried, only to be prosecuted together for their respective acts of bigamy.[21] They claimed to have married twelve years before the prosecution, which took place in 1448. They parted, or so the sentence reads, after four years of marriage. The husband was to have spent eleven years married up to the time of his arrest. That would have required as short time to find and marry his second spouse but could have been possible. His first wife, more plausibly, was to have been married to her second husband for seven years before her arrest. We can perhaps assume that the eleven years of marriage is the number most likely to be correct, as most recent, but as to the four years of marriage cited in the sentence or the first marriage having been entered into twelve years before, claimed by both individuals, we cannot say if one or both might be off by at least a few years.

In short, these numbers, I think, must all be taken as rather vague, or even quite vague. They must have been of some importance to the court, however, as every man's confession included some reference to the duration of each marriage, but the exact number of years married does not seem to have been a crucial issue. Most important, probably, was how clearly it could be established that a first marriage had in fact taken place and that it had taken place before the second marriage.

Taking the information on these marriages as offered in the sentences, we can seek out another clue that helps us to understand something of the identity of these bigamists. By counting these years, however vaguely and seemingly improbably presented in the sentences, we can acquire an idea of the ages of these men, which turns out to have considerable significance. While the ages of these men at the time of their sentencing are not given, we can make some assumptions if we count up the number of years they were supposed to have spent married to both wives before prosecution. What we find, on the whole, suggests that these men were mature, above all if we assume that most of them married for the first time at twenty, which is a safe and low assumption for this region of Europe.[22]

Seven of these men married their first wives roughly fifteen to twenty-seven years before the date of prosecution. These could not have been young men. If we assume they first married at twenty on average, or even at the more unlikely age of fifteen, they were at the very least thirty or forty years old, or probably even older at the time of their prosecutions. If the men first married in their mid- to late twenties, which is closer to what we would expect, then they were at least forty, probably fifty or fifty-five, and possibly even over sixty at the time of prosecution. Seven more men had first married ten to fifteen years prior to sentencing. We thus find once more men who might have been at the youngest in their thirties or perhaps twenties, if they had married their first wives at exceptionally young ages.

Indeed, unless there is some reason to suppose that the people of Troyes violated the usual northern European marriage age pattern, these fourteen men may well have all been over forty or fifty years old. The remaining five men, who had first married three to six years before the sentence, could have been in their twenties or thirties.

I suggest that the age of these men, however vague our sense of it, sheds some important light on these prosecutions. If they were not young, it is not reckless and defiant youth that the community and court of Troyes chose to prosecute in this spectacular fashion, but older men. These mature adult men may have in fact seemed more deficient in their standing as good Christians than a flighty young man who affianced himself to three women in as many months. These nineteen mature men had almost all abandoned first marriages of some significant duration. Given the chance, they seem to have treated the second marriages with considerable seriousness as well.

In any case, before the revelation of a bigamous past, many of these men may have seemed quite respectable and responsible in their second marriages, which may well have made their fraudulence all the more offensive. Before the bigamy came to the attention of the court and the community, they had looked as if they were behaving as husbands should behave. In reality, however, most had left behind other marriages and other wives. As we shall see, however, even those whose first wife had done the abandoning of their marital domicile were considered to have failed to live up to the expectations fifteenth-century northern French Christian society set for husbands. A man whose wife left him had failed in his responsibilities and had failed even further if he could not succeed in gaining her return. Seeking out a new wife in a new place, however well he might have treated her, only added fraud and the mistreatment of another woman and any children they might have to his failures. The maturity of these men may well have contributed a great deal toward their prosecution. Before we examine that point in further detail, there is a final feature of their criminal behavior we should study: the fraudulent actions these men engaged in that allowed, for a time, these bigamous marriages.

To explore this fraud in more detail, let us now examine precisely how these mature married men, these artisans, clerics, and journeymen, went about making their second marriages. The many ways in which these men set about breaking the law were not always described in any detail in the records. Where present, however, this information serves as a crucial element in the court's understanding of their behavior as criminal and as a criminal distortion of Christian identity. Indeed, these men almost all sought, one way or another, to distort their identity.

These nineteen men went about making the second, illegal marriages in a variety of ways. When they remarried in Troyes, as most of them did, a judicial apparatus, which seems to have at least sometimes served to prevent such marriages, stood in their way. As mentioned in the first chapter, synodal legislation in Troyes ordered parish priests to investigate carefully the background of any "strangers" hoping to marry in their parishes. These strangers should have been asked to prove that no prior marriage or other impediment threatened the validity of the match. Such proof could have taken more than one form, both written and oral.

We begin with written proofs. The synodal statutes of Troyes and of many other dioceses required proof of freedom to marry from newcomers to the diocese or from men and women with absent spouses. The statutes do not always explain what acceptable proof may have been, but they often asked for letters from the parish priest of "the foreigner." The requirement that such letters be provided was so routine that form letters for the use of parish clergy were included in a synodal statute collection of Troyes.[23] The sworn testimony of witnesses to the death of a spouse was another acceptable form of proof, one that had been designated as satisfactory in the decretals. A third type of proof occasionally accepted by the courts was a sworn oath from the aspiring spouse himself. Nowhere in the decretals or in synodal statutes from Troyes or the neighboring dioceses is a sworn oath of one's own freedom to marry described as a sufficient proof. Nevertheless, in some cases, the bishop's official accepted an oath swearing freedom to marry as sufficient proof to allow remarriage.

Some would-be bigamists may have been deterred by the requirement that they prove the death of their first spouse. But the nineteen men whose history we seek to uncover in this chapter resorted to fraud. Married men, they sought first of all to present themselves otherwise. The most common first step in the distortion of identity engaged in by these men was to claim widowed status. Interestingly, few seem to have severed themselves so completely from their past as to present themselves as single, as bachelors. Instead, they largely claimed that they had been married, but that their wives had died.

For example, around 1400, Casini, called "le Noble" of Challey-sur-Marne in the diocese of Soissons (Chailly-en-Brie), had contracted espousals and then marriage *in facie ecclesie* with Jeanette Rouselle, of La Ferté Bernard (Sarthe), in the city of Chartres.[24] Abandoning that marriage some dozen years later, Casini traveled to Nogent-sur-Seine, in the diocese of Troyes, and contracted espousals with Melina, the daughter of Jean le Seurre of Conflans-sur-Seine (Marne), in the diocese of Troyes. At this point, Casini was asked for proof of freedom to marry. He went to the city of Troyes and swore an oath before the bishop's official that nothing impeded his marriage. Permitted to marry Melina, he stayed with her up to the time of his arrest in 1425.

Similarly, in 1448 Jean le Nieps, a cooper from Rongueil, in the diocese of Langres, made his first marriage *in facie ecclesie* in the village of Chevigney, also in the diocese of Langres.[25] Jean's wife was one Ginotte, the daughter of

Guillaume le Roy of Chevigney. Jean stayed there with her for 22 months or more, and they had two children together. Afterward, in 1450, he left her and swore an oath in the city of Troyes that Ginotte had died. Thus falsely claiming that he was free from any prior marriage bonds, Jean married Perrette, the daughter of Jean Motian. He had a daughter with Perrette and stayed with her for about sixteen months. Thereafter, exceptionally, Jean returned to Ginotte and spent six days living and sleeping with her. No other bigamist studied here seems to have done so. In any case, Jean did not stay long. After those six days, Jean returned to his second wife, "as a dog returns to its vomit," and stayed with Perrette until his arrest.

While some bigamists swore a false oath that they were free to marry, other men produced witnesses who lied on their behalf. These bigamists may have needed third-party witnesses because the official would not accept their own oath. It is also possible that they were reluctant to perjure themselves, preferring to find others willing to lie for them.[26] Here, in any case, are two examples of men who made use of false witnesses in their efforts to prove their freedom from existing marriage bonds.

In the case of Pierre de Louay, alias Galey, also described above, Pierre was asked to provide proof of his freedom to marry before he would be granted permission to marry with ecclesiastical sanction in Preize, in the diocese of Troyes. Perhaps some people in the diocese remembered the first wife Pierre had brought home with him, who had abandoned Pierre after a few months some three or four years before he began to try to remarry. In any case, Pierre complied with the request for evidence, producing witnesses who were willing to falsely swear that his first wife, Colette, had died.[27]

Étienne, called "Languedoc" of Langres, described in the first chapter, had abandoned his first wife in Langres after about ten years of marriage.[28] He then set out to contract a second marriage to a widow of Bouilly, in the diocese of Troyes. Instead of looking into whether his wife was still living or not, Étienne found witnesses willing to give false testimony that she had died.[29] Indeed, it seems likely that he knew she was alive, as he had abandoned her not long before his arrival in Troyes, where he began his efforts to remarry. Successful for a time, he lived with his second wife for three years before he was caught and imprisoned. For this perjury, for suborning witnesses, for his many offenses against matrimony, and for deceiving his second would-be wife, his crimes were to be punished, along with nullification of the second marriage, by one day of public exposure and six months of imprisonment.

Offering false testimony and swearing false oaths did not exhaust the repertoire of fraudulent tactics used by these resourceful bigamists. Another tactic was to assume a false name. This stratagem was one of the devices used by Renaud des Maraulx in his efforts at bigamy.[30] Renaud, whose professional and social status we explored above, had married one Denise about ten years before his sentencing and had lived with her in the diocese of Langres for five years. During that time they had four children, Jean, Jeanne, Clément, and another Jean. Afterward, Renaud abandoned his wife and traveled to the village of Courtisot in the diocese of Châlons-en-Champagne, where he changed his name. Renaud now called himself Jean Juignet, having already established an affinity for that name in the names he had chosen for his children. After the adoption of this pseudonym, Renaud contracted and solemnized a marriage with one Marie at the Church of Blessed Mary of the Thorns, in the parish of Courtisot. Four months later he was arrested and imprisoned.

A layman, Antoine Bonnart, also changed his name in the course of his efforts to find and marry a new spouse.[31] Born in St. Martin de Campis, in the diocese of Auxerre, Antoine also married his first wife there but then abandoned her after only three months of marriage. Antoine left the diocese and changed his name to Jean Bourdon of Blaigineau. He moved to the town of St. Leonard in the diocese of Troyes, where he contracted marriage with solemnities.

As we have seen, a number of men made false oaths or bribed or otherwise encouraged witnesses to give false testimony in their efforts to prove their freedom and fitness to marry in a new diocese. Another strategy was to bribe clergymen to assist with necessary proofs or with the ceremony itself. Clergymen with enough Latin could, for a price, produce false documents attesting to the death of a spouse or the freedom to marry. An aspiring bigamist might also seek the complicity of clergy in the performance of a marriage ceremony. Rather than provide fraudulent proofs, a bigamist might pay a bribe to a priest or chaplain to bless a marriage without requiring any proof that the couple was free to contract. The complicity of parish priests, chaplains, and other members of the clergy must have abetted a number of illegal marriages, even as other clergy required the proofs that would-be bigamists had to find means to provide. Bribed with wine, cheese, or gold pieces, a poor rural priest or a city chaplain might agree to bend the rules and dispense with the formalities and inquiries that ought to accompany every marriage that they blessed and celebrated *in facie ecclesie*.

For example, Barthélémy Bouvier, of Troyes, compromised two chaplains in his efforts at committing bigamy.[32] Having married one Paquette Gareva in 1444 in Autun, he had four children with her, of whom two survived. He then took Paquette to Orléans and abandoned her there. On arrival in his hometown, the village of Fontvannes in the diocese of Troyes, he claimed that his wife had died and sought to marry Jeannette, the widow of Jacques LeClerc and evidently a widow of some means. Here, however, Barthélémy's way was barred, as the official of Troyes became involved, refusing to accept Barthélémy's oath and requiring proof of the death of Barthélémy's first wife.

As we saw earlier, in other cases the court official accepted an oath as a substitute for written proof or witness testimony.[33] Barthélémy's offer to swear an oath, however, was refused. We are given no reason for this refusal, unfortunately, but Barthélémy's subsequent behavior certainly justified the official's response.

Needing proof of the death of his first wife and unable to convince the official of Troyes to accept his oath, Barthélémy traveled to the diocese of Sens, where he bribed a chaplain with wine and cheese to forge letters attesting to the death of his wife. It is unclear if Barthélémy tried to use the letters in Troyes. It seems that he may have suspected that the court would not have accepted the letters as valid proof. Perhaps Barthélémy had gotten as good a letter as he had paid for.

Still leery of his chances in Troyes, Barthélémy then took Jeannette to the diocese of Auxerre, where he bribed a second chaplain with a gold écu to marry them in secret in his chapel. These precautions, however, did not prevent Barthélémy's first wife, Paquette, from coming to look for him. She confronted Barthélémy and claimed him as her husband. He responded by publicly declaring that he did not know her and that she was not his wife, and that if he had ever slept with her it was only as a prostitute or a concubine. He then privately acknowledged Paquette as his wife and offered to bribe her with some of Jeanette's property if Paquette would swear that she had been his maid and not his wife.

As the case of Barthélémy shows, some of these bigamists not only bribed witnesses and clergy but also—if rarely—their first wives. Barthélémy's case allows us the opportunity to observe instances of fraud and bribery, as well as some nasty treatment of a first wife. One other man, Mathieu Rancin, does not seem to have bribed any priests or first wives, but like Barthélémy he similarly denied his marital status and claimed that his accuser—his wife—might only have been known to him as a concubine or a whore.

These two confrontations, the only cases we know of in which the abandoned wives came looking for their errant husbands, offer extreme examples of caddish acts of fraud and rejection of responsibility toward a first wife. That both men are alleged to have rejected their first wives in the same manner, with the same language, is curious to be sure. Certainly their denial may have had some truth to it, aside, of course, from the claim not to know the woman at all. We know only too well how vague and complex marital status was in many cases, and these men may well not have considered themselves married to their first wives, even if the court ultimately decided otherwise. In any case, such a public rejection of a spouse after years of marriage certainly seems gratuitously cruel.

Indeed, some of these men seem to deserve a description as swindler or adventurer, or at least inconstant and seemingly unfeeling. In one example, Bertrand, called Bourroche, a barrelmaker from the town of Moselme, in the diocese of Langres, had first married sixteen years before, around 1410.[34] At that time he had married Alison, the widow of Colin de Boyes, at the doors of a church in the city of Troyes. Bertrand and Alison stayed together in Troyes for fourteen years, after which he took Alison to live in Verdun with him. Once there, Bertrand and his wife both fell ill, an illness that kept Bertrand in bed for about three months. He recovered and left his wife behind, who was herself lying prostrate in bed. Bertrand then returned to Troyes and claimed that Alison had died. Worse yet, as the record proclaimed, Bertrand claimed that both she and their daughter had died of plague. A reasonable assumption, perhaps, but not one that reflects the sort of behavior one might hope for from a husband and father.

All this said, we might expect that fraud, abandonment, and efforts to distort identity were the behaviors that set apart these men's crimes as deserving of public punishment and incarceration. The degree of fraud, however, and even which spouse abandoned the other first—husband or wife—seemed to play no discernible role in determining the severity of the punishment—that is, the number of days on the scaffold and the number of months of imprisonment meted out by the court.[35] All these nineteen men had done damage enough just by acting as if they were free to remarry when in fact they were not, and they knew they were not. Moreover, and as the next chapter will show, women who similarly sought to change their identities, who offered the court false or at least dubious witness to their status as widows, did not meet the same end as did these bigamous husbands.

In sum, we can identity only three characteristics that these men shared. They were all bigamous, male, and more mature than youthful in years. These men were mostly but not all exclusively "foreign" to the diocese, and in any case the prosecution often took place only after many years of residence. Finally, these men often but not always engaged in considerable fraud to remarry. Why, then, did the officiality of Troyes attribute such importance to prosecuting these men? Why was it so important to the court that these husbands face public punishment on the ladder of the scaffold?

Here it is important to insist that the officiality of Troyes and the community it served, whose denunciations and rumors the court acted upon, seem to have identified the crime of bigamy with male behavior. It is men, and not women, who were convicted of the more serious forms of criminal remarriage. It is men, and not women, who were subjected to public punishment on the ladder of the scaffold. That male bigamists, and only male bigamists, found themselves made public example of in this way is of great significance. It was their behavior, and not that of bigamous women, that required this public display of punishment to expiate the sense of sin and scandal such marriages provoked in the community.

It seems, then, that the officiality of Troyes, and perhaps the community of Troyes as a whole, set high standards for what they considered appropriate husbandly behavior. Husbands whose marital habits violated these norms faced denunciation, prosecution, and conviction for bigamy. To better understand this behavior, it is helpful to look to a variety of sources: comparative evidence from the social history of other regions; and the contemporary culture, as found in sermons and devotional literature, as well as in prose romance and even popular stories. Indeed, a number of scholars have identified the fifteenth century as a period in which theologians, judges, and even writers of romance literature seemed to call for higher standards for husbands' conduct.

Let us begin with the evidence of comparative social history. The treatment of husbands in Troyes is not without its contemporary parallels. Consider fifteenth-century England, for example, as investigated by Shannon McSheffrey. In studying marriage litigation and the prosecution of sexual offenses in England, McSheffrey identifies a heightened sense of importance attributed to male—and especially husbands'—morality. She links this emphasis on male morality to communal values of patriarchy, governance, and reputation. As part of the patriarchal system of fifteenth-century England, McSheffrey argues, men, and especially husbands, had a duty to govern and to set an example by their own behavior, in which sexual morality, meaning marital chastity, played an important role.[36] In this context, a wife's adultery certainly mattered, but it could reflect as negatively on her husband's character as on her own, if not even more so: "while it was the wife who committed the sin of adultery, the insult highlighted the husband's inability to control and govern her."[37] Although the prosecution of wives found guilty of adultery persisted in the fifteenth century, McSheffrey also points to a number of cases in which husbands, rather than wives, husbands both rich and poor, were prosecuted and imprisoned for adultery.[38]

A similar fifteenth-century moral economy, setting high standards for

Christian husbands, has also been described by Leah Otis-Cour, in her work on southern France. Otis-Cour argues that fifteenth-century handling of adultery in Toulouse marked a decisive shift away from previous practice. Prior to the fifteenth-century, adultery prosecutions largely involved only the prosecution of wives as adulteresses, while husbands committed adultery without risk of judicial punishment.[39] Beginning in the fifteenth century, however, husbands also faced prosecution for adultery. In fact, they may have been prosecuted even for adultery committed with an unmarried woman, not only for adultery committed with a married woman. Moreover, Otis-Cour finds that couples and families increasingly handled wives' adultery as a private family matter, favoring reconciliation over judicial or extrajudicial punishment and publicity. These inhabitants of the south of France seem to have shared with their contemporaries in fifteenth-century England the sense that an act of female adultery reflected the failures of her husband and her family. With such an understanding of adultery, husbands and families preferred to conceal the matter and handle it privately rather than expose their failure to prevent this adultery to the community by means of public prosecution and punishment.

It seems, then, that at least in the realm of morality and moral offenses men, especially husbands, more often faced prosecution and punishment than in prior centuries. However, this fifteenth-century emphasis on the primacy of husbands as heads of household did not necessarily always have a negative impact on these men. In fifteenth-century royal French court prosecutions, husbands and fathers might also enjoy advantages as a result of their status as such. Here we can turn to the work of Claude Gauvard. In her analysis of royal justice in Paris, Gauvard finds evidence of this interest in shielding husbands and fathers from more severe punishment in the later Middle Ages. Gauvard found that married men with children stood a much better chance of being forgiven their crimes than bachelors. Gauvard associates this interest in forgiving husbands and fathers with the state's interest in keeping those men alive and out of prison, in hopes that they would find (better) means of supporting their families.[40]

Such status as husband with wife and children certainly was little help, however, to the bigamists convicted in Troyes. Indeed, their offenses seem to have been considered more reprehensible than adultery alone, and more offensive than similar acts committed by married women. To ask once more, why was so much being asked of these husbands—and more, indeed, than was asked of their wives?

Cultural sources offer another useful means to explore this question. Like the findings from English and southern French courts, romance literature of the Burgundian court offers yet another example of evidence for new standards for good husbandly behavior in the later Middle Ages. As Rosalind Brown-Grant explains, fifteenth-century Burgundian romances called upon men to be good husbands as they had never before been asked in French romance.[41] Husbands reading fifteenth-century romances would learn that they were expected to act as upright Christian husbands just as much as twelfth- and thirteenth-century wives had been called upon to observe the models of good wives in twelfth-century French romances. How to explain this development? Brown-Grant has argued that these new standards for married male behavior can be linked to the preaching efforts of clerics such as Jean Gerson, whose sermons contributed to this new development in the field of medieval romance, as cultivated in the court of Burgundy.[42]

Can looking to sermons, such a fruitful means for unpacking the meanings and lessons of fifteenth-century Burgundian romance, also help us to understand the prosecution of male bigamy in Troyes? Can these sermons help us to understand what expectations for husbandly behavior were, and why the bigamous husbands' behavior was considered such a gross violation?

Let us examine these sermons. When presenting models to follow for husbands, whom did preachers put forward as an example? What qualities did these model saints exemplify in the preachers' vision of a perfect husband and father? One natural place to look is to the writings of Jean Gerson, one of the most influential writers of sermons in the fifteenth century, whose sermons remained popular and important guides for preaching long after his death. The celebrated Gerson also has a place in our inquiry as a *champaignois* who rose to be chancellor of the Collège de Navarre in Paris, where so many of the Troyes ecclesiastical officials received their training in theology.

Studying the sermons of Gerson, we find ourselves, once again, in the world of biblical theology. For Gerson, the ideal husband was none other than Saint Joseph, husband of the Virgin Mary and "adopted" father of Jesus. Prior to Gerson's efforts, Joseph had a shoddy reputation as a saint in northern France. Previously, artists had depicted Joseph as an old man standing in the shadows of his glowing holy family. Joseph, as cuckolded by God Himself, was often depicted as so old as to presumably be incapable of sexual intercourse, to make the point more clearly. In short, Joseph was something of a figure of ridicule before Gerson and others championed his cause.[43]

This idea of Joseph would change, however, and had begun changing even before Gerson took up the cause of the promotion of Saint Joseph. David Herlihy recognized the developing importance in medieval culture of Joseph as self-denying husband, as ideal husband and father; now the goal was "taming men to become like Joseph," as Susan Mosher Stuard wrote.[44] A husband had obligations to preserve a wife's dowry and to look after her interests generally: "Because a man was a husband, he bore responsibility for both."[45]

Beginning in the early fifteenth century, plagued by the Hundred Years' War and the struggle between the Orléans and Burgundian factions, Gerson began to write and preach on Saint Joseph.[46] Gerson argued that husbands should follow Saint Joseph and, as did Joseph for the Virgin Mary, "have such love, such faith and loyalty toward their spouses, and love them, nourish them, and protect them."[47] Gerson depicted Joseph as a just man and protector of his spouse, whose discretion and good faith helped him. When hearing of the virgin birth, he sought to protect her reputation. All spouses, Gerson urged, should follow this example and remain together in spite of false rumor or doubts.

If the choice of Saint Joseph as model husband seems strange to us, a seemingly curious choice of model spouse or parent is not at all without precedent in the Middle Ages. Abraham, who expelled from his home one son and nearly sacrificed the other—albeit on God's orders—often served as the model father in medieval imagery, especially between 1150 and 1250.[48] The patriarchs and saints chosen as models in the Middle Ages often offered such deeply ambiguous lessons. This ambiguity aptly reflected the often complex and contradictory position of married and parental Christians, with the rights and obligations they owed each other, their neighbors and lords, their churchmen, and God.

If Saint Joseph supplanted Abraham as model husband and father (or one or the other), we can perhaps begin to understand how Joseph, who did not sleep with his concubine or even his wife and who did not pretend his wife was his kin on his travels in Egypt, as, of course, did Abraham, might be taken as a better model for ideal Christian husbandly behavior.

However strange the interest in Joseph as a model seems, it marks an important change in medieval perceptions of Joseph. In this new order, Joseph was no longer to appear as the elderly cuckold, a marginal and comical figure in the trinity of the Holy Family. Instead, Joseph is to be revered as a great, generous patriarch, the earthly father of Christ and the husband of Christ's mother, Mary, first among women. This was not a matter for scorn but for admiration and even emulation.

As presented by Gerson, Saint Joseph was in fact the perfect Christian husband: self-denying, raising God's child as his own, and not ever consummating his marriage (nor indulging in any extramarital liaisons). It is an awful lot to ask of a husband. Now Christian husbands could of course sleep with their wives when they wished, and indeed essentially had to render the sexual debt to their wives upon demand. They were urged to increase and multiply their legitimate Christian offspring. But they were not supposed to sleep with anyone other than their wives. Additionally they were considered responsible for the behavior of their wives and their children. It was their responsibility to keep their wives at home, to prevent them from straying to other men or to less than respectable wifely behavior.

In being instructed to act like Saint Joseph, husbands had quite a lot to live up to. If Saint Joseph was in fact the model for a good husband, we can certainly understand that mature adult male bigamists in particular fell far short of the mark. And indeed, court records do seem to reflect an attitude that resembles the promotion of Joseph as model. As we have seen, secular and ecclesiastical court records of England and southern France suggest that a husband's adultery was not tolerated to the degree that it had been in previous centuries, and that a husband might be considered responsible for his wife's adultery. If adultery and sexuality served as contested grounds for defining Christian male identity, I would argue that bigamy offered a still more stark example of behavior that was seen as firmly outside both what Christian doctrine and what popular culture might tolerate from Christian husbands. Reading these court records, then, in the context of theology and culture, reveals important lessons as to why bigamous men, why bigamous husbands, faced such relatively harsh prosecution and punishment at the hands of the Troyes officiality.

Examining the sentences passed against the nineteen bigamists revealed four important features of the nature of the crime that the officiality of Troyes prosecuted with such severity. First, almost all of the people prosecuted and punished for bigamy were male, and all of the bigamists subject to public prosecution and imprisonment were male. Examining these men as a group, all but five were outsiders, not native to the diocese. Their status as "foreign" seems to have had at least some role in their prosecution, if a smaller role than the second and third pieces of these men's collective identity that we can extract from the sentences. Third, it seems important that these men, whatever their economic or social status, were on the whole older men, mature adult married males, and as such perhaps particularly deficient in having so grossly violated their responsibilities as husbands. These were, like Joseph, mature or even old men, but they were older men who fell far short of Joseph's example. Fifteenth-century preachers and fifteenth-century culture seem to have developed new benchmarks for morality, calling for high standards for husbands, whose conduct as Christians should have followed the model of Saint Joseph.

In a sense, of course, these bigamists were trying to present themselves as upstanding men, as honorable and responsible husbands (to their second wives) on the model of Saint Joseph. However, if these men presented an outward appearance of morality, seeming to emulate Saint Joseph in marrying and staying with their second wives, they did so only fraudulently. These pseudo-Josephs sought to distort their identity, engaging in a variety of fraudulent behaviors in their efforts to take second wives. This is what emerges as a common thread in the sentences passed against them. These husbands publicly denied being married to living wives, and sometimes even publicly spurned these wives, claiming that they had never been married to these women. They were presenting themselves to their communities as good Christians. Yet such distortions of identity, such rejections of the obligations of Christian husbands, were behaviors that the officiality of Troyes found deeply offensive and deserving of public punishment and imprisonment. Husbands could not be permitted to masquerade as good Christians in a manner so contrary to the laws of Christian marriage and so alien to the standards of husbandly behavior that had come to prevail. Mature married men, who should act like Saint Joseph, could not be allowed to so violate the rules of the order of matrimony.

CHAPTER 3

Abandoned Wives

In 1448, the official of Troyes found that Perrette, the wife of Jean "le Gros" Jehan, had remarried "de facto" despite knowing her husband still lived.[1] For this crime Perrette was sentenced to one year in prison. She was the only woman, out of all the thirty-three women investigated on suspicion of bigamy, whom the Troyes officiality so punished. Meanwhile, her husband Jean, who had also bigamously remarried, was sentenced to an even harsher punishment. Jean was sentenced to both imprisonment and public punishment on the ladder of the scaffold. What can explain this difference in punishment? Why imprison only one woman for bigamy? Why punish the bigamous husband more harshly than the bigamous wife?

To answer these questions we must address the role of gender in the prosecution and punishment of bigamy in the diocese of Troyes.[2] We must examine the marital behavior of wives, just as we examined husbands' behavior in the previous chapter. Moreover, if we hope to understand both how and why married women remarried, and also how and why the community and the court responded to their actions, we must also study the cultural and social context for the behaviors of these wives. Such are my aims in this chapter, which offers a description of how women committed bigamy and how the court and community responded to their actions. In order to deepen our understanding of the circumstances and context of the court actions preserved in the archives of Troyes, I will conclude the chapter with a broad consideration of the place of women, and wives in particular, in the diocese of Troyes. As in Chapter 2, I will draw upon a wide range of cultural sources in addition to legal records.

To begin, we must try to understand the marital behavior of these women, these would-be widows. I must try to establish what precisely these wives did that attracted the attention of the court. I do so, however, under considerable constraint, working from limited sources. Suspected female bigamists appear only rarely in the records, and usually the case is only described in a few words. The fact that relatively few female bigamists show up in the records, however, does not imply that relatively few women entered into bigamous marriages. The scant offerings in the register tell us instead that the court officials in Troyes do not appear to have found many women whose behavior, to their minds, called for prosecution, and especially punishment, as bigamists.

Indeed, as we will see, this court focused far more on regulating the marital behavior of potentially bigamous husbands than that of bigamous wives. Even on the rare occasions that a bigamous wife came before the court, court officials concerned themselves as much—and even more—with the men involved in her remarriage. Would-be husbands, suborned witnesses, and priests all often shared in the punishment of a bigamous wife. Moreover, in many cases the bigamous wife herself was not punished at all. Meanwhile, the second wives of bigamous men almost never faced fines or other penalties for having married or affianced themselves to a man with a living wife. In short, female bigamy did not greatly provoke the court. When cases of female bigamy did come before the court, men often received a considerable share of the blame.

To be sure, the court was not completely tolerant of female bigamy. The court did investigate and prosecute bigamous wives in and of Troyes, and many of these women the court punished with fines and, on one occasion, even imprisonment. But there were other, considerable consequences as well. If the court found a living husband, the bigamous second marriage was dissolved. If the court could not clearly establish the status of an absent first husband, the second marriage might be suspended, placed on hold as a union that would become recognized as a marriage if it could be proven that a first husband had died before the marriage took place. Until the missing man's status was known, the bigamous wife and her would-be husband were left in a sort of limbo, required to live apart with no recognized marriage. Sometimes the court further ordered that neither could marry other spouses without proof that the absent first husband lived or had died. The court handled the marriages of bigamous men in much the same way.

Out of the hundred cases examined in these chapters, in only thirty-three cases was the suspected bigamist a woman. The quantitative difference between number of men and women prosecuted alone reflects a predominance of male suspects (67/100). The difference is magnified, however, in a qualitative context: only Perrette faced a prison sentence. The court punished the rest of the women with fines ranging from a pound of wax to 100 sous.[3]

The greatest difference lies in the use of punishment, the terms of imprisonment, and in particular the use of the ladder of the scaffold as a tool of public punishment. The court did not make a public example of any of the wives it prosecuted. These women's crimes did not somehow call, as did those of nineteen bigamous husbands and one bigamous monk, for public punishment. This distinction, this exclusion of female bigamists from the scaffold, was made so starkly by the court that it excluded the bigamous wife, Perrette, while exposing her bigamous husband, Jean. However much of the year of imprisonment Perrette may have served, her punishment, and that of the other wives, was not in public.

In determining the appropriate punishment for an offender, the Troyes officiality applied the notion of public crimes. So-called public crimes called for public punishment, recompense for the scandal caused in the community.[4] The Troyes official subjected a number of men to punishment on the ladder for such public crimes: not only for bigamy but also for blasphemy, perjury, heresy, and brigandage committed by members of the clergy.[5] They also used the scaffold in condemning one woman, convicted of idolatry, to public burning at the stake.[6] The absence of public punishment for bigamous wives suggests that the court did not see these wives' behavior as public crimes. The bigamous husbands had committed public crimes, but somehow the bigamous wives had not. A key task of this chapter is to explain why. How, if at all, did these wives remarry in less scandalous or public a manner than did bigamous husbands? Indeed, in what ways, if any, did the female behavior differ from male behavior? Or was it that female bigamy, no matter how publicly celebrated, was regarded as less of an offense to the public communal order?

Certainly a difference in behavior, in the kind of bigamy committed by these wives, as opposed to that of the husbands, would explain a difference in punishment. Based on what little evidence we have for female bigamy, however, we have no reason to suppose that the bigamous marriages of the wives were somehow less criminal or scandalous than those of the men sentenced to the stand on the ladder of the scaffold. As I will argue, the exclusion of wives from the public scaffold implies not that women remarried in different, less criminal ways than men but rather that the court distinguished between seemingly similar activities based upon the gender of the actor. In fact, if the records of the officiality of Troyes offer a window on the values of court and community, the diocese of Troyes had strikingly different expectations for how husbands and wives ought to be held to account for their own conduct and that of their spouses.

When prosecuting and punishing bigamy, the Troyes officiality treated the remarried wives it encountered not as willful bigamists but as irresponsible and foolish abandoned wives. Hence the title of this chapter. In late medieval

Troyes, court and community responded differently to the same behaviors, depending on the gender of the offender. When it came to bigamy committed by women, any punishment was mitigated on account of the imbecility attributed to their sex: "infirmitas sexus."

Such "infirmity" certainly seems to have shielded women suspected of bigamy, but the court's treatment of women as weak and foolish does not fully explain the relationship of gender to bigamy prosecution and punishment. Concepts of female inferiority, to be sure, did not save the woman that the Troyes officiality condemned to burn for idolatry. Clearly there was something about the crime of bigamy in particular that led the court to treat female bigamy more leniently than male bigamy.

It is my contention that the exclusion of bigamous wives from the ladder of the scaffold offers a crucial clue. It is highly revealing that husbands like Jean "le Gros" faced public punishment while even more severely punished women like Jean's wife Perrette were not. It suggests strongly that male bigamy was regarded as more scandalous, more of a public crime. Female bigamy, then, was more of a private matter, something for the husbands and fathers of these women to handle or a matter for the confessional.

Additionally, the court and community tolerated female bigamy for another, related reason. As we saw in the last chapter, one of the main reasons male bigamy was regarded as so offensive was because it so grossly violated a man's responsibilities and obligations as husband and head of household. Female bigamy was a less egregious offense. A wife who was separated from her husband and who remarried in some ways chose a more respectable path than an abandoned wife who remained alone. Medieval society may well have preferred to see a woman enter into a potentially bigamous marriage rather than remain free, unattached, a likely candidate for prostitution, for concubinage with a parish priest, or at any event for sexual license and general license to act outside the circle of familial rights and obligations. For a woman to commit bigamy was for a woman to seek family, home, male headship. All these things medieval society might forgive its women.

Let us begin by seeing what we can learn about the women in and of Troyes whose remarriages were subject to investigation by the officiality. As a result of the court's focus on male behavior, we know almost nothing about these women and only slightly more about how they went about remarrying. Nevertheless, the court records describe, if most often only in scant detail, enough efforts at remarriage undertaken by women in and of the diocese of Troyes to offer at least a rough sketch of female bigamy as practiced there.

To return to Perrette, the court records describe her as an inhabitant of

Barbuise, in the diocese of Troyes. Perrette had married Jean, who came from Ancerville in the diocese of Châlons, about twelve years before her sentencing, *in facie ecclesie*, in Dijon. Some time afterward they went to live together in Nogent-sur-Seine. They stayed there as man and wife for four years. If any children were born during this time, the register makes no mention of them. Subsequently, or so the couple later claimed, because of the war and the incursion of troops in that area, Jean left Perrette. That people might flee troops certainly is not surprising. We are not told why they did not flee together. It appears that they decided to separate.

They also decided to remarry. First Jean, in Lorraine, married a widow called Hélène and stayed with her for eleven years and had children with her. All this time, it seems, he knew that Perrette was still alive. Meanwhile, Perrette, at the village of Malle in the diocese of Laon, married Feliset Arnoul, a man from her hometown, Barbuise. She lived with Feliset for seven years. We do not know if they lived together in Malle or in Barbuise.[7]

In any case, somehow, and indeed most mysteriously, Perrette and Jean both found themselves detained in the bishop's prison, investigated, convicted, and sentenced to punishment for their respective acts of bigamy. The fact that they were prosecuted together and yet punished differently makes their case a remarkable piece of evidence demonstrating gendered difference in the court's treatment of bigamy. The only difference we know of in their behavior is that Jean married some years before Perrette—yet they received different punishments. Why was Perrette not sentenced to public punishment on the ladder alongside her husband? Was her bigamy somehow less a public crime than his?

Nothing in the record suggests that Perrette's marital behavior was substantially different from, or substantially less blameworthy than, that of her husband Jean. We are told that she married *in facie ecclesie*, lived with her husband Jean for some years, separated from him, and "in contempt for the sacred state of matrimony" married again, staying with her second husband for seven years, up to the time of her arrest.[8] We do not know the details of how Perrette went about taking a second husband. But certainly, if she married *in facie ecclesie*, Perrette must have falsely presented herself in the diocese of Laon as free from prior marital bonds, perhaps as a widow. Even had the diocese of Laon maintained less strict rules for marriage than found in Troyes or Rouen, Perrette would have had to lie, if not necessarily to go so far as to present false testimony or false witnesses. Somehow or other, Perrette must have married under false pretenses in order to celebrate her second wedding. Moreover, after the wedding, she subsequently falsely acted as if she were the wife of another man than her first (and only legitimate) husband, Jean. However much fraud

Perrette engaged in, however many ways she distorted her identity, the court in Troyes responded by dissolving her "de facto" marriage and by sentencing her to prison. Something other than the criminality of her conduct must have motivated the court to spare her public punishment. To better understand both Perrette's case and other acts of female bigamy prosecuted in Troyes, let us see what we can deduce about other women's marital histories as recounted in the court records.

The earliest evidence we have of prosecution for female bigamy, usually described in the records as either "marriage with two men" or "marriage made with a first husband still living,"[9] dates to the second decade of the fifteenth century. In 1412, to offer a few examples, two women were ordered to pay fines of 20 and 45 sous, respectively, for having "contracted with two men."[10] What sorts of contracts? Engagements or marriages? Publicly and *in facie ecclesie* or more informally? As the registers have examples of "contracting marriage" as well as "contracting bethrothal," we do not know. The court records describe the woman allotted a fine of twenty sous as "Joanne, daughter of Colin called Houger." That the record refers to her as a daughter rather than someone's wife suggests that her contracting did not leave her bound to marry either of the men. Unfortunately, as we will see, however, the officiality offered far from clear or consistent declarations of female status in these matters. In other cases the officiality sometimes refers to women as daughters when they have not yet established for certain if a woman is married or to whom. At the same time, occasionally and inconsistently, the officiality refers to women as the widow of a certain man when the whole point in prosecuting these women was failure to prove the death of the husband in question.[11] In any case, the second woman prosecuted in 1412 was also described as a daughter rather than someone's fiancée, wife, or widow. We are left, therefore, far from any clear sense of the status of these women, what precisely these women's marital behaviors had been, and why the court decided to fine them.

Other records are at least somewhat more forthcoming. In 1414, Jeanette, the daughter of the deceased Feliet Auberon and the wife of Jean Vallet of Longsols in the diocese of Troyes, was found to have previously contracted marriage by words of the present tense with Simon Jacquet. For having made these two marriages she was assessed a fine of 60 sous. Jacob, curé of Longsols, admitted to announcing the banns for Jeannette and Jean's wedding two times at most (instead of the requisite three) and was fined 45 sous. The story that we might be able to tell about this effort at a second marriage, presumably annulled once the first marriage had been revealed, suggests that Jeannette or others sought the complicity of the curé in allowing the couple to marry with less than the full required publicity of no less than three banns in hopes of concealing the marriage from too much undesired attention.[12] Nevertheless, Jeannette certainly celebrated this second marriage publicly, and with at least some banns, and this does not as a result seem like a great deal of concealment. As we will see, publicity mattered to these women in making their marriages. Even more, marrying on the steps of a church and with a priest's blessing seemed to have held great importance for them.

Skipping ahead to the 1420s, we find one of our earliest and most detailed accounts of the efforts at remarriage made by a would-be widow. As we saw in Chapter 2, claims of widowed status appear with considerable frequency in the efforts at remarriage practiced by male bigamists, who presented themselves in new communities as widowers. This trend is also found with many of the women studied here. Abandoned women often seem to have presented themselves as widows. In fact, a woman who claimed widowed status, presenting herself in a community as a widow, is found in court records beyond Troyes as well. The abandoned wife who claimed to be a widow is found also in the archdeaconal court records of Paris.[13] As we saw in Chapter 1, wives of uncertain status, would-be widows in Paris, Rouen, and Cambrai, also sought to remarry and asked for approval from the officiality.[14]

Returning to Troyes and turning to a register of sentences beginning in 1423, we find another such case, involving one Colette, described as the widow of Jean de Feuges.[15] As recounted in the sentence passed against her, Jean, whom she had married many years before, had abandoned her. Colette is the first of many women explicitly described in the records as an abandoned wife. We do not know why Jean left her or where he had gone. We do not know if Colette or Jean's family also lived in Troyes and what support networks Colette might have drawn upon in the absence of her husband. We might assume that Colette and Jean had no children, or at least that no children survived, as they are not mentioned in the court records. We know only that Colette and Jean, wherever they had been born, had come to live and be married in Troyes, and that Jean had at some point left Colette and had not returned for some years. We do know that Colette came to the decision that she might be a widow, or at least that she might try to pass as a widow.

What would Colette stand to gain by taking on the status of a widow? What social, economic, or spiritual benefits might have arrived for Colette with the assumption of this title? We can make some guesses. To be sure, we know almost nothing about her marital property or her social status. Nevertheless, there are reasons to suppose that being a widow brought advantages in both regards. Becoming a widow, if she sought such legal status from a secular court, would have granted her the return of her dowry, if there was one, and her dower lands, if there was any such thing among her possessions. If she sought to be named a widow by an ecclesiastical court and succeeded in her efforts, she could have been granted the right to marry again, a *licentia nubiendi.* The social importance and honorable status accorded publicly married wives in late medieval Troyes was a boon for many women. To obtain license to remarry in Troyes, however, Colette would have had to prove that Jean had died. She may well in fact have done so, offering the testimony of a few witnesses or some documentary evidence, evidence that would have been intentionally fraudulent or at least ultimately found incorrect. The sentence passed against her, however, makes no mention of such efforts.

In any case, we have no reason to assume that Colette approached either secular or ecclesiastical officials to attempt to change her legal status to that of a widow. Instead, what Colette may have worked to bring about, or what may have simply happened more organically for her—without a great deal of effort on her part—was a shift in the community's perception of her marital status. Based on rumor, on the passage of time, or on some other unknown circumstances, people began to think of Colette as something other than Jean's wife, something other than the wife of a living man, their neighbor. One way or another, the community in Troyes came to regard her as a widow. It seems to have been assumed that Jean was dead, or as good as.

Colette at any rate decided to remarry, and she does not appear to have sought permission from the officiality to do so. As explained in the court records, after an unspecified number of years with no news of Jean, Colette assumed he had died and married Feliset Naalot. What was quite important was that Colette did not do so informally or in a private chapel or outside of the diocese. She does not seem to have sought to conceal her remarriage at all. Instead, this wedding took place at the doors of the church with a priest's blessing, *in facie ecclesie,* and with banns announced beforehand. Evidently, neither Jean's family nor any of Colette's neighbors nor the priest who blessed the marriage offered any opposition to the match. Jean was thought to have died, and this was accepted in the community, or at least not considered worth the trouble of making a complaint to the bishop's official. If anyone objected to Colette's behavior, no trace of this opposition remains.

However, at least as far as the law was concerned, this marriage should not have been so easily allowed. As stated in the earliest surviving synodal statutes for Troyes, promulgated in 1374: "No priest should join in marriage a woman married to an absent husband until the death of the husband, by testimony, is made clear. And the same for men whose wives are absent."[16] Nevertheless, the court records mention neither the presence nor the lack of an investigation, nor any other precautions beyond the announcement of banns. Instead, the record simply describes Colette's intent in remarriage as without fault. Colette had reasonably, or plausibly, "verissimiliter," believed her husband had died. In light of the law whose history we traced in Chapter 1, such a belief should not have satisfied Colette's priest, the community, or the officiality. Nevertheless, Colette's belief that her husband had died, and certainly her gender, seem to have shielded her from prosecution as a bigamist. As for Feliset, he claimed that he did not know Colette had a still-living husband at the time of their marriage and so had married in innocence of any wrongdoing.

But Feliset and Colette would soon lose that presumed innocence. After the celebration of nuptials, Feliset and Colette lived together for three years and had a daughter. At this point, however, the missing husband, Jean, returned to Troyes and found his wife remarried. Remarkably, Jean moved in with the couple and their child, dining and drinking together with them over a period of about fifteen days before leaving Troyes once more. While one imagines this scenario with some difficulty, that is, at any event, how the court record described Jean's return.

Certainly we find no evidence of any acrimony or conflict at all, on either side. At any rate it does not seem likely that Jean ever denounced the couple for their illegal union. We have no reason to suspect that Jean wanted to resume married life with Colette. If he had gone from Feliset and Colette's home to the bishop's official and lodged a complaint about the doings of his wife, one would assume that the official would have dissolved the second marriage and ordered the pair to separate. Additionally, the official would have required Colette to leave Feliset and resume married life with Jean. But for whatever reasons, Jean seems to have done no such thing. Whatever he wanted, he went away from Troyes after those fifteen days and was not seen again.

The court did hear rumors, however, about Jean's visit home and ordered Colette and Feliset to separate. We might suppose that a malicious or virtuous neighbor observed the visiting husband and denounced Colette. Nevertheless, Feliset and Colette somehow managed to stay together as man and wife for another five years. Perhaps the court had some distractions, more political or military than marital. Or perhaps the rumors were not sufficiently clear to provoke the court to detain Colette and Feliset and launch a full investigation against them. Perhaps the court did investigate and sanction them, but Colette and Feliset ignored these efforts and resumed life together regardless. Somehow or other, married life continued in spite of rumors and evidently weak efforts on the part of the court. At this point, Jean did die. How the court came to learn of his death, or indeed how Colette and Feliset learned Jean had died, we simply do not know.

It is soon after Jean's death that we find the couple in court again. They appeared, perhaps on their own initiative, in seeking ratification of their marriage now that Colette's husband really had died. It is also possible, if somehow less plausible, that Colette and Feliset no longer wished to live together and confessed the illegal union on their own initiative. Or finally, and most likely, a promotor had compiled enough evidence to bring a case against them. However the case came to be brought before the official, the court found the couple guilty of adultery and concubinage. Their crime was to persist in a pretense of marriage, a so-called marriage, despite knowing Jean lived. In addition to dissolving the marriage of Colette and Feliset, the court determined that the couple had incurred the impediment of crime. Such an impediment might arise when a man and a woman committed adultery and promised to marry if their spouses were to die. Interpreting the impediment of crime with some severity, the court determined that Colette and Feliset, having willfully committed adultery while Jean was alive, could never marry each other.[17] The court further punished them with the promotor's legal costs and an unspecified penance.[18]

Such heavy penalties suggest that if Colette and Feliset, had they brought the court's attention upon themselves, would have been foolhardy indeed. It is possible that they decided they wanted to expose their illegal union in order to gain a desired dissolution. Such certainly seems to have been a relatively common practice found in English and Italian records.[19] It seems unlikely, but at least possible, that Colette and Feliset could have become desperate to find a way to separate themselves, desperate enough to do so whatever the legal consequences. On the whole, it seems more probable that Colette and Feliset were more unwilling participants in the official's justice.

As a result of this court decision, Colette, the so-called widow of Jean, now his widow in fact and in law, had lost a second would-be husband, the father of her daughter. Thankfully, the court treated this daughter as legitimate. Conceived with the presumption that a valid marriage existed between the parents, the child was recognized as the legitimate daughter of Feliset and Colette, even if their marriage no longer had any legitimacy, presumed or otherwise. We might then suppose that the daughter would have kept her father's name and could expect to inherit from him as one of his heirs. It is less clear who would have had custody of the child.

All this, of course, assumes that Colette and Feliset obeyed orders to separate this time, as opposed to their defiance of the earlier warnings. However, especially considering their prior history, this need not necessarily have been the case. Depending on their economic, social, and spiritual circumstances, flight from the diocese may well been another option. Whatever judgments the court in Troyes made concerning Colette, Feliset, and their child, we cannot assume that this family obeyed orders. In any case, to our knowledge, neither Colette nor Feliset appeared before the official again.

Colette was far from the only self-designated widow whose marital designs the officiality interfered with, sooner or later. While Perrette and Colette both managed several years of married life before the dissolution of their marriages, other investigations seem to have taken place more precipitously. These cases reflect the eagerness on the part of the court to dissolve or suspend any potentially bigamous marriage. Male or female, a spouse who had remarried too hastily, without documentation or proof, might find that the court required an end to their marriage until the status of a missing first spouse was known for certain.

For example, Étienne bon Cheval and Philippa de Beaufort, first described as his wife, appeared before the official on 15 May 1456 and swore to return again before the court on the Thursday after Corpus Christi, that is, twenty days later, on penalty of excommunication and ten livres.[20] The couple did reappear on that date, and the court addressed them in different terms.[21] This time the promotor brought an action against Étienne and Philippa, now described not as Étienne's promised wife but as his fiancée. The marriage tie between Étienne and Philippa was untangling rapidly: Philippa already had a husband. The promotor accused the couple of having contracted an engagement by words of the future tense *in facie ecclesie* and having consummated their bond, all without first proving that Philippa's husband had died. The court ordered the couple to separate and fined them 20 sous each. On the same day, the court also made an entry in the register of sentences where Philippa was now described as the wife of one Jean Asseline of Ramerupt.[22] Étienne and Philippa were warned not to persist in cohabitation, adultery, and scandal, on penalty of excommunication and ten livres tournois.

Clearly, in the twenty days that passed between the first and second appearances of Étienne and Philippa, the court had established that a good deal seemed to be wrong with this near-marriage. We have, however, very little information to go on. We do not know how this marriage first came to the attention of the court, nor how the court established that Philippa was already married to a living spouse. The most glaring absence in the case is Philippa's husband, Jean. We know only that he was the husband of Philippa and the designation "de Ramerupt." We do not know what role if any Jean played in these court proceedings. If Jean appeared before the court we have no record of it. We also do not know how Philippa, married already to one man of Ramerupt, managed to marry another man of Ramerupt, and *in facie ecclesie* no less. We do not know anything about Jean's marriage with Philippa—when, where, or how it had taken place. Nor do we know what had happened between Jean and Philippa before she came to marry Étienne. It seems plausible to assume that Jean was absent from the diocese at the time of Philippa's attempted marriage and perhaps also the court prosecution. Another reason to suppose that Jean played no role in the prosecution of Philippa is that the court did not order her to resume married life with him.

Indeed, as Sara Butler has also found for England, in many other cases where a wife had strayed from her husband or the reverse, and when the abandoned spouse brought suit in court, errant spouses were urged in no uncertain terms to return to their conjugal domicile and resume married life, on penalty of a fine or excommunication, or even imprisonment.[23] We have nothing of the kind with Philippa. We do have, however, a fine and an order to separate. The fine that Philippa and Étienne were ordered to pay, twenty sous each, was not so large. The real burden they faced was that despite their efforts to contract an engagement, even having consummated this promise, the officiality of Troyes did not permit this woman, who was evidently married to a still-living man, to take another husband.

Even in cases of less certainty, when the court did not claim that an absent husband necessarily lived, the court ordered would-be widows to abandon marital projects and quasi-married life until they could prove the missing man dead. Such was the case with one Isabelle, described almost always in the court registers as the widow of Jean Pot. Having contracted espousals in the future tense with Guillaume Vincent, of Chapelle-Lasson (Marne), and having consummated the union, Guillaume and Isabelle nevertheless had to separate. They were fined an écu apiece and were ordered on penalty of a fine of ten silver pieces not to attempt to proceed with their marriage unless they could prove Jean Pot had died. Finally, Guillaume paid the fine for himself and for Isabelle, described here as his maid (*pedisecca*), and they disappeared from the sources.[24]

Many of these cases offer an imbalance of information, focusing more on the men involved than the women, even in cases in which it was the woman who had tried to marry two men. To give one example, on 28 December 1442 the official ordered Jean de Sermizelles, of the diocese of Auxerre, a man-at-arms, and Glandine, described only as Jean's fiancée, not to continue to cohabit until they could prove the death of Glandine's (unnamed) husband, on penalty of excommunication and ten livres. The official ordered further that neither could marry other spouses unless the court granted them permission.[25] We learned very little about Glandine in the course of this investigation, save that she had been married to someone. We have a similar imbalance of information in many other cases.

As alluded to earlier, while we know so little about these women, we do learn something of the many ways in which they married and the ways the court responded to their behavior. The claim of widowed status is found throughout, as is a good deal of publicity and church solemnity. To be sure, we do not know how Jean and Glandine had affianced themselves, but most of these couples do not seem to have married informally or secretly. If these would-be widows did distort their identity in claiming widowed status, they did not seek to conceal their new marriages but instead sought to celebrate these unions at the steps of a church and with the blessing of a priest.

In another example, also from 1442, the court records reveal that Colin Cardun, of Fontvanne, and Perrette, the widow of Floret de Lemire, had contracted espousals (*sponsalia*) by words of the future tense and *in facie ecclesie* and that they had slept together, consummating the marriage. They had done so despite the death of Floret not being indisputably known. The official ordered them to separate and in no way to further associate with each other, and above all not to have sex again, on pain of a penalty of twenty livres tournois and excommunication.[26]

This ruling brings us to the question of how the court responded to these marriages. These last few couples are left in a sort of marital limbo: this judgment meant that they could not live together as man and wife unless they could prove Floret had died before their marriage. It also meant that Colin could not marry anyone else until Floret's status was known. If Floret still lived, this would annul their marriage, presumably leaving Colin free to find another wife. If Floret had died before the marriage, however, Colin and Perrette were married. Finally, if Floret had died after their marriage, they were not married and would need to seek special permission to marry each other, having earlier contracted in what might be determined to be bad faith, or at least in circumstances too uncertain to be fully licit.

Strikingly, in many of the cases of this type, the would-be husband and the would-be widow both faced sanctions from the court. The focus on the men in these cases, even as the would-be husbands of bigamous women rather than as bigamous men themselves, is borne out in the court's allotment of fines. Men were ordered to pay fines for their marriage, even though it was only the would-be widow who might have had a living husband. That the nonbigamous men faced legal penalties for making these marriages, as well as the priests who celebrated the unions rather than preventing them,[27] reveals something of how the court conceived of responsibility in marriage. The court seems to have held the men, the husbands and would-be husbands, more accountable for their actions and the actions of the women they tried to marry than the reverse. We will return to this idea of male accountability.

What more can we learn about how some of these would-be widows went about remarrying? To a certain extent we can assume that a number of these women were asked to document their marital status, as was so often the case with men. We have little by way of direct evidence of these efforts, however, and it is at least possible that fewer women than men were asked to provide proof before marriage. It seems safer on the whole, however, to argue that men and women both were asked to provide proof of their marital status, and at more initial stages of engagement or marriage as well as after several years of married life.

In 1468, Jean de Terre, of the diocese of Clermont, living in the diocese of Troyes, and Jean Chatelonge, of Granche in Troyes, were both punished with imprisonment and the *scala* for falsely swearing that they had witnessed the death of Jacques Passe. They had so sworn in an attempt to establish that Jacquette, Jacques's wife, was a widow. The two Jeans did so, they claimed, at the instigation of the man who wanted to marry Jacquette and also with the support of Jacquette's mother, who was in favor of the marriage.

Most markedly absent from the record of this prosecution is Jacquette herself, as well as her mother and the suitor who had allegedly encouraged the false testimony. What had happened to them? Of course, the record of their prosecution by the officiality may simply not have survived. The evident absence of legal consequences for Jacquette, however, who may well have had little directly to do with the subornation of false witnesses to her husband's death, fits into a larger pattern of absence. The story of bigamy prosecution in Troyes is a story in which males faced the brunt of the court's prosecutorial energies. Women, prosecuted alongside these men, faded into the background, ordered to separate from illegal spouses and to pay fines rather than sharing in the harsher punishments allotted near-exclusively to male bigamists.

That a woman might do as much as a man, but might better manage to avoid full punishment at the hands of the officiality, is a supposition that is given some support by the court records that detail an extraordinary sequence of litigation instigated by one Isabelle, known in Troyes as the widow of Simon Vautier.

Isabelle first appeared before the court to seek enforcement of a clandestine promise to marry that she claimed to have made with a cleric (in minor orders, and so not an ordained priest, and as a result free to marry) called Manchin le Jon.[28] As Manchin denied the charge, witnesses were produced, who claimed that the two had promised to marry each other numerous times, over dinner and in general conversation. As this testimony reveals, Manchin promised to marry with evident reluctance. Isabelle appears throughout the records as the aggressor in this relationship, seeking to compel Manchin to marry her.[29] According to this testimony, Isabelle demanded her rights as his promised fiancée at every turn: "you promised me that you would have no other wife but me!" or "you know that you are my fiancé and you can't have any other wife but me." To these claims Manchin grudgingly consented, with his consent ranging from a conditional: "yes, as long as you behave properly" to raising his head from his hands and saying, simply, "Yes."[30] That all of the witnesses remembered one occasion or another when Isabelle so pressed Manchin to reaffirm his promise speaks volumes about their relationship. Whatever the other reasons for Manchin's reluctance to commit to Isabelle, one reason emerges from the testimony of a priest, one of Isabelle's neighbors. Manchin had hopes of advancing in the ecclesiastical hierarchy one day, and marriage to Isabelle, a widow, would render him forever ineligible. However, if Isabelle could prove both promises to marry and subsequent sexual relations, Manchin and Isabelle were man and wife.

For the first several sessions in court, Manchin did not appear. Eventually, Manchin answered the summons and admitted to a relationship with Isabelle but denied the marriage. Meanwhile, witnesses continued to testify that they had seen Isabelle and Manchin in bed together in Isabelle's home. Witnesses also reported that four months after the relationship had gone sour, Manchin had broken into Isabelle's home one evening and taken a purse from her "with violent force." She called for help, and Manchin sought sanctuary at the nearby church of St. Remi.[31] This alleged theft, it seems, was resolved by Manchin's appearance in court, where he promised not to harm Isabelle or any of her property on penalty of excommunication and a heavy fine.[32] Suffice it to say, things were not going well for Manchin.

In an evident effort to turn the tables, Manchin began to seek some way to prove that Isabelle was not his wife. At some point, presumably at Manchin's instigation, Isabelle's marital status came into question. She duly presented three witnesses, men from her former husband Simon's hometown. These men testified to their presence at her husband Simon's death and burial, which they all maintained had taken place in Brittany, where Simon had been working as a fruitpicker.[33]

However, a few months later, one of those witnesses returned to the court as a prisoner. He confessed that he had previously given false testimony.[34] The witnesses to Simon's death, he now claimed, had all lied at the instigation of Isabelle, who had promised to pay them well for their efforts. We do not learn, however, which time, if either, this witness told the truth.

It is worth observing that Isabelle, had she wanted to prove Simon dead, would probably have needed to hire witnesses whether her claim was true or not. Many widows and widowers, however strong their claim to widowed status, may have had to exert a great deal of effort to come up with some form of proof of death, written or oral, above all in the context of the Hundred Years' War. Paying witnesses may have been necessary in any circumstances. False testimony may have cost much more than truth, but we do not know which kind of testimony Isabelle may or may not have paid for, as the one imprisoned witness was eventually released and the matter was evidently not ever resolved.

As a result of this contradictory evidence, however, the court was thrown into considerable doubt over Isabelle's marital status. In subsequent litigation—as Manchin accuses Isabelle of a sexual relationship with a Franciscan and a variety of other sexual offenses—the court refers to Isabelle not as a widow but as the daughter of her deceased father, the only status relationship, it seems, that they could assume to be correct. Soon after, however, Isabelle is referred to in court documents as the wife of Simon Vautier. This would suggest that the court had been somehow convinced that Simon still lived. They would not, however, persevere in this conviction. In the last entries in the court registers that make mention of her, Isabelle is called the widow of Simon Vautier once more. Additionally, Isabelle is fined for contracting a clandestine union with Manchin and for consummation of that promise.[35] Such a combination of promises and consummation was usually enough to render a couple married, and so Isabelle and Manchin, for better or worse, may well have been considered married by the court.

One cannot easily imagine this couple living happily ever after, however. Indeed, Manchin seems to have fled the diocese entirely. As for Isabelle, she was not prosecuted for marrying without first proving her husband had died, nor for suborning witnesses. However, another wrinkle remains. If Isabelle was married to the now absent Manchin, she found herself once more married to an absent spouse.

Based on the extensive testimony that accompanies this litigation, Isabelle had exchanged promises to marry with Manchin a number of times. Perhaps she planned or at least hoped to convince Manchin to exchange vows with her at the doors of the church, even the nearby church of Saint Remi, such a short distance from Isabelle's home, for example. The public promises she alternatively cajoled and demanded from Manchin gave her grounds to assert that the couple should be recognized by the community as engaged and on their way to being married. When Isabelle's projects failed to convince Manchin that he should be her husband, she went to court. These court proceedings reveal, among other issues, how tenaciously a woman might have had to work to retain her status as a widow; that is, legally recognized as the former wife of a dead man and free to contract new marriages.

What have we learned from this examination of the bigamous behavior engaged in by women? We have seen that these wives, like the bigamous men, often claimed widowed status. Women did so perhaps most often by merely presenting themselves to their community as such; or their friends, family, and neighbors colluded in this effort, perhaps convincing even the woman herself that her missing husband had probably died or at any rate would not return. In such circumstances, the abandoned wife might as well declare herself a widow and remarry.

We have also found little evidence that these would-be widows married with great secrecy or informality. Even Isabelle, the one would-be widow found in these records who did not marry in church, hardly seems to have lost an opportunity to tell all and sundry that Manchin had promised to marry her. Isabelle seems likely to have been in the process of attempting to drag Manchin to the altar. When she could not manage that mechanism of marrying, she tried her luck in court instead.

On the question of false testimony and false witness, it must be said that we have only scant evidence of these women bribing priests to marry them, asking for forged letters affirming the death of a spouse, or seeking out others to give false witness. We do have some evidence, however, and that evidence offers some important lessons. First, at least some women did engage in this behavior, and second, they seem to have largely gotten away with it. On the whole it may have been the case that women more often presented themselves as widows by means of more informal and less legally dangerous strategies, but we have no means of knowing without doubt.

That said, bigamous wives and husbands alike distorted their identity in an effort to remarry. We know of more men than women who compounded their fraud by changing their names or by using false documents, false witnesses, and false oaths in court. Such exacerbations of the crime of bigamy, however, were only that. Many of the men punished on the ladder faced no such accusations as the use of false testimony. It was enough, it seems, to know that one's spouse lived, to say that one was a widower, and to remarry for the court to recognize the behavior as criminal and subject to prosecution and punishment.

This analysis of the behavior of bigamous wives cannot provide a number of important details that we could, by contrast, find out about the bigamous husbands studied in the last chapter. To begin with, we track the movements of women with far greater difficulty, or even not at all. We do not usually know where they came from, and so we cannot say if they left their home parishes and dioceses to remarry. It seems largely possible that many women did leave home and husband—or one or the other—behind; we certainly know of husbands abandoned by their wives.

We do know that Perrette, Jean Jehan's wife, came from Troyes. Colette the widow (eventually) of Jean and Isabelle Vautier were both probably but not certainly native to Troyes, as was Jacquette, the woman on whose behalf two men went to prison for offering false testimony. As for the rest of the women, however, we know only what they did, and very little about it at that, as opposed to any information about who they were or where they came from. We know only rarely how many years either of the two marriages engaged in by these women lasted. As a result, we also do not know anything about the ages of these women.

We even know very little about how they went about marrying and remarrying, though publicity and *in facie ecclesie* seem to have dominated. We can suppose that they, like the bigamous men, largely sought to marry publicly and with a priest's blessing and only sought to marry in more privacy and secrecy—if still with the presence of some priest and in some sacred space—when their efforts at public marriage went wrong. Also, we know how many of these wives often presented themselves as widows. Both these behaviors they shared with the bigamous men punished on the ladder.

Studying these cases in detail has thus offered mixed results. We can certainly observe that contrary to what one might assume, while men served as the main subjects of bigamy prosecution, they were not the sole practitioners. Many women did marry despite being already married. We have also found that one of the reasons these cases are so difficult to document is that the court itself seems to have preferred to ignore or at least pass quickly and quietly over female bigamy, thus to have treated these wives differently from husbands. Despite the relative inattention of the court to women, we can nevertheless assemble a rough picture of the ways in which these women went about committing bigamy. In so doing we have not found any great difference in the behavior of bigamous wives as compared to that of the bigamous husbands examined in Chapter 2. How, then, can we understand the difference in the way in which the court—and perhaps the community—handled these cases of bigamous marriage?

An analysis of the court records in isolation does not fully explain this difference. Nevertheless, we can also seek out explanations by studying the cases in context and in a variety of contexts. The pastoral theology of sermons, the law, and the social norms we can extract from court records all offer opportunities for further consideration of this problem. What, then, can theology, and sermons in particular, teach us about why bigamous husbands and wives met with different treatment? If husbands, as we saw in the last chapter, were asked to emulate Saint Joseph, and male bigamists in particular fell so short of the mark, what was being asked of wives? What can we learn from the law? Did the canon law or secular law ask different things of wives than husbands? What about social practice in the community—what ideas can we find about appropriate wifely behavior? What expectations did the court and community of Troyes have for wives?

A survey of late medieval theology, law, and social practice reveals three main differences between the roles of husbands and wives in marriage. First, wives and not husbands had to obey their spouses. Conversely, husbands and not wives had responsibility for their own behavior as well as that of their wives. Second, while both husbands and wives were obliged to cohabit, it seems in practice that the onus of cohabitation and staying at home lay heavier on wives than on their husbands. Finally, women's sexual morality, and not that of the husband, was closely associated with honor, the honor of both the husband and the wife. In what follows we will briefly examine each of these differences in more detail and conclude by asking what answers these differences offer for a difference in the treatment of male and female bigamy.

When we read the records of the officiality of Troyes alongside sermons, one recurrent theme emerges: the importance of wifely obedience. Again and again the officials instructed wives to obey their husbands.[36] We rarely learn the cause or details of the difference or difficulty that brought the wife and husband to court, but the outcome almost always followed the same lines: wives should obey their husbands. Such obedience, we are told, should meet with the reward of domestic peace. Meanwhile, husbands should treat their wives well, sleep with them when their wives wished it, care for them, and not beat them excessively or without cause.[37] This recipe for a good marriage conformed with the pastoral instruction offered by preachers.

In particular, the importance of wifely obedience emerges in the descriptions of model wives offered by preachers. Thus, Jean Gerson portrayed the

Virgin Mary as an example of the ideally submissive wife. According to Gerson, just as husbands should imitate Saint Joseph, wives should follow the example of Mary. Above all, wives should emulate Mary's obedience to Joseph, her submission to Joseph as head of household. As Gerson explained, Mary recognized Joseph's authority as her "seigneur" and lived peaceably with her spouse.[38]

Preachers invoked other scriptural texts for the same purpose. The importance of husbandly lordship is found, for example, in the New Testament, in the Letters of Peter. Here, the model wife is Abraham's Sara. The main way in which this Sara seemed to serve as a good model for Christian wives was her submission to Abraham's authority. As described in 1 Peter 3, Sara is praised above all for her recognition of Abraham's authority, for calling Abraham lord. In the Christian liturgy of model wives, obedience seems to have held an essential role.

In pastoral sermons of the thirteenth century, in the works of Robert de Sorbon, Gilbert de Tournai, Jacques de Voragine, Vincent de Beauvais, and others, the model wife is another biblical Sara, the wife of Tobit or Tobias. As recounted in the Old Testament, Sara's efforts at marriage began with seven failed and fatal—for the would-be husbands—nuptial beddings. Sara had a successful wedding night for the first time because divine intervention, her prayers, and the upright nature of Tobias, aided by Raphael, drove off the demon who had been killing Sara's would-be husbands. Humble and devout, Sara served as the model wife in thirteenth-century sermons because she followed the admonishment given in Tobias 10:13—to honor her father-in-law, to love her husband, to take care of the family, to govern the household, and to behave irreproachably.[39]

In accounts of good wifely behavior, a wife's obedience did have limits. According to Gerson, if a husband asked his wife to violate divine law, she could disobey, or at least seek mediation from her confessor. Wives should consider themselves free, for example, to attend mass on Sunday and feast days despite their husband's objections. Their husbands could not reasonably forbid them to go.[40] If a husband persisted in adultery or other sins, it was even the wife's duty to urge him to behave better.[41]

In addition to obedience, cohabitation, a subject of some importance for a study of bigamy, was a central issue in sermons on marriage. The requirement that spouses live together, not traveling for lengthy periods without the permission of the other spouse, was based upon the rule that spouses must be available to render their spouses the conjugal debt upon demand.[42] According to canon law, in marrying, husbands lost ownership of their bodies, which belonged to their wives. Wives gained possession of their husband's bodies and rendered their own. As a result, spouses had a mutual obligation to be present in the conjugal domicile, ready to supply the conjugal debt when needed. Cohabitation thus held considerable importance in canon law in principle. Nevertheless, the enforcement of cohabitation in ecclesiastical court practice seems to have been rather lukewarm or is at any event difficult to assess.

In sermons, we find a considerable difference in the length of time a spouse might appropriately be away from home. In particular, preachers urged wives to stay at home at all costs, day and night, as such behavior became a good Christian wife. Displaying oneself on the street seemed an invitation to adultery.[43] The importance of staying home appears in sermons on Sara such as those discussed above, in sermons venerating the marital comportment of the Virgin Mary, and also in sermons praising the attributes of Mary's mother, Saint Anne. Before and after the Annunciation one finds the Virgin Mary at home, not on the street.[44] Outside of the home, women might be found gossiping or worse. Thus a good wife tended to her household and remained in the home. Just so, the angel appears to Anne to announce her miraculous pregnancy not on the street but at her home.[45] After many years of sterility, Joachim, Anne's first husband, had faced ridicule at the synagogue and departed the city of Jerusalem in shame. Anne, meanwhile, stayed home, where she had remained in prayer, and where the angel who announced Mary's miraculous birth found her.[46]

The notion that a wife belonged at home, of course, has other sources than late medieval sermons. Roman legal tradition and Byzantine law required that wives not only stay close to their husbands but also stay quite close to home. A wife who spent a night away from home without her husband's permission could be prosecuted as an adulteress.[47] Western canon law did away with these additional strictures. Nevertheless, custom and social norms seem to have relegated honorable wives to the confines of home, measuring female honor by proximity to her hearth.

At least in theory, under canon law both husbands and wives needed the consent of their spouses to abandon the conjugal domicile for lengthy periods of time. Pope Innocent III made an exception for crusaders, allowing men to leave on crusade without the otherwise necessary permission of their wives. Such license, however, appears to have played an extremely limited role in the law.[48] The law may have technically required spousal permission for any lengthy absence, as for vows of celibacy, temporary or permanent. Our evidence for implementation or enforcement of this rule, however, is slender.

Court records do not show much by way of widespread efforts to enforce cohabitation rules unless one or the other spouse initiated a complaint. This certainly did not mean that spouses stayed as close together as the law required. Officiality records reveal widespread informal separations or extended absences.[49] As Anne Lefebvre-Teillard observes, both husbands and wives abandoned the conjugal domicile relatively often, but apparently the Church did not fight very strongly against this tendency.[50] Indeed, the registers from Troyes offer little evidence of any interest on the part of the court in punishing those spouses who lived apart, as long as they did not engage in any suspicious or scandalous relationships. The vast majority of cases in which the court ordered a wife or husband to return home and resume conjugal life were cases that also alleged that one or the other spouse, or both, had engaged in an adulterous (or bigamous) relationship. If separated spouses could remain continent or at least above suspicion or accusation, the courts do not seem to have troubled them.

In practice, and in keeping with the exegesis on Mary and Anne discussed above, the requirement of cohabitation lay heavier on wives than husbands. Unsurprisingly, wives who left the conjugal domicile seem to have been subject to more negative attention from their neighbors than were husbands. Reminiscent of Byzantine and Roman laws on adultery, local custom voiced by at least some members of the community in Troyes held that women should not leave their homes if they did not want to be considered prostitutes. In the process of a suit in 1464, one man of the diocese claimed that it was commonly said that a woman who left her home, even for only one day, was considered a prostitute.[51] However extreme this one example, it may well reflect higher standards for wifely morality than those expected of husbands.

We can find as well a third important difference that emerges not so much from theology or from law as from social practice, a practice policed by the officiality. Turning to the court records, we find that the community of Troyes engaged in seemingly constant disputes over the sexual morality of their women. As so often the case with medieval defamation and slander, the bulk of the insults levied in Troyes had to do with the sexual conduct of women. Impugning a woman's sexual morality, of course, was a way to attack husbands and wives alike. Men might be called thieves, but they were more often called cuckolds.[52] Slander made directly against a wife almost always featured an accusation of sexual availability for men other than their husband. Insults included "whore," "adulteress," or "priestess" (that is, the mistress of a priest), or "concubine" or "prostitute." One woman was even called a quadrigamist.[53]

Violence seems to have been considered an acceptable, or at least typical, method of redress for such an insult. Or, the violence was the appropriate reaction and the summons to court a common next step to seek to establish if the accusation had any merit or not. Here the evidence is in agreement with Daniel Smail's work on the secular court of Marseilles: the episcopal courtroom could also serve as an arena for disputes over honor, for efforts to defend one's good name and seek recompense.[54] These battles for honor sometimes divided spouses but more often seem to have united them in defense of their marriage against external opposition. Many of these women launched themselves into violent disputes to defend their honor with their husbands fighting by their sides.

All of this evidence points to a central issue in the cultural perception of wives, bigamists or not. A wife's sexual behavior reflected not only on her but also on her husband. The same could not be said for a husband's behavior. If a wife left her husband or was left by her husband, her sexual behavior sullied his honor. If a husband left a wife, she was abandoned, to be sure, but would not have shared in the same degree of disgrace. There was, after all, no feminine equivalent for the word "cuckold" in Old French. This necessarily implies that male and female or, more narrowly, wifely and husbandly behavior meant different things.[55] The sexual morality, the marital chastity, of a wife was of utmost importance for the honor of her husband, who might even fall subject to the neighbors' scorn, it seems, if his wife left the house for more than a day.

In this cultural world, husbands were held responsible for the misbehavior of their wives. Female bigamy, like male bigamy, may have ultimately been understood as more about the failings of a husband to keep his wife than anything a wife did or did not do. After all, if a wife strayed into adultery, Jean Gerson attributed the blame to her husband, responsible for her behavior as head of household.[56]

However powerful the social pressure on wives to stay at home and main tain the honor of the marriage, it was the husbands' responsibility to keep their wives there. That wives should obey and husbands take responsibility offers, in the end, the strongest explanation we have for the difference in prosecution of male and female bigamy. Cohabitation was not what mattered most to the court. If it was, wives who left their husbands would have met with more prosecution and punishment than they seem to have received. Also, husbands whose wives had abandoned them and who later committed bigamy would have received more lenient punishment than bigamous men who had abandoned their wives. Nor was it the sexual morality of the wife that mattered most. If it had been, would not her marriage, and presumably her sexual relations, with two different men have more greatly bestirred the officiality against her? In fact, bigamy prosecution had very little to do with sexuality and a great deal to do with marriage. And when it came to marriage, what mattered most was that the success of a marriage was ultimately a husband's responsibility.

There was a fundamental difference in how the court and community of late medieval Troyes thought about the behavior of husbands and wives. The would-be widows, the "abandoned" wives of Troyes, were not held responsible for their behavior in the same way as bigamous husbands. Husbands and wives were not legally or theologically responsible for their actions in the same way or to the same degree. A husband was responsible for his wife's adultery and not the reverse. A wife had a moral obligation to try to prevent her husband's adultery, as well as her own, but she was not responsible. If a wife abandoned her husband, it was his fault; if a husband abandoned a wife, it was also his fault. A husband, as head of household, was accountable for the behavior of every inhabitant of that household in ways that an irresponsible wife could never be.

As a result, when it came to bigamy in fifteenth-century Troyes, wives who remarried could anticipate being treated as abandoned and irresponsible, rather than criminal and culpable. Their community expected wives to stay at home and protect their own sexual honor. If wives fell short, it was their husbands, wherever they were, who were to blame. If wives remarried, they could be seen as having acted in accordance with cultural norms, which so honored both marriage and married persons. A wife's duty in marriage was to provide a husband with children and to submit to his authority. Better for an abandoned wife to submit to a second husband than to have no husband at all.

CHAPTER 4

Why Commit Bigamy?

Men and women alike committed bigamy in late medieval Troyes. Whether abandoned or abandoning, separated by circumstance or design, by mutual consent or a unilateral desertion, men and women who found themselves at some distance from their spouses found new spouses to marry. Subsequently, at least some of these men and women found themselves at odds with ecclesiastical courts. The scattered surviving court registers include records of these proceedings for modern scholars to puzzle over, and scholars have identified and analyzed bigamy cases found across medieval Europe.[1] However, none of these scholars offer much by way of explanation of why late medieval men and women committed bigamy.

Why commit bigamy? In the fifteenth-century diocese of Troyes, at least, one did so at great risk. The bishops and ecclesiastical officials of Troyes, in addition to at least some law-abiding parish priests, made a sustained effort to prevent bigamous marriages throughout the fifteenth century. Certainly, many bigamously married couples may well have managed to avoid prosecution. We do not know how often bigamists accomplished their second, illegal marriages without coming to the attention of the court, and we have no way of assessing how often bigamists were caught or not.

However, we have seen how spectacularly and harshly those men found guilty of bigamy were punished, a public example to all who might attempt to marry despite being already married. The possible consequences for such behavior were clear, proclaimed by the diocesan officials in the subjection of convicted bigamists to public punishment on the ladder of the scaffold. Additionally, court officials confined bigamists to prison, dissolved their second, bigamous marriages, and upon release from prison ordered these men and women to return to their first and only lawful spouses, on penalty of a return to confinement. With such risks, why commit bigamy? Even without such risks, why marry when already married to a living spouse? What was there to gain in remarriage?

Having examined the behavior of male and female bigamists in previous chapters, in this chapter I ask why these men and women remarried when already married to a living spouse. As I will argue, based on the evidence we have, the best explanation I can offer has much more to do with theology and with the culture of marriage in late medieval Troyes than with any other reasons. Before coming to that explanation, however, I will review the existing scholarship on bigamy and explore other possible explanations for these behaviors.

The picture of the practice of bigamy that we can garner from prior scholarship offers a mixed and complex account of very different court practices and marital behavior. We know that people seem to have gone about bigamy in different ways, and we certainly know that courts handled it in different ways. Nevertheless, we are left with few ideas as to why medieval people committed bigamy.

English and Italian sources, for example, include a large number of bigamy cases processed on quite different terms than those found in northern France. Modern scholars, following Donahue and Helmholz, usually describe English and Italian cases involving double marriages as pre-contract or three-party cases.[2] In cases of this type, one party alleged that two marriages (or engagements) took place; that is to say, one of the parties bound him- or herself to two spouses. The court then determined which union, if any, took precedence and dissolved any second, and therefore invalid, union. Shannon McSheffrey located a large number of such bigamy prosecutions in England, but as she herself argues through some fascinating detective work, these cases are far from what they seem on the surface. While the cases she examined from fifteenth-century London turned on the allegation of a bigamous marriage, this first marriage was often a convenient fiction, offered up to the court in hopes that the court would dissolve the "second" or in any case no longer desirable marriage. Such "confessions" of bigamy, found in both English and Italian court records, reek of fraud.[3] Often enough in these cases, the alleged first spouse had (conveniently) died, leaving those in the "second" and therefore invalid marriage free to take new spouses.[4]

In fact, in these English and Italian cases the ban on bigamy seems to have done the same sort of service for these nonnoble men and women that the ban on incestuous marriage did for nobles. As we saw in Chapter 1, the Church's ban on incest afforded royal, noble, and wealthy litigants a de facto route to divorce. We also saw that there is no evidence that nonnobles used the same strategy, contrary to Maitland's speculation that they may have done so. In these three-party cases we discover an answer to Maitland's implicit query: (how) did ordinary men and women manipulate canon law to terminate unwanted marriages? The answer, at least at some times and in some places in England and in Italy, is that ordinary men and women exploited the ban on bigamy in ways similar to the exploitation of incest rules that had been used by kings and nobles, who were also known to make use of the impediment of a prior bond in seeking an end to a marriage.[5]

This is a fascinating discovery of a practice that may well also be found in Spanish and German court records. Unfortunately, it is not a discovery that answers the question this chapter poses. First of all, it does not seem likely that many cases of this type can be found in northern French or Burgundian court records. Certainly, some of the bigamists in Troyes may also have wished to bring an end to a second marriage by confessing to a prior bond. If so, however, they acted in different circumstances and faced considerably higher risks and much higher costs.

Bigamists in England might in principle be punished with whipping, a whipping "around the market," a punishment somewhat reminiscent of the southern French custom of punishing by whipping offenders and subjecting them to a humiliating procession, often at a run, around town.[6] This also has some resemblance to the penitential processions that had a role in secular and ecclesiastical punishment in northern France. However, bigamists in England, like most offenders in most ecclesiastical courts, were usually punished only with fines. Often enough, in England and Italy courts did not even fine bigamists.[7] In Troyes, if bigamists exposed their own crime they risked far more serious and even potentially fatal punishment. Perhaps it may still have been worthwhile to them, if it meant an end to a truly terrible marriage, but we can probably assume that far fewer of the bigamy cases in Troyes were brought at the (duplicitous) instigation of the bigamist him- or herself. While some unhappily married men and women might be willing to risk their own death or that of their spouse to bring about an end to the marriage, we can assume that the threat of extremely shameful and potentially fatal punishment would have acted as a deterrent to false claims of bigamy. Probably married persons who in less stringent circumstances might have attempted an admission of bigamy to get out of an unwanted marriage would have looked for other options in Troyes.

In any case, these three-party cases can offer no answer to the question addressed in this chapter: why commit bigamy? That some people posed as bigamists in order to escape an unwanted marriage offers an important example of the importance of monogamy and indissolubility to the judges in England and Italy, who dissolved any second marriages made known to them, but does not explain why other men and women actually married themselves to multiple living spouses.

Turning to northern France, the records of the Paris archdeaconal court reveal a number of cases in which men and women were accused of having committed bigamy in a context wholly unlike the fraudulent or at least convenient "precontract" suits discussed above. Léon Pommeray characterizes the practice of bigamy found in fifteenth- and sixteenth-century Paris as a common response to the abandonment or disappearance of a spouse.[8] Pommeray describes and transcribes several cases in which wives and husbands remarried once or twice and were sentenced to pay fines, undergo public punishment, and go to prison.[9] Women also often appeared before the court on allegations that they had not provided proof of their freedom to marry when as alleged widows or as strangers to the diocese they should technically have done so.[10] If, as Pommeray suggests, bigamy was often practiced by abandoned spouses, he offers no reasons why.

Returning briefly across the Channel, Philippa Maddern and Sara Butler offer further evidence for the practice of bigamy in medieval England, making use of both ecclesiastical and secular court records.[11] Each offers descriptions of behavior that led to or was accompanied by acts of bigamy. Maddern pointed to high levels of geographical mobility of both sexes, which she linked to serial monogamous behavior,[12] while Butler studied the movements of wives who ran away from their husbands.

As for why these men and women committed bigamy, both Maddern and Butler see the prevalence of illegal remarriage as evidence that outside of the ecclesiastical courtroom English marriage practice involved a great deal of deviance from Christian marriage law. As just discussed, even inside the courtroom some Englishmen and -women declared their marriages bigamous in hopes that the ecclesiastical court would duly dissolve these marriages. As we have also seen, however, most people went to court seeking to confirm a marriage, not to get out of one. That said, as Maddern asks, was marriage really "a relatively stable institution, and divorce or marital breakdown rare, in late medieval England?" Or did many people's marriages in fact fall apart, and did these people prefer to eschew the courts and resort instead to extrajudicial means: "informal separation, followed, sometimes, by unlicensed remarriage"?[13] In her analysis of English court records Maddern found ninety-one allegations of bigamy, in which men and women faced accusations that they "had gone from one partnership to another without benefit of legal process."

Such unlicensed serial monogamy, Maddern argues, may have been far more common than scholars had previously realized—"the tip of a much larger iceberg." Other scholars, such as Michael Sheehan, share in this supposition.[14]

However common or uncommon, we remain with the question of why. Why commit bigamy? Maddern and Sheehan do not directly answer the question, but by implication they give a kind of answer. Bigamy took place because people practiced "self-divorce" or a "de-facto" divorce, rather than appealing to the courts for an annulment when their marriages fell apart. This, then, somewhat describes how some people committed bigamy. It explains, at least, why people left a first spouse behind. But once again, why did these people remarry?

Sara Butler, in studying "runaway wives" who fled their homes and husbands and sometimes remarried, does offer an explanation for the behavior. As Butler explains, drawing on the work of anthropologist Laura Betzig, such incidence of self-divorce and remarriage reflected ordinary people's attitudes toward marriage and especially monogamy. These cases of husband desertion and remarriage, she argues, reflect a failed Christianization of the laity, the Church's failure to instill the ideal of monogamous marriage.[15] Butler understands widespread desertion and remarriage as evidence of a conflict between the Church's efforts to "impose its idea of marriage as a permanent monogamous institution," on the one hand, and the laity on the other, which "had a much more fluid perspective of marriage and the acceptability of divorce.[16] The Christian definition of marriage as monogamous and indissoluble had not become accepted among these people, who preferred and practiced a more flexible and even breakable form of marriage. For Butler and Betzig, medieval marriage is therefore best understood in terms akin to those expressed by Georges Duby in his study of noble marriages.[17] Just as Duby saw marriage as a conflict between competing noble and clerical models, Butler and Betzig posit a conflict between popular and clerical models of marriage.

It is my purpose in this chapter to argue that such an interpretation fundamentally misconstrues the meaning and practice of bigamy in late medieval northern France, and perhaps in other places as well. Serial monogamy, or bigamy, was not a sign of the Church's failure at encouraging the laity to value marriage, but the reverse. An examination of self-divorce and remarriage through the lens of bigamy prosecutions in Troyes shows not a failed Christianization but instead the exact opposite. Monogamous marriage, celebrated at the hands of a priest, was exactly what these men and women convicted of bigamy wanted. Indeed, they wanted this concurrent, illegal marriage so badly that they were willing to perjure themselves and risk imprisonment, all to partake in an only outwardly licit form of marriage. This clearly shows that Christian monogamous marriage, far from being rejected in popular culture, had become a desirable commodity for which people would pay a high price. Marriage norms and symbols had disseminated and been assimilated in popular culture, much as David d'Avray has argued that they did.[18] This form of lawbreaking reveals, in short, not the failure on the part of church officials to instill ideals of Christian marriage, but if anything too much success. Christian marriage had become worth breaking the law to obtain, even if only obtainable in a superficial form.

Before making such an argument, I first explore a number of other possible motivations that could have provoked an act of bigamy. Focusing for the most part on the twenty detailed sentences passed against men sentenced to public punishment and imprisonment for this crime, the chapter will also make use of the more limited information we have on female bigamy.

Before we begin with these potential explanations, we must recognize the limitations of the data used in this chapter. The behaviors and stratagems we will examine here were those of many men and a few women convicted by the Troyes officiality for their crimes. We should not assume that these men and women exhibit behavior typical of bigamists, generally speaking, but rather that of the men and women whom the Troyes officiality prosecuted as bigamists. As a result, these cases are instructive for what they can tell us about the behavior of unhappily married men and women, but only to a certain extent. These cases are most instructive for what they demonstrate about the priorities of the officiality of Troyes, the subject of the following chapter. However common or uncommon the behaviors and strategies of these convicted bigamists were, they were certainly the behaviors and strategies that the court found most offensive and criminal out of the many marital crimes committed in the diocese. This is why the court sent them to prison and to the ladder for public humiliation. This is also why they left behind a careful record of the crimes each man and woman was accused of. All that said, in light of these limitations we should be cautious about drawing firm conclusions about how medieval bigamy was practiced.

With that caveat in mind, let us turn once more to Sara Butler's rich analysis of husband desertion in medieval England. Butler suggests a number of motivations that may have led the women she studied to quit their husbands. As Butler observes, wives in medieval England faced a number of difficulties and disadvantages, legal, economic, and social. Turning to the cases of actual desertion, Butler identifies a handful of potential explanations for the behavior of these wives, explanations offered by the wives themselves. Some of the reasons for desertion given by these wives had to do with physical defects, others with defects in character. One woman may have decided to leave her husband because he was blind. Other wives alleged impotence against the husbands they had deserted. Many wives claimed they abandoned the conjugal domicile because their husbands had committed adultery. The other common motivation for desertion claimed by a wife, often part of the instigation of a suit to seek a legal separation from a husband, was that the husband had been cruel and "excessively" beaten his wife.

Another question is, having left one spouse behind, why take another? Butler's sources shed little light on this question. She suggests economic vulnerability as one of the real problems a runaway wife might face if family and friends did not offer shelter and support, and we can imagine that economic needs might well lead a woman to remarry. Butler also posits that wives may have remarried based on more recent or longstanding personal attachments, relationships that began as adultery and became bigamous marriages. We could suppose, then, that financial incentive or romantic attachment might provoke bigamy.

Why else might a wife, or a husband, first of all abandon a marriage and second of all enter another? Looking to the records from Troyes, what possible reasons can we find? Some of the few reasons given to the court by the bigamists themselves resemble the reasons given by the runaway wives studied by Butler. These bigamists, like the women studied by Butler, had every reason to dissemble if they hoped it would protect them from the court. Nevertheless, we should make a careful study of the explanations offered by these bigamists themselves. It is one of the few scraps of information we have, and it offers at the very least evidence of what these bigamists hoped might count as an acceptable or at least a plausible reason for their behavior.

The few men who offered any information on why they had left a first wife behind claimed very personal reasons. One said he left because of rancor. Two other men claimed they had acted in response to their wives' alleged adultery. Beginning with the stated reason of "rancor" we learn that Hugh, called "Chenilloy," of the diocese of Autun, had married one Marguerite, a widow, in that diocese.[19] Subsequently, soon after their marriage, because of "rancor" between them, without seeking authorization from the Church, Hugh left his wife, living first in the diocese of Meaux. Then, about six years before his sentencing, he had come to the city of Troyes. There, regardless of the fact that Marguerite was still alive, Hugh sought to marry a widow of Troyes called Robin. From the perspective of the court, rancor, obviously, however violent or disturbing, was not a sufficient cause to leave a wife without first seeking from an officiality permission to separate and thus no reason to commit bigamy.

Two men claimed that adultery had precipitated the rupture of their first marriages. Simon Lugnet's wife fled their marriage in the company of a tailor, quitting the diocese in favor of Metz. Only after this flight did Simon move to a new place and seek a new bride.[20] The second bigamous husband, Guillaume Pomier, a cleric from the diocese of Besançon, had married Jacquette, daughter of Jean Nuelle, *in facie ecclesie* with solemnities, some twenty-five years before his sentencing in 1449, so roughly in 1424. Then, in 1447, after over twenty years of marriage, Guillaume left his wife "on the pretext that she had sinned against the law of marriage by committing adultery, as [he was] told by others."[21] Soon after, Guillaume found another woman to marry.

Adultery certainly offers an important example of grounds on which spouses have often wished to end a marriage. There is no reason not to take these claims seriously, either as genuine or as at least plausible reasons to leave a wife. Adultery, rumored or real, certainly brought hundreds of marriages to an end throughout the Middle Ages. Nevertheless, the crime of adultery did not terminate a marriage, which would allow for a divorce in which the "innocent" party retained the right to remarry. Legal separation on the grounds of adultery can be found in both ecclesiastical and secular legal traditions.[22] The idea that adultery could mean an end to marriage with a right to remarry was banned in the West but remained in use in Byzantine tradition. The right to divorce an adulterous spouse, usually a wife, and to remarry may well have kept a place in popular consciousness even as both ecclesiastical and secular law of western Europe firmly opposed such a belief. Certainly in Troyes, and also in England, as we saw with the work of Butler discussed above, and in Italy, as Cecilia Cristellon has shown, people often considered adultery sufficient grounds to terminate a marriage.[23]

What else might have motivated a man to first leave behind his first wife, second not to return to her, and third to remarry? Some men may well have not intended a full rupture with the first wife, while others left with the intent never to return. Still others, with their wives having left them first, may not have known if their wives planned to return or would eventually return, but decided nevertheless to move to a new place where they found new brides.

Some men may have left a first wife behind with the full intention of remarrying and fully intending to remarry the woman they did marry. While it is not clearly stated in the records, we can certainly read this scenario into the story of Mathieu Rucin and his efforts to remarry. Mathieu had lived with his wife for three years before he tried to marry another woman. Around the time of Lent in 1446, he left his wife behind and traveled to Sens, a distance of about forty miles. Once there he prepared to contract an engagement at the doors of the church with banns announced beforehand. These banns, however, were rudely interrupted: the first wife arrived just in time.[24]

These personal reasons for abandonment of a marriage, few as they are, offer the only predominant pattern we find in the reasons given by the bigamists themselves. The court does not seem to have pressed them to explain, at least not in the records we have. None of the men prosecuted for bigamy were asked to explain why they chose to take a second wife. Neither do the court records reveal that any explanation for this behavior was asked for or offered by women who remarried. Without any further such admissions or explanations to build upon, we must seek out the potential motivations elsewhere.

Allowing that husbands and wives might have chosen to abandon a first spouse and remarry for personal reasons, what reasons other than general incompatibility, rancor, or adultery might have led to the abandonment of one marriage in favor of another?

One common supposition is that medieval people, and perhaps men in particular, might seek to remarry if their first marriages did not produce heirs. While Christians celebrated the biblical stories of the miraculous birth of children after many years of barrenness, children such as Isaac, Samuel, and the Virgin Mary, medieval Christians could not alter their marriages to accommodate a need for heirs. Spouses in a childless marriage, grounds for either the taking of a concubine or for a divorce and remarriage in many other traditions, had no such recourse in medieval Christian doctrine.

Nevertheless, childlessness, and the lack of legitimate heirs in particular, clearly troubled kings and nobles who often sought annulments of their marriages, annulments that allowed them to remarry and attempt to ensure their succession. The problem of childlessness must also have troubled a good number of ordinary men and women who wished for children but could not necessarily afford an annulment nor find grounds that an ecclesiastical court might recognize as sufficient to nullify a marriage.

Can we find any evidence that such concerns as childlessness motivated any of the men or women prosecuted for bigamy? In fact, we find nothing at all in support of this supposition. If seeking heirs served as a motivating factor in the act of bigamy, not only do none of the accused bigamists admit to such a motivation, but the court does not show any concern or interest in asking about the presence or absence of surviving children from the first marriage.

Out of all the cases of bigamy, eleven make no mention of any children at all. In these cases, either the court did not inquire or these twenty-two marriages all really resulted in no children, or at least no children born to those marriages survived. We have no sure way of knowing but might confidently assume that at least a few children had been born and lived, but their birth and lives did not appear in the court records.

The sentences do occasionally mention children born to the first or second marriages. Six cases mention children from the first marriage only, and often a number of children. In one of these cases a man had ten children by his first wife, of whom six survived, before he left his wife and remarried. Out of the remaining sentences we find a smattering of more children. Only one sentence mentions children born to a second marriage and not a first. Two men had children by both their second and first wives. All this information seemingly amounts to very little, but it is worth something in that it offers not the slightest indication that any of these men or women remarried in search of heirs. Nothing here shows that childlessness caused many or most of these men to leave their wives and seek new spouses. Certainly, childlessness remains a possible incentive for bigamy; nevertheless, with no evidence for that potential cause for bigamy, we must continue to seek out other motivations.

The previous examples looked almost exclusively to the few motivations attributed to male bigamists and focused only on emotional explanations. What of women? And what of more practical reasons for separation and remarriage?

Why did Perrette, Colette, and Isabelle, three of the women whose marital practices we studied in the prior chapter, remarry? Why did they and other would-be widows commit bigamy? Did any of these women complain of violence, adultery, or the physical incapacity of their husbands, as found in Butler's work on runaway wives? In short, we do not know why Perrette remarried, why Colette remarried, or why Isabelle tried so hard to remarry. Nor do we know why each woman married one man or another in particular. We know nothing about what might have led each woman to make her choice.

Did Colette marry because she wanted a child? Perrette because she hoped for financial security? Isabelle because she wanted to be a respectable wife? And love? Or did these women remarry because they feared the desires of the flesh, because Saint Paul had taught it would be better to marry than to burn?

If we cannot locate any specific motivations for why these men and women remarried based on the individual court records, what of their more general circumstances, living as Christians in fifteenth-century Champagne? We can certainly assert that the Hundred Years' War, which all too often included the burning of entire towns and villages to the ground, may have led to the separation of some spouses. Men left their wives behind and joined the armies or gangs of bandits who roamed the Champagne region throughout the first half of the fifteenth century and well into the 1460s. Women, too, left their husbands, seeking economic or emotional comfort with soldiers or clergy.

In times of war and peace alike, men left their wives on business, to find work, to fight, or to make a pilgrimage. Wives left their husbands on similar grounds. We have no evidence of any of these reasons for departure from a first marriage, aside from the peculiar statement from one bigamous couple, Perrette and Jean Jehan, who had decided to leave their home in Burgundy and go separate ways, "on account of the war."[25]

One final incentive that combines both personal and practical motivations returns to the question of children. If childlessness does not emerge as a clear reason for bigamy, legitimacy does. For in all cases in which children are discussed, the bigamous marriage is dissolved, but the children born to that bigamous marriage are recognized as legitimate.[26] On the presumption that at least one of the partners to the marriage believed that the marriage was valid and legitimate, the court treated the children as legitimate. Such legitimacy could not have been obtained for the children of an adulterous relationship, at least not without great difficulty and an appeal to the papacy.[27]

Remarkably enough, an act of bigamy thus may have served as a guarantee of legitimacy for any offspring. If the court's recognition of the children of bigamous marriages as legitimate was in fact regularly granted, and if this practice was commonly known, we find, then, a considerable incentive to commit bigamy. Whatever the personal risks, at least the children would be legitimate. Regretably, we do not have a strong sense of what being legitimate or illegitimate would have meant to commoners living in the diocese of Troyes in the fifteenth century, but one can imagine that it must have counted for something, and so bigamists certainly had at least something to gain, even if the court detected the bigamy and dissolved their marriage.

Finally, rather than looking for reasons why they remarried, what can we learn by asking how they remarried? What might we learn of any underlying motivations in committing bigamy in looking to how bigamists went about their marriages? How one does something often has some bearing on what one hopes to do as a result. These men and women do not seem to have remarried in hopes of keeping either their first or second marriages secret or easily abandoned without friends or neighbors ever knowing a marriage had taken place. Indeed, quite the opposite. Here, to offer one sample, are the marriages and remarriages of the twenty bigamists we know the most about:

1. fol.6 1. fac. ecc. (Langres)	2. de presenti Bouilley (Troyes)
2. fol.7r 1. fac. ecc.Joyaux (Autun)	2. de presenti (Troyes)
3. fol.11r 1. de presenti (Troyes)	2. fac. ecc. (Lausanne)
4. 2fol.11 1. fac. ecc. (Sens)	2. banns Preize (Troyes)
5. 2fol.16 1. fac. ecc. (Troyes)	2. solemnities and acc. to custom (Troyes)
6. fol.17v 1. fac. ecc. (Chartres)	2. contracted marriage Confent (Troyes)
7. fol.38v 1. unk.	2. secret and clandestine in chapel with no banns
8. fol.60r 1. fac. ecc. (Chartres)	2. fac. ecc. de futuro with banns interrupted (Sens)
9. fol.63r 1. fac. ecc. (Dijon)	2. contracted marriage (Lorraine)
10. fol.63r 1. fac. ecc. (Dijon)	2. contracted marriage (Laon)
11. fol68 1. fac. ecc.Besançon	2. contracted marriage Longeville (Troyes)
12. fol82v 1. fac. ecc. Pontaber (Autun)	2. fac. ecc. banns Fontvanne (Troyes)
13. fol.85r 1. fac. ecc. (Langres)	2. solemnized marriage (Troyes)
14. fol.98v 1. fac. ecc. (Troyes)	2. solemnized marriage (Troyes)
15. fol.106 1. fac. ecc. (Toul)	2. solemnized marriage (Troyes)
16. fol.120 1. fac. ecc. (Troyes)	2. solemnized marriage acc. to custom (Vauds)
17. fol.124v 1. fac. ecc. (Langres)	2. solemnized marriage (Châlons)
18. fol.125 1. fac. ecc. (Toul)	2. fac. ecc. (Troyes)
19. fol.133 1. solemnized marriage (Autun)	2. fac. ecc. (Auxerre)
20. fol.149 1. fac. ecc. (Auxerre)	2. solemnized marriage acc. to custom (Troyes).[28]

Out of all of these thirty-nine marriages, only one took place explicitly "clandestinely"—and, at that, in a chapel with a chaplain bribed not to perform the banns. Whatever else we might say about this group of men and women, they do not seem to have married informally very often. The participation of a priest had universal importance for these marriages; publicity seems to have been at least generally desirable, if not always attained.

Looking closer, we have a number of puzzling details to work out. Almost all of the first marriages are described as contracted "in facie ecclesie," with only three exceptions. The second marriages are almost all not described as marriage contracted "in facie ecclesie," with only five exceptions. Can we tease out any difference between marriages contracted "in facie ecclesie", and marriages contracted "with solemnities" and "and according to custom"? The two second marriages contracted "de presenti" may have taken place without banns or solemnities or the presence of a priest. The prosecutions of these two cases appear one immediately following the other, in 1423. While the second marriages are described as "de presenti" only, both men are accused of public perjury in making the second marriages and, more important, accused of having deceiving the church in which the second marriages were made. Either rhetorical flourish overrode facts or these marriages also took place on sacred ground and with a priest's participation.

The majority of the descriptions suggest at least some publicity and also the presence of a priest and the doors of a church. "Solemnized" almost certainly means that however a marriage was initially contracted, there was in the end the ceremony at the church door, possibly preceded by banns, and that the couple had their marriage blessed by a priest.

What this analysis of the different descriptions we have of the marriages and remarriages leaves us with, then, is a strong sense that all of these people lived in a society that prioritized both publicity and proximity to a church and priest in marrying, with an emphasis on the latter.

This behavior is perhaps the most significant finding that we can extract from these cases in our effort to understand why these men and women chose to commit bigamy. That they sought the blessing of the church and publicity tells us something. It tells us that they chose to commit bigamy because they lived in a time and place in which marriage mattered a great deal. Already married, but to a distant or undesirable partner, these men and women had found another, more present or more desirable partner. They wished to sanctify this second union by marriage, to gain recognition as married in their communities, but perhaps also they hoped that the ritual might bless their union, even if the law did not.

There is certainly a great deal that the records examined here do not tell us. Many of the circumstances and causes for these marriages and remarriages remain concealed from our view. What we have learned, however, is suggestive. That these men and women sought out the doors of the church and the blessing of a priest in their remarrying offers an important indication of the cultural environment of marriage, of Christian identity in late medieval northern France.

Some of the information we seek and cannot find in the court registers does emerge from other sources. Turning briefly from legal records to literature, we find that the classic bigamy stories of the Middle Ages invoked the timeless problem of a man who went away to war and who might discover on return that his wife had remarried in his absence. We find our medieval predecessors of Martin Guerre and Bertrande de Rols, or our medieval Odysseus lacking a steadfast Penelope. Medieval stories also reveal the converse tale of a husband who remarries in the course of his own travels, regardless of the wife left behind. Both situations play on the anxieties that must have accompanied periods of separation in the premodern world. Men who went away to war might not return and might have taken another wife. Women left behind might have given up on their missing husbands and decided to marry again. The law, of course, demanded otherwise, at least in theory. Nevertheless, one imagines that spouses may have had their own understandings regardless of the law, and indeed, stories of such private arrangements can be found in medieval literary traditions.

One story of such a private arrangement between spouses is found in the writings of Caesarius of Heisterbach (ca. 1170–ca. 1250), whose exemplar concerned a devotee of Saint Thomas who traveled to India on pilgrimage.[29] This tale reemerged in a new setting and new interpretation at the hands of Boccaccio. While Caesarius used his story as an example of how devotion to Saint Thomas would work miracles for a follower who otherwise would have lost his wife to another man, Boccaccio's setting offers hospitality and friendship as the merits that are rewarded.[30] Both stories address concerns over men who go on pilgrimage or to battle and disappear. As with many stories of war and separation written during the later Middle Ages, Boccaccio's story is set vaguely during the crusading efforts of Frederick I.

One Messer Torello, a nobleman of Pavia, offered hospitality to Saladin, who was disguised as a merchant and touring Europe to see what provisions the Christians were making for war. Messer Torello entertained his guest to the best of his abilities, in both his country estate and his Pavian mansion. His wife gave out sumptuous robes and other clothes as a present, her husband topped off the offerings with fresh horses, and Saladin left, determined to one day repay the bountiful hospitality of his host and hostess.

Afterwards, Messer Torello decided to join the Crusade, seeking, as he said, both fame and salvation. He asked his crestfallen wife to promise that if she had no proof that he still lived, after a year and a month and a day she should consider herself free to find another husband. They parted; he boarded a galley in Genoa. Subsequently, he and the rest of the army fell ill with a deadly fever. Nearly all the survivors were captured and imprisoned by Saladin. Messer Torello became a falcon trainer while in prison in Alexandria and so came to the attention of Saladin. Saladin recognized his onetime host, revealed that he had been the merchant in disguise, and promised to repay the hospitality he had been shown. Meanwhile, another Messer Torello, this one of Dignes rather than Pavia, had died on Crusade, and this news traveled to Italy, where our Messer Torello's wife and family brokenheartedly accepted that their Torello was dead. Her family eventually forced his wife to agree to a second marriage, though she insisted on waiting until the year, month, and day had passed. A week before this marriage, our Messer Torello realized that his wife had most likely given up on him and had decided to marry another. This devastated him and he took to bed, resolving to die of grief. Saladin heard of this and had one of his magicians transport Messer Torello home in time to prevent the wedding. Messer Torello materialized in the church of San Pietro in Ciel d'Oro of Pavia, on his bed of finery and surrounded by jewels. Messer Torello asked the abbot to keep his miraculous return secret for the moment, so he could observe his wife at her nuptials. He and the abbot attended the nuptials, but no one recognized Torello with his long Saracen beard and Saracen clothing. Torello was pleased to see his wife looking despondent, and so slipped a ring she had given him into her cup. She recognized the ring and her husband, and the second marriage was swiftly called off; the return of Messer Torello was celebrated instead.

Both the stories told by Boccaccio and by Caesarius of Heisterbach offer a cultural expression of anxiety over how indissoluble monogamy might be threatened by separation, even when spouses wished to stay married to each other. Such stories reflect the uncertainties of the time and the ways in which couples might have attempted to deal with this uncertainty.

Notably, stories from the fifteenth-century Burgundian court reflect a different attitude toward bigamy.[31] In the anonymous historical romance of Gillion de Trasignes,[32] Gillion, a knight and nobleman of Hainault (now part of Belgium) embarks on pilgrimage to the Holy Land, leaving his wife behind. He is immediately captured by the sultan and would have been executed in the manner of Saint Sebastian, tied to a stake, bare-chested, and pierced through with arrows, had such an arresting sight not conquered the sultan's daughter—for, of course, the sultan has a daughter, and of course she falls in love with Gillion. His life spared, Gillion nevertheless manages not to marry the princess until he has first heard a false rumor that his wife had died in childbirth. Believing the sad news, Gillion attempts to console himself by converting the sultan's daughter to Christianity and marrying her, while also fighting as many battles as possible for the sultan, which allowed Gillion the opportunity to kill as many Muslims as his angry Christian heart desired.

Gillion's wife, however, lived still, waiting patiently and refusing all offers of remarriage, and so when Gillion learns this he rushes home with the sultan's daughter in tow, and all three, the husband and the two wives, are so horrified at the sin of bigamy, however accidentally committed by Gillion, that all three enter monasteries and take vows of celibacy.

The overwhelmingly pious manner in which the accidental bigamy of Gillion is handled in this tale is matched by another fifteenth-century bigamy story found—of all places—in the normally salacious *Cent nouvelles nouvelles*, written, once more, for the Burgundian court and presented to the duke of Burgundy in 1462.[33] In story sixty-nine we find the tale of a woman bigamist. The story seems out of place amid the ninety-nine others, all treatments of adultery and farce in the style of Boccaccio. Nevertheless, here is this story of bigamy and of piety and virtue. The story concerns a virtuous noblewoman, the wife of a knight of Flanders.

The knight had gone off to fight for John of Burgundy and the king of Hungary against the Turks. In the battle of Nicopolis, in 1396, the Turks capture the knight and many other knights and nobles, killing some and leaving others to languish in prison. Meanwhile, years pass while the virtuous, beautiful, and pious wife waits for news of her missing husband. Her friends and relatives, anxious on her behalf, urge her to accept that her husband had died and to remarry. She resists all logic for some time, but in the end feels obliged to obey her friends and family, with great regret; after nine years with no news of the missing man, she remarries. However, no less than six months later, the knight and many of his fellows are ransomed and begin their journey home, the news of their release preceding them. The noble lady, so horrified and broken-hearted that she had betrayed her husband, drops dead of grief.

However far the culture of the Burgundian court distanced itself from the ordinary men and women of Troyes, a study of both the Burgundian court literature and the Troyes court registers offers the same lesson: marriage mattered, and mattered a great deal. To return to the bigamous men and women of Troyes, we have found that they committed bigamy, insofar as we can see, largely because they valued marriage. Obviously, the sources that allow this assessment have some limitations that leave wide open the possibilities for other motivations, more difficult for us to discern.

One final story, one final product of late medieval culture, offers perhaps the most compelling lesson of all in our efforts to understand why the men and women in and of fifteenth-century Troyes committed bigamy. In an attempt to assess the behavior of late medieval men and women who insisted on remarriage at church door and in spite of the law, where better to look than to the most famous remarrying widow of the Middle Ages, Chaucer's Wife of Bath?[34]

In writing the story of a pleasure-loving widow who insisted on her rights to remarry as often as her husbands died, Chaucer brought to life one of the central problems of monogamous marriage that many married persons faced. Christian doctrine encouraged, of course, celibacy above all. Marriage also had a place, but widowhood a still better place in the Christian hierarchy. Chaucer's Alison describes herself as subject to two basic attacks on her identity as a good Christian wife: first, as a remarrying widow she violated the ideal of monogamous and indissoluble marriage, and second, as a woman, she should have submitted to the authority of her husbands.

Chaucer's Wife of Bath's Prologue and Tale is deeply engaged in dialogue with Church doctrine, and above all the writings of Saint Jerome on remarriage and authority.[35] Chaucer's Alison first of all claims a right to remarry as often as she pleases and second asserts the possibility that a laywoman, even a wife, might pick and choose whom she will consider authoritative, what authority she will submit to.

Chaucer's Wife of Bath claimed her right to remarry as often as she pleased. Her engagement with authority, picking and choosing what she would endorse and claim as her rightful path as a good Christian wife and which authority she would reject namely her last—or at least latest—husband's overexertion of authority over her offers important lessons for our efforts at explaining the curious behavior we find practiced by the husbands and wives of the diocese of Troyes who married too often.

True, in so marrying they violated the law in ways that Chaucer's Wife of Bath did not. They rejected legal authority in ways that she did not. Their claim, however, their efforts to create new lives and new marriages for themselves, new Christian identities, has a great deal in common with Alison's assertion of authority against Jerome and against her would-be domineering husband, whose authoritative book she burned. They wanted a Christian marriage, blessed by a priest and at a church door, but a marriage of their own making.

The men and women of fifteenth-century northern France described in the sentence register from Troyes are surprising in many ways. They traveled a good deal and exerted much energy to see that their marriages were made publicly and blessed, even if the marriage itself was invalid and illegal. Their circumstances are also surprising. They seem to have lived in a time and place with high standards for written proof of participation in sacraments such as marriage. Not only were the requirements strict, but they seem to have been enforced to a surprising degree.

Perhaps the most important conclusion involves the mentality of these bigamists. It is easy to think of bigamists as people who had contempt for marriage.[36] But that would be wrong. Far from displaying contempt for marriage, these errant Christians showed a remarkable willingness to take great risks in order to present themselves to their communities as married. They risked public humiliation, imprisonment, and no doubt social disgrace. They also took the financial risks involved in abandoning their established homes. They did all these things, not in the effort to avoid marriage, but in the effort to contract marriage with the spouse of their choice. Their behavior is evidence, not of the weakness of the Christian norm of marriage, but of its surprising strength.

In the course of the Middle Ages, the Church sought to induce all Christians who did not choose a life of celibacy to choose marriage instead, rather than living lives of lustful fornication and sin, risking damnation. Better to marry than to burn. Having learned that lesson, popular interpretation might also extend the tradition farther: better to remarry than burn.

The women whose cases Sara Butler studied clearly felt the importance of marrying a second time, even though doing so exposed them to great risk. That several of these women left their husbands only to marry a second time offers an example of marriage's importance in these communities. To value marriage so much as to enter into it illegally is a strange form of praise, but a high form of praise nonetheless. Such behavior reflects the great success the ideal of indissoluble monogamy had in late medieval Western society.

In ways that parallel the manipulation of canon law on marital impediments by nobles and kings seeking to repudiate unwanted spouses, these ordinary men and women living in the diocese of Troyes also sought to manipulate rules governing how marriages could be contracted in order to seek out illicit marriages. Instead of asking for an annulment, however, they fraudulently proceeded with marriages that were legally impossible but that outwardly conformed to the canonical requirements. In the fifteenth century, marriage was of great importance to commoners as well as to nobles and kings, even as they each engaged in different strategies for ending one marriage and beginning another.

CHAPTER 5

Why Prosecute Bigamy?

In September 1448 the officiality of Troyes condemned two men to the same punishments: public exposure on the ladder of a scaffold in front of the cathedral one Sunday and six months' confinement in the bishop's prison.[1] The first man, a Dominican friar, had been convicted of brigandage. He had taken up arms in the Hundred Years' War and in so doing took part in more pillaging, murdering, and stealing than fighting of pitched battles. Such behavior, even if restricted to the field of battle, was an egregious violation of his clerical status, which prohibited both carrying weapons and shedding blood. As for the second man, a layman, he had parted from his wife and married another woman some years later, a crime we would call bigamy.

One question I will pose in this chapter is how and why the second crime came to be punished at all, and above all on the same level as the first. How and why did the bishop's court in Troyes come to regard the crime of bigamy as an offense comparable to that committed by a friar who fought in battles and killed? Why punish bigamy with the same severity as clerical brigandage?

To answer this question, I studied the court that inflicted these punishments: the bishop of Troyes' judicial court. In part it is a study in prosopography. Information about the identity and education of the court officials offers some indication of why the court took such interest in regulating behavior in the diocese. But we must also consider the particular historical context and circumstances in which these men lived. The clergy on the bishop's court served in a time of great calamity, living as they did in a time and place that suffered great hardship as the Hundred Years' War swept again and again across Champagne, a time of troubles that lingered long after treaties were signed and peace finally declared in 1453. As I will argue, the experience of these troubles shaped their attitude, not only toward clerical brigandage, but also toward bigamy. In the midst and aftermath of the Hundred Years' War, these men made use of their training and their positions in the bishop's court to impose order upon a desperately disordered society. Driven by a sort of "moral panic" of the kind Millard Meiss described in postplague Florence,[2] provoked by the devastation, upheaval, and social unrest of the Hundred Years' War, this court came to regard itself as an agent of reform.

Indeed, the two crimes that this chapter begins by describing are not unrelated. Both crimes were to some sense provoked by the Hundred Years' War. War may well have provided the occasion—or necessity—that led a Dominican friar to take up arms and fight. War may also have provided the occasion—or necessity—that drove a married man to leave his home and to take another wife. Also, war arguably drove the court to undertake a program of reform. As Claude Gauvard has argued, the Hundred Years' War and the many other misfortunes that had overcome late medieval societies—dynastic upheaval, papal schism, famine, and plague—drove many communities to call for the prosecution of heinous crimes in an attempt to restore order.[3] Ecclesiastical courts shared in these prosecutions. Vincent Tabbagh argued that war, epidemics, and a "brutal" rise in prices around 1438–39 provoked the archbishop of Rouen's officiality to act to regulate behavior in the diocese, in particular to prosecute and punish superstition and sorcery, as well as usury.[4] Tabbagh also points to similar prosecutions of witchcraft and sorcery in the Dauphiné between 1432 and 1435.[5]

If similar to the courts in Paris, Rouen, and the Dauphiné in efforts at instilling order by means of regulation and punishment of crimes that seemed to both reflect and perpetuate crisis, the court in Troyes was seemingly unique in such active regulation of marriage. The Troyes officiality was far more aggressive in its handling of bigamy than other officialities that scholars have studied thus far. The prosecutions described in the Troyes officiality records, while in keeping with the letter of the law, far exceed any known practice in any other time and place of the Christian Middle Ages. Only in the fifteenth century, and in northern France, have scholars found any such concerted effort to investigate both marriage formation and intact marriages.[6] In fact, the surviving court records of Troyes reveal a degree of regulatory behavior that invites comparison to the famous registers of Jacques Fournier, the bishop whose inquisitorial proceedings in pursuit of Cathar heretics yielded such unexpected fruits as Le Roy Ladurie's *Montaillou*.[7] Heresy, however, was not the most important matter at hand in Troyes. Chief among those subject to the harshest punishments in the officiality's (limited) arsenal were the two sorts of offenders described at the beginning of this chapter: clergymen found to have taken up arms in the Hundred Years' War and men who had married despite being already married to living spouses. My aim in this chapter is to understand why.

Let us begin with an overview of the court's activity. Drawing, perhaps, upon local knowledge and local connections, and certainly drawing upon their legal and theological training, these officials set out to enforce Christian norms in the diocese. That said, they did not act against all possible deviations from proper Christian morality. Nor did they perceive all sinful behavior as deserving the same punishment, or even necessarily any temporal punishment at all. Some matters, however grudgingly, the court left to secular justice; other sins the officials left to the confessional or to God. There were only certain particular sins that they would not tolerate.

A bishop's court, especially a bishop's court in northern France, could claim competence over a wide range of offenses. Anne Lefebvre-Teillard lists abortion, incest, sodomy, homicide, failure to pay child support for an illegitimate son or daughter, perjury, blasphemy, sacrilege, heresy, rape, arson, usury, and failure to pay tithes as examples of offenses over which a bishop's officiality might claim jurisdiction.[8] We could append to this list violence committed by or against clergy, bestiality, adultery, fornication, concubinage, clandestine marriage, failure to make annual Lenten confession, and defamation.

Reading through the records of the court, we find examples of cases involving many, but far from all, of these infractions. We cannot imagine that the court—however proactive—moved to prosecute and punish every type of offense committed against Christian norms in the diocese over which this court held jurisdiction. It must be the case that some behaviors—words and deeds—were passed over. We find, for example, no cases of abortion or infanticide. Obviously such things could have taken place, and indeed probably did take place. Also, we find no prosecutions for sodomy. It is at least remotely possible that no homosexual acts took place in the diocese, but it is extremely hard to believe. The same might be said for bestiality. We find as well no prosecutions for other sexual offenses, such as masturbation or heterosexual sex in inappropriate—meaning nonprocreative—positions.

The men and women of the diocese of Troyes found occasion to denounce each other for a wide variety of (other) infractions. Constantly in and out of each others' homes, the people of Troyes, and especially those married to each other or engaged in sexual relations with each other, could have revealed to the court any of the above offenses just as much as they did in fact denounce blasphemous or injurious speech or suspicious or scandalous sexual relationships. Choices were made, in denunciation, in investigation, in prosecution, and in punishment. But we cannot allow these choices to overly influence our understanding of what people were "really" doing in the diocese. They are only evidence of what mattered to the court and of what people of the diocese thought mattered to the court. However, my goal in this chapter is to understand precisely that: what mattered most to this court and why.

Restricting ourselves to the record of prosecution and the information it offers, we find that the court identified and responded to a number of perceived problems, a number of specific violations of Christian doctrine. Clerical concubinage, as well as less established suspect or scandalous relationships involving clergy, predominates. That clergy of all ranks kept mistresses or engaged in casual relationships with women had long served as source of complaint in the diocese. The officiality included in the registers a record of a number of general warnings against such malfeasance made at the behest of the bishop of Troyes or the cardinal of Bar.[9]

Fornication and adultery as practiced among laity also reflected a widespread failure at maintaining proper Christian continence in the diocese. Those men and women, clergy and laity, suspected of involvement in forbidden relationships faced a summons and a warning to separate and avoid each other's company. Those found guilty and accruing fines, as well as the occasional excommunication or suspension, were especially those who ignored the warnings and persisted in their relationships. Spouses who had strayed into other relationships faced orders to return to the conjugal domicile and resume married life.

Still more often, again according to the court records, violence and violent language played a predominant role in social exchanges in the taverns as well as the churches and cemeteries. Men and women of Troyes exchanged words and blows, occasionally even fatal blows, which led to their summons before the officiality. The officiality most often fined these offenders, apart from the murderous, who were usually imprisoned. Hundreds of violent but nonhomicidal men and women were also asked to swear not to harm another person or their family or goods on penalty of excommunication, imprisonment, and heavy fines.

In quantitative terms, violence, insults, and sexual offenses take up most of the pages of the case registers of the officiality. In qualitative terms, however, between 1423 and 1468, a hundred cases received special treatment. Instead of a few jotted lines of text, we find a full folio or even pages of text describing the misdeeds of a man or woman whose behavior called for special attention from the court. These men and women had committed serious crimes, crimes that called, it seemed, for harsh punishment.

Why some crimes and not others? Why, in particular, bigamy? For indeed, bigamy is among the offenses that received such special attention. Our first instinct might be to suppose that the court aimed to reestablish normalcy after the disorder of the Hundred Years' War by beginning with the family. With the war over, with absent spouses returning home, order could be instilled in the community by the court's efforts to adjudicate over who belonged with whom. Yet any such interpretation is inadequate. The efforts of the court divided families at least as often as it united them. The court dissolved a large number of intact marriages, throwing the marital status of some into uncertainty and ordering others to resume married life, somehow, with absent and long-missing spouses. It its own way, the court was creating disorder as much as it was creating order. We can understand, therefore, that order through family may have been a goal, but it was not the primary objective. The primary objective must have been different. It must have had far more to do with the salvation of souls and with an effort to protect the purity of marriage and to uphold the sacrament of marriage in the diocese. Condemning and invalidating all potentially bigamous marriages forced marriage practice in the diocese to better comply with the requirement that Christian marriages be monogamous and indissoluble, as they, as Christian marriages, had to emulate the monogamous and indissoluble model marriages of Adam and Eve and Christ and the Church.

To gain a more complete understanding of why the court acted as it did, we must look more closely at its personnel. We should begin by observing that this court had a distinctly local and learned character.[10] The bishops, judges, and officers were local men, the sons of the wealthy merchants, mercers, and artisans of Troyes and the surrounding region.[11] This group, united by blood and by marriage, dominated both ecclesiastical and secular offices in the city and diocese. Rather than absentee clergy seeking only to accrue whatever benefits, if any, their offices provided, these men served at their posts among their families, neighbors, friends, and surely enemies. They were involved in their community and they had, in short, great interest in the diocese.

They were also men of considerable and distinct Christian learning. Related by blood and by marriage ties, they also shared a common education. Several had studied theology at the Collège de Navarre of Jean Gerson's Sorbonne, founded by Jeanne de Navarre in 1305 for promising young men of the Champagne region.[12] These men were also learned in law, having been students and members of the law faculty in Paris, where they studied canon law, and students and faculty in Orléans, an important center for the study of Roman law.[13] To be sure, we know very little about their theological training. Nevertheless, there is good reason to suppose that theology studies at Paris flavored their program of reform and emphasized a strict adherence to the promotion of marriage as indissoluble and monogamous.

Certainly the sermons offered by preachers of every denomination who trained in Paris alongside the bishops and officials of Troyes and who came to preach in Troyes espoused this strict view of Christian matrimony. As explained not only in canon law texts but also in these sermons, no married person could remarry without first obtaining proof of death of their first spouse. Acting otherwise was to marry as did pagans, Jews, and Muslims.[14] Such lessons, offered in sermons, may well have also played a prominent role in the lectures offered in Paris. If the laity sometimes ignored or overlooked these rules, their court officials encountered them as students and instructors in Paris and certainly implemented them when they returned home to serve as bishops and judges in Troyes.

These men thus shared an educational as well as a social and cultural background. Many of these ecclesiastical officials also shared, as I will argue, an interest in reforming their devastated diocese. The instruments of this reform included the officiality and its rural courts, visitation, and the enforcement of strict synodal legislation.

Four bishops served Troyes during the period studied: Étienne de Giverny (bishop from 1395 to 1426), Jean Leguise (1426–50), Louis Raguier (1450–83), and his nephew Jacques Raguier 1483–1518). They appointed several officials, including Thomas Domanche (1395–1413); Jean de Foissy (1413–15); Jean du Chene, licensed *in utroque,* that is, in canon and Roman law (1424–26); Étienne Grappin (1426); Lambert Milon (1426–50); Étienne Colin, bachelor *in decretis* 1436, licensed in canon law 1438 at Orléans (1441–49); Pierre du Fresne (1470); Nicolas Coiffart, who studied Roman law at Orléans (between 1475 and 1488), and Nicolas le Bascle (between 1490 and 1499).[15]

The education and achievements of these bishops, their officials, and even a number of the promotors was often quite impressive. Jean Leguise was born in Troyes to a cloth merchant and *teinturier* (dyer) and his wife, Guillemette de la Garmoise, members of the high bourgeoisie of Troyes. The eldest of many children, Jean studied at the Collège de Navarre in the Sorbonne beginning in 1404 and received his baccalaureate in Roman law (presumably, but not necessarily, in Orléans) and was later licensed in canon law.[16] Leguise was appointed as the morning lecturer on the decretals at the canon law faculty in Paris from 1423 to 1426, and his colleagues voted in favor of his promotion to professor just before he assumed the episcopate of Troyes.[17] The holdings of the municipal library of Troyes include some of the canonical texts he owned.[18] In addition to his legal learning, while serving as bishop he frequently gave sermons. His political career was no less distinguished. A famous opponent of the Burgundian party in the Hundred Years' War, he played no small part in welcoming Joan of Arc to Troyes.

A fellow supporter of the French king against the Burgundian faction, the official Étienne Grappin was born in 1390, the son of a poor furrier. He went on to be licensed in law, served as a member of the city council of Troyes at least in 1432, was named archdeacon of Margerie in 1440, and in 1447 curé of St. Jean in Troyes.[19] His nephew, Étienne Plaisance, another cathedral canon, studied law in Orléans (1440–45) and then taught as rector at the university.[20]

Bishops and officials of a common background and education, they also developed and implemented a common plan of reform. The bishops promulgated synodal statutes in 1374, 1427, 1441, 1465, and 1501.[21] They issued these statutes issued in Latin and in French, to facilitate the parish priests' comprehension and to ensure proper instruction of parishioners. In a related effort to educate and foster the spiritual welfare of the community, the city council, often chaired by the bishop, hired Paris-trained preachers to give sermons during the Lenten period and other important feast days or in times of fear of an epidemic.[22] This edification was to be supplemented by annual confession and frequent attendance at mass. To encourage compliance, those found to have failed to confess or to receive the Eucharist were occasionally fined by the officiality.[23]

The caliber of these bishops and their officials, their presence in Troyes, and their interest in their home diocese offer a striking contrast to much of what one generally finds in late medieval episcopates. The disparity is most marked in its contrasts with the complaints subsequently issued by sixteenth-century reformers who deplored the general problems of absenteeism, the lack of education, and the lack of interest in the flock exhibited by many bishops, archbishops, and cardinals of fifteenth-century Christendom. What information we have about the episcopal court in Troyes suggests a very different scenario indeed. The officiality of Troyes offered the diocese a well-trained and deeply committed court, dedicated to a program of reform.

What we must try to understand is why these bishops chose to reform behavior in the diocese, and to reform behavior in the manner in which they did. We have two main means of gaining any sense of what motivated the officiality: first, the sources that describe when and how the court inflicted punishment, and second, the sources that offer a record of what the official, in judging these cases, said about the crimes the court so punished. These two topics will serve as the main subjects of this chapter.

Before treating in further detail why the court in Troyes prosecuted bigamy, it is worth briefly considering a basic preliminary question in formulating what we know of how the court went about prosecuting bigamy: how these marriages came to be investigated in the first place. Who, if anyone, denounced the bigamist? Who aroused the suspicion of one of the promotors, the court-appointed prosecutors, who for their part initiated investigations, issued summonses, imprisoned, and prosecuted the bigamists?

On this subject we have very little information. As we learned in Chapter 2, "Bigamous Husbands," two men's wives seem to have come looking for them. These wives probably denounced their husbands to the officiality once their husbands had publicly spurned them and persisted in their efforts at remarriage, if not before. As for the other seventeen men, we have no way of knowing how they fell under suspicion. Most of their wives seem unlikely sources for denunciation. Most often these wives seem to have not taken part. Indeed, a good number of them would have been most reluctant to participate, as they had, at least according to their first husbands, often themselves remarried and preferred to stay with their second husbands.

If not the first wife, who? One could easily imagine denunciations instigated by neighbors or family members of the first wife who happened upon the bigamous husband in his new setting. We have evidence from other dioceses of denunciations made by the second wife herself or her family.[24] Finally, we find some bigamists who came forward seemingly "spontaneously" to confess their own crimes and ask for the nullification of the second, illegal marriage.[25] Considering the risks of humiliating punishment and possibly fatal prison sentences, however, self-identification as a bigamist seems an unlikely means for exposure in Troyes.

We find ourselves, then, with a court and a community that prosecuted bigamists acting presumably upon accusations or denunciations. We do not know the identity of the denouncers or their relationship to the accused. We do know that the court presented itself as receptive to allegations of marital, sexual, and violent conduct. Indeed, the court seems to have regularly sent out its many promotors and other officers in search of just such information, a level of activity that did not pass without complaint, an issue we will return to.

This sort of regulatory behavior appears, however, to have been exceptional: English courts, especially before the fifteenth century, have been described as more receptive than proactive. Fifteenth-century Italian courts, as Silvana Seidel Menchi has argued, adopted a more pastoral than regulatory attitude toward litigants and accused.[26] As for northern France and Burgundian lands, regulatory is the word that best describes much of the court action for which we have surviving sources. Clearest evidence of this manner of ecclesiastical justice is found in Rouen, Brussels, Cambrai, Paris, and Troyes. However, even in this grouping Troyes stands apart. This was an exceptionally regulatory court.

The instruments of punishment deployed by this officiality were the bishop's prison and the scaffold before the cathedral of Troyes, both maintained by a cohort of men employed to repair the prison walls, to attend to the prisoner's chains, and to erect the scaffold and its ladder and place prisoners upon it. No other court but Troyes is known to have made such concerted use of its scaffold and prison. Between 1423 and 1468, in addition to condemning twenty bigamists to the ladder and prison, the Troyes official further condemned fifty-seven others to fixed terms of imprisonment. Other punishments included the ladder of the scaffold alone without additional penalty, penitential procession into church and the presentation of a candle at the altar, pilgrimage, banishment, and the burning at the stake of a woman accused of idolatry.

Throughout our period, much to the evident displeasure of some royal officials, three to six promotors investigated throughout the diocese.[27] They were assisted by a host of notaries and advocates who would collect testimony, copy out citations, and serve as assistants on visitations. This team of law enforcement officials included members of the cathedral chapter, subdeacons and deacons of the diocese, and laymen. Their labors led to the summons and processing of thousands of suspected offenders in the course of the century.

This highly proactive judicial behavior did not go without reproof. On the contrary, it called forth an angry response from royal officials. These complaints were voiced amid a broad struggle over jurisdiction and privileges in the course of the fifteenth century. This struggle resulted in a royal mandate issued by Charles VII, the *Ordonnance de Montil-les-Tours*, promulgated in 1453, ordering the compilation of local customary laws. These efforts resulted in a broad and successful assertion of royal jurisdiction. To return to the local conflict between royal and ecclesiastical authority in Troyes, since 1434 at least the bishop's official and the king's bailiff were at odds, reciprocally excommunicating and imprisoning various members of the other party's staff.[28] The matter came before the Paris Parlement, a *procès* that began in 1455 and was not resolved until 1461. In the course of this litigation, royal representatives took the part of the beleaguered people of the city and diocese of Troyes, claiming that these men and women suffered excessively under the sway of this overly active court.[29]

More broadly, contemporary and sixteenth-century critics of officialities accused the courts, and this court in particular, of acting on less principled motives. Agents of the Crown criticized the officiality of Troyes, accusing the bishop and his officials of encroaching on royal jurisdiction and excessively burdening the people of Troyes with heavy and too-frequent fines. The court had gotten too big, argued the representative of the Crown, and was doing too much.

But why had the bishops of Troyes and their officials so surpassed their colleagues elsewhere in their efforts to regulate marriage? We address, in effect, two different questions. First, why do so much? Second, why do such things? One can certainly attribute financial motivations as an explanation for court activity. Power-seeking, aggrandizement, and financial gain are certainly reasonable charges to levy against the fifteenth-century officiality of Troyes. Such incentives may well explain employing more staff, claiming broader jurisdictional powers, and scouring the diocese in search of people to prosecute and fine. Such incentives, however, do not explain the way in which the court chose to handle marriage in general and bigamy in particular. Why bigamy?

An explanation for the court's preoccupation with bigamy emerges in part from the historical context. Donahue has observed that in the fifteenth century ecclesiastical judges in northern France, and particularly the Burgundian territories, seem to have shared a real sense that marriage was in crisis.[30] The history of Champagne, as discussed earlier in this chapter, offers one plausible explanation for this. This region had suffered great devastation, especially as a result of famine, plague, and most recently the Hundred Years' War and its aftermath. Large-scale suffering may well have brought a sense of need, to the bishops and their officials, at least, for renewed moral and religious rigor.[31]

The most obvious objection to this argument is that not all bishops everywhere in all dioceses that saw the worst of the Hundred Years' War similarly motivated themselves. Further, the Hundred Years' War had no such negative impact on Burgundian lands. In contrast, Champagne and Normandy are known to have especially suffered, and it is in Troyes and in Rouen that we find the most proactive, the most regulatory, of officialities.[32] Of course, and most important, devastation in itself is not enough to provoke reform. There must also be active and willing reformers ready to act to promote the salvation of souls in the diocese and the restoration of order. This combination of hardship and will, not to mention education, can certainly be found in Troyes.

When we turn to the language used by the court itself in its handling of bigamy, this impression is reinforced. We have access to two of the ways in which the court communicated its understanding of bigamy. First, there is the metaphorical language of the punishments the court meted out, and second, the literal language used by the court to describe bigamy in the sentences read out in the condemnation of offenders.

The language of punishment, when employed by an ecclesiastical court, had a quite limited vocabulary. Ecclesiastical officials could not spill blood, even indirectly, and thus could not punish by mutilation or execution, as practiced in secular courts.[33] Barred from these forms of punishment, the Troyes officiality made use of fines, imprisonment, and public exposure, and also, if extremely rarely, banishment and penitential pilgrimages.

Even with such a limited vocabulary, the court seems to have classified crimes into different types of offense and punished them accordingly. For the officiality of Troyes, the crime of bigamy required both public punishment and imprisonment. Few others crimes also met with this combination of public exposure on the ladder of the scaffold and confinement in the bishop's prison.

The ladder, an instrument of public punishment, was intended to punish public crimes, crimes made against the body public. In the hands of ecclesiastical judges, public penance and public punishment intertwined. Public sins causing public offense, such as adultery or incest, required public punishment. When so administering public punishment in fifteenth-century Troyes, the officiality invoked a centrally important concept in medieval legal thought on crime, the idea of public crimes. The notion of public crimes and public punishment has a long history. The relevant maxims are derived from a legal tradition that medieval canonists extracted from Roman law, in particular the *Digest*. As Richard Fraher argues, public interest was a central principle for regulation of crime in the Middle Ages. In the early years of Innocent III's papacy, the papal chancery produced an important decretal, "Inauditum," arguing that it was in the public interest that crimes not go unpunished. Reforming ecclesiastics adapted this conception of public interest in the thirteenth and fourteenth centuries to justify the prosecution of "notorious" and "manifest" crimes with a lower standard for proof than other crimes.[34]

When first invoked by Innocent III and other reforming ecclesiastics, the concept of public crimes was intended for use in the prosecution of clerics suspected of concubinage, heretics, and usurers. By the later Middle Ages, however, bigamists would also come to be prosecuted as notorious and thus subjected to public punishment.[35] Indeed, most of the sentences passed by the Troyes officiality against bigamists include the phrase "Ne crimina remaneant impunita." Associated in particular with public crimes, this phrase served to justify prosecution of notorious crimes even without denunciation or definite proof. With the use of such terminology, we see the legal context in which the Troyes officiality considered bigamy cases and their consciousness of a mandate to combat activity that violated Church laws and morals in their diocese.

Public crimes, offenses to the body public, merited public punishment. Bigamy, above all a bigamous marriage that had been celebrated publicly and *in facie ecclesie*, fell under this rubric of public crime.

As we have seen, the ladder appears in the synodal legislation of Tours as the officially prescribed punishment for bigamy. We arrive with some difficulty, however, at an idea of exactly what this edifice looked like or how it worked. The bishop's scaffold evidently consisted of a raised platform with a ladder, and it seems most likely that the man or woman subject to the punishment was placed on or in between the rungs of the ladder.[36] This, at least, is how medieval illuminators and sculptors would depict the *échelle* as found by Barbara Morel in her survey of images of punishment from medieval France.[37] To be placed upon any of these structures was a deeply humiliating and shameful punishment for a culprit and for his or her family.[38]

The officiality of Troyes, like a number of other ecclesiastical courts, used the ladder to punish bigamy, false testimony, blasphemy, heresy, and serious violations of the sacrament of orders by clerics. Thus bigamists were punished in ways similar to perjurers, but also to heretics and felonious clergy. The ladder, however, only represented the public half of the punishment inflicted upon bigamists in Troyes. What of the prison?

Between 1423 and 1468 the officiality issued no less and probably more than seventy-seven fixed prison sentences ranging in terms from one month to perpetual confinement in the bishop's prison on bread and water and in chains. The crimes that called for such punishment, to use the language of the court, included bigamy, homicide, brigandage, sacrilege, performing mass without a license, heresy, blasphemy, perjury, forgery, arson, sorcery, and the baptism of a stillborn. Members of the clergy predominate, only twenty-three of the offenders had lay status. That members of the laity found themselves subject to lengthy detention in a bishop's prison at all is fairly surprising, as such was not usually their fate elsewhere.[39] Heresy served as the general exception to this rule, with the mass imprisonments of suspected Cathars in thirteenth- and fourteenth-century southern France offering a well-known example. We must, however, append bigamy to heresy in our short list of reasons why a layperson might be confined in a bishop's prison. Almost all of the laypersons imprisoned in Troyes were bigamists, and the same might be said of the archdeacon's prison in Paris. The punishment of prison, then, ranks bigamists alongside felonious clergy, sorcerers, and heretics in the eyes of the officiality.

The combined punishment of ladder and imprisonment we find most often, and indeed almost exclusively, used against bigamists and against blaspheming or felonious clergy. The language of punishment, while a blunt instrument, set bigamists apart from other members of the laity. Bigamists, like clerical brigands, had violated their status. To commit bigamy was to violate the most essential rules of the order of matrimony in a way not unrelated to the shedding of blood by a man sworn to renounce violence and serve God.

The language of punishment, carefully read, offers a possible means of understanding how the officiality thought about the crime of bigamy. What these punishments communicate is that that the officiality regarded bigamy, at least when committed by men,[40] as a grave public offence. The language of the sentences used to condemn these bigamists reflects a great deal more of why the officials of Troyes found bigamy in particular such a grave violation, why the court could not tolerate bigamy.

The language of the sentences passed against these bigamists and other serious offenders offers the strongest evidence of moral panic on the part of the judges and a special concern with matrimony, with the sacrament of marriage. These sentences include descriptions and definitions of the various offenses and the reasoning behind the punishments allotted. These sentences thus offer direct evidence of the specific crimes the judges deemed deserving of such punishments, and further, they offer evidence of the reasons given by the judges for so punishing such crimes. To fully understand these sentences, however, we cannot confine ourselves to cases of bigamy alone. We must compare the language used against bigamists to that used against other offenders. After identifying a number of these descriptions of the offenses found in sentences passed against bigamists, we will see if similar language can be found in the sentences passed against felonious clergy or heretics.

Before we turn to examining the sentences, some explanation of the background and function of these sentences is required. As Donahue explains, "—we know that the tradition of writing sentences in highly formal and rhetorical language was characteristic of Romano-canonical procedure as it was practiced in the ecclesiastical courts in the later Middle Ages . . . They give an impression of seriousness and solemnity, an impression that was clearly their purpose to produce."[41] This was true for the sentences Donahue studied from the registers of Cambrai and Brussels and is certainly true for Troyes.

We assume that these sentences were read out in court by the judge, for the offender and all else present to hear. If the court did not read out the sentence in the vernacular, however, this must have had a somewhat limited impact on many of those men and women convicted by the court, although the reading of the sentence aloud may well have had a ritual effect and have made an aural impression on the convicted offenders regardless of their presumably limited comprehension of Latin, as Donahue suggests.[42] One can also understand, however, why late medieval plays performed by guilds of law clerks mocked ecclesiastical court officers for "jabbering in incomprehensible Latin."[43]

At any rate, these sentences were presumably read aloud. They are addressed to the offender, comprehending or not, who is called "Tu." The sentences begin by invoking the Lord's name, usually giving the date and listing the names of the promotor and other officers present; then the status, origins, and occasionally the profession of the offender are listed. The sentence next offers a chronological list of the crimes the offender has "confessed" to, along with the court's judgment. The language is highly formulaic and repetitive, drawing on "stock phrases" routinely deployed by the official to describe and condemn various crimes and events.[44]

Read aloud in Latin or in the vernacular, the sentences from Troyes that involved the most serious offenses display the same sort of "heightened rhetoric" described by Donahue in his assessment of sentences from the registers of Cambrai and Brussels: "Like the formulae of a Homeric poem, a repertoire of stock phrases and half-phrases can be stitched together to fit the circumstances of the case."[45] This rhetoric, however formulaic, is of great importance, as it helps us to understand how the court perceived these various offenses. Indeed, the court's reliance on *formulae*, on stock phrases derived from the decretals, from biblical, patristic, and canonical procedural works, offers a lens of real importance through which to view the court's assessment of these crimes, the contexts in which these crimes were viewed.

The earliest conviction we have for a bigamist, a sentence passed in 1423, concerns a man whose case we have examined previously, that of Étienne, called "Languedoc," from the diocese of Langres. To review, Étienne had confessed to a fourteen-year-old marriage made with one Isabelle in his home diocese. He had subsequently left Isabelle and come to the village of Bouilly in the diocese of Troyes. His efforts to marry a widow, Marguerite, in that village were repeated in his sentencing by the court as a list of crimes.[46]

First of all, having abandoned his wife Isabelle in Langres, he had come to the village of Bouilly and contracted marriage "de facto." This marriage was considered a de facto union—rather than a de jure union—because Isabelle had been living at the time, and still lived. That is the first crime, a crime because willfully and knowingly done. Second, in order to make this marriage, Étienne had falsely asserted that he had heard news of Isabelle's death, and he had sworn a false oath: "without being in any way informed that Isabelle had died, and having made no diligent inquiry as to her status."

Here, the court began to offer its interpretation of these crimes. We come to an example of the "heightened rhetoric" described above, a lesson in how the court perceived these crimes. With these deeds, Étienne had "vilified the state of marriage," a thing instituted, as the court reminded Étienne, "in the terrestrial paradise" and "by Jesus Christ."[47] Further, "he had shown contempt for the people of the holy church militant, above all the duped second wife." Having deceived her, having deprived his first and only true wife of the marital debt, he had also committed perjury and many other crimes to the detriment of his soul and salvation. These crimes had been committed publicly and against the body public and thus, implicitly, deserved public punishment. All this, then, offers an account of the court's perception of his crimes, crimes deserving public punishment and incarceration.

"The state of matrimony, instituted in the terrestrial paradise" is certainly a phrase that could have been inspired by reference to countless medieval theological and canonical writings describing marriage in Paradise and at Cana. The phrase could also have stuck in the mind of a judge or could have been thought to affect an offender in an aural context as well. It is a phrase that might easily have been heard in church, perhaps even in a Lenten sermon.

From the middle of the fourteenth century the city council of Troyes was in the practice of hiring preachers for the Lenten season. These preachers had trained at the Sorbonne in Paris, as had many members of the officiality and other ecclesiastical officials in Troyes.[48] This phrase appears in the Lenten sermons, for example, of Jean Cleree, one of the preachers known to work in Troyes.[49] Born in 1455, Cleree's preaching postdates this sentencing but offers an example nonetheless of the stock phrases repeated in Parisian-trained Dominican preaching from well before his time.[50] Nor was the phase unique to Dominicans, the Franciscan Saint Bonaventure had also preached along similar lines.[51] We have, therefore, the possibility that both judge and offender had heard this phrase before, perhaps even in a vernacular Lenten sermon.[52]

Many of the same phrases were used against a bigamist whose case was recorded in the register immediately following that of Étienne "Languedoc." Both sentences were rendered on the same day but with two different promotors.[53] From this second sentence we learn that Hugh, called "Chenilloy," of the diocese of Autun, had married one Marguerite, a widow, in that diocese.[54] Subsequently, without seeking authorization from the Church, Hugh had "recklessly" left his wife, living first in the diocese of Meaux and then, about six years before, he had come to the city of Troyes. There, regardless of the fact that Marguerite was still alive, he had sought to marry a widow of Troyes called Robina. Just as Étienne had sworn that his wife had died despite having no information or reasons to suspect her death, so did Hugh swear. Once more, these crimes were offenses against the state of matrimony, created in the terrestrial paradise by God. Again, just as with Étienne, Hugh had shown contempt for the people of the body church militant, deceiving above all Robina but also committing perjury and risking his own salvation.[55]

In a subsequent case of bigamy, we learn that Jean Ferrand, likewise, "against God and the ordinances to the Church committed perjury, *stuprum,* adultery, and other crimes against the sacrament of marriage, Christ's creation."[56] Looking next to the case of Pierre de Loray, we find that in 1427 Pierre was condemned for a remarriage made without any reasons to suspect that his first wife had died, committing adultery with his second wife in bad faith, many crimes against the state of matrimony, contempt for the church militant and above all for the second wife, Jeanne, perjury, and many other crimes—all threats to his salvation.[57] Bigamists were also frequently accused of showing contempt for the statutes of the Holy Fathers,[58] an important accusation to which we will return.

As for Casini, called "the Noble," of the diocese of Soissons, he had sworn a false oath in order to marry one Melina in Nogent-sur-Seine, in the diocese of Troyes. Three years before his sentencing, his first wife, Jeanne, had in fact died, but this was well after his marriage to Melina. Such were his many crimes: vilification of the sacrament of marriage, deceiving the Holy Church Militant, depriving his true spouse of her rights, deceiving Melina, adultery, injury, and other crimes, including dissimulation.[59] It is interesting that perjury is not included in this list, at least not explicitly. This must be a simple oversight, since the sentence clearly states that Casini had given a false oath, claiming that no prior marriage bonds prevented his marriage to Melina, his so-called second wife.[60]

Skipping ahead to 1442, we find the sentence and punishment of Jean Pietrequin, a layman from the diocese of Châlons-en-Champagne living in the village of Chauchigny, in the diocese of Troyes. At the instigation of the devil, as Jean's sentence read, knowing that his first wife was alive but seeking to avoid publicity or any investigation of his background, Jean contracted a clandestine marriage in a chapel in Verdun. As we have seen, Jean paid the chaplain 12 *grossi* to celebrate the marriage without banns or any other solemnities. Afterward, he persisted in adultery, to the damnation of his soul.[61]

Acting "dyabolica sugestione" or "instigante dyabolo" was an important component of many of these sentences passed against bigamists. This is another stock phrase used in these sentences, used not only against bigamists but also against virtually all serious offenders. In these sentences we find as well an additional phrase: acting to the detriment of one's soul or salvation "in sue anime detrimentum." As we will see, both phrases were a feature of the sentences passed not only against bigamists but also against clerics who had murdered and laity guilty of heresy or sorcery. With these phrases, an emphasis on salvation emerges, an emphasis that stands out in these sentences.

One final example of rhetoric used against bigamists was certainly unique to these offenders but has important resonance above all in comparison to cases of criminal clergymen. Most interestingly, bigamists were told from time to time that they had violated the order of matrimony, "ordo matrimonialis." Just as with our initial rhetorical example of marriage instituted in the terrestrial paradise, we have another example that has resonance with medieval sermons.[62] Before turning to the sermon, however, let us see how the phrase was used in passing sentence against bigamists. Here, to give one example from the Troyes sentences, is the condemnation of Barthélémy Bouvier: "And so that such crimes and marriage contracted *de facto* do not remain unpunished, nor such dissimulation be tolerated, but publicly and in such a way that the honor and reverence of the Holy Mother Church and the order of matrimony are vindicated they are to be punished, and set out as an example and to inspire fear."[63] This "order of matrimony" may well have been seen to resemble in some ways the order of clergy. "Ordo" could certainly also refer in a more general manner to a way of life, as in the three orders of medieval society: those who fight, those who labor in the fields, and those who pray. However, there is precedent found in medieval sermons for considering an "order of matrimony" as a religious order.

Nicole Bériou and David d'Avray found an example of the "order of matrimony" in a sermon written by Dominican preacher Henri of Provins as part of a collection from 1272–73.[64] This sermon explicitly compared the Order of Preachers and the Order of Matrimony. Drawing upon this and other examples from other sermon collections, Bériou and d'Avray argue the following: "When these passages are taken together, they lead us to think that the idea of matrimony as the oldest 'religious' order, founded not by a saint but by God Himself deserves to be called one of the commonplaces of thirteenth-century preaching."[65] This high praise for matrimony would bring high expectations for behavior, as found in these cases where bigamists are condemned alongside those who had violated the sacrament of ordination.

In sum, bigamists were accused almost always of adultery and often of perjury. They were told that they had vilified the statutes of the Holy Fathers and that they had scorned marriage, instituted by Christ in the terrestrial paradise. They had all offended the church militant, the holy church, and Christian people. They had offended above all either the second spouse they had deceived or the first spouse they had deprived of the conjugal debt and other rights owed a spouse. Misled by the devil, these men (and one woman) were guilty of "vilification of the state of matrimony, showing contempt for the Church Militant, deceiving Her, that is; the Church, and your wife, depriving her of the conjugal debt, and damnably incurring perjury."[66]

These cases thus offer a consistent account of the ways in which the court of Troyes perceived these crimes of willful and deceitful bigamous marriage. These crimes were all described as being against the Church, against its teachings and sacraments. According to the court, these crimes abused vows, the Church, and the Christian people. As we have seen in earlier sections of this chapter, the punishments inflicted on these bigamists resemble most closely those inflicted upon clerics guilty of murder or desecration of the mass or the Eucharist. Does the language of these sentences similarly resemble the language of those or any other crimes?

In answer to this question, we begin with the group whose punishments matched most clearly and consistently those punishments inflicted on bigamists. We begin with criminous clergy, whose sentences certainly included rhetorical devices similar to those used in describing the offenses of bigamists. The sentence passed in 1423 against Friar Pierre Mignon of Paris, for example, offers much by way of recourse to the same level and tone of rhetoric. This vagabond friar, who had left his monastery without permission, was only a subdeacon, not ordained a priest, but nonetheless celebrated mass more than sixty times in the town of Ramerupt. He was thus accused of having "deceived the Church Militant, offended the divine and indescribable majesty, vilified the sacred priestly order, shown contempt for the keys of the Church, and committed unspeakable crimes and sins."[67]

Jean Alegres, alias "Gaillart," was a priest who had given out unconsecrated hosts at mass and had in so doing threatened the salvation of his parishioners. The response of the official was scathing.[68] The court described his actions not only as foolish but also as scandalous, dangerous, and inexcusable. Jean was suspended and banished from the diocese.

Clerics guilty of homicide faced slightly different rhetorical treatment. While bigamists were told that they had deceived the church militant and shown contempt for the statutes of the Holy Fathers, these murderers were told that they had broken a divine commandment: thou shalt not kill. Such was the language used against one Jean Creney, an unmarried cleric. Misled by the devil and unmindful of the commandment, Jean had killed a certain Deniset, from Burgundian lands, a layman and servant (*famulus*) of Nicolas le Roy.[69] So, too, did the court describe the homicide committed by Jean de Metz, married cleric of the diocese of Troyes, who, "out of excessive anger and at the suggestion of the devil," killed a man, regardless of the Ten Commandments.[70]

A cleric who stole from churches was also reminded of the Ten Commandments in his condemnation.[71] Another cleric and thief, who persisted in stealing from churches after already facing punishment for prior thefts, was condemned as a recidivist: "like a dog who returns to its own vomit and as incorrigible, unmindful of your salvation you backslid (recidivisti) into evil."[72] So too was described a bigamist who returned briefly to his first wife, only to go back once more, falsely and adulterously, to the second, illegal wife.[73] Found in Proverbs 26:11, this evocative depiction of caninelike recidivism has been applied in many such contexts. For example, the First Council of Nicea so described Christian clergy who entered military service,[74] a reference that the bishop's official in Troyes failed to echo in his own castigation of clerical brigands. The phrase was also made use of by Augustine to describe morally lapsed Christians and subsequently used throughout the Middle Ages to condemn recidivist heretics.[75] The Troyes court thus participated in this tradition in its condemnation of some of its criminal recidivists.

Having seen the rhetoric used against murderers and thieves, what of perjurers? Jean de Terre, at the "suggestion" of the mother of one Jacquette, presumed wife or widow of Jacques Passe, had sworn that he had seen this Jacques buried and that Jacquette was thus free to marry. "At the instigation of the devil," Jean had testified falsely that he had been in Burgundian lands and in the village where Jacques, as Jean falsely claimed, had died and was buried.[76] This perjury, a crime against the body public, could not, according to the court, remain unpunished. Jean and his accomplice in this false testimony met with much the same punishment as passed against bigamists in Troyes.

Coming finally to cases of blasphemy and heresy, we find rhetoric as charged as that passed against the bigamists. These men and women certainly all acted "at the instigation of the devil." Adelaide, guilty of baptizing a stillborn baby who had been dug up for this purpose, had been misled by the devil in her violation of the sacrament of baptism: "and you knew the baby was a dead cadaver, but nevertheless, instigated by the devil, you abused the holy sacrament of baptism."[77] Midwives could certainly baptize infants, and should, in fact, baptize them if they suspected that the infant might die, but a stillborn could not be baptized, and to do so was to abuse the sacrament.

For Adelaide, and for the other men and women suspected of blasphemy or heresy, a delegated inquisitor of heretical depravity joined in the sentencing, occasionally accompanied as well by theologians and other experts. Hugh Milot, accused of speaking in public "against the honor of the Immaculate

Virgin,"[78] met his sentence at the hands of not only the official but also Friar Nicolas de Rotaria: Dominican, bachelor in theology, and inquisitor delegated by the pope for matters of heresy in the city and diocese of Troyes.

Other accused heretics and blasphemers also faced harsh rhetoric alongside harsh punishment. Jean Barbier, alias "Petit," was condemned in 1462 for sorcery.[79] He was accused of divination and practicing magic, an egregious crime above all for his abuse of the Eucharist. An "apostate," this sorcerer was condemned to perpetual imprisonment.

As we have seen, the language of sentencing offers more distinctions among the serious crimes than the more limited language of punishment. The worst crimes, those that resulted in some of the harshest "heightened rhetoric," were those that in addition to causing scandal, risking salvation, and causing offense, also violated in some way a sacrament—be it the sacrament of marriage, of ordination, or of baptism. The sacraments of the Church were to be protected by the vigilance of the court. So too were violations of divine precept and the teachings of the Fathers.

Such is the picture that emerges from our records. In the midst and aftermath of the Hundred Years' War, the fifteenth-century bishops of Troyes did not hesitate to make use of episcopal jurisdiction to impose order upon a disordered society. This action took place above all, it seems, by means of the officiality.

To conclude, we must recognize once more the exceptionality of this regulatory behavior. While the vast majority of sources do not survive, and much of what remains has yet to be examined on this question, outside of northern France and the Burgundian lands, other courts across Christian Europe do not seem to have shared the zeal of the court in Troyes for regulation of marriage until the sixteenth century or even the seventeenth.

In the fourteenth and fifteenth centuries, most English courts handled marriage litigation as civil suits initiated by one of the parties rather than at the courts' own initiative. Nor do southern German courts seem to have sought out offenders in marital behavior. The Italian courts, with many criminal records only recently unsealed and not yet studied, remain a mystery. But it seems unlikely and out of character for ecclesiastical courts in Italy to show this regulatory character before the sixteenth century, and we have a good deal of evidence that the regulation of marriage and prosecution of bigamy only begin in the sixteenth century in Italy, and in some cases not until well after the Council of Trent. Much the same could be said for Spain. As for the rest of France, southern French courts do not seem to have had the means or ability to exert a great deal of authority over marriage practice. Only in Rouen, Paris,

Cambrai, Brussels, and the Champagne region do we find anything like the degree of regulation of marriage found in the records of the diocese of Troyes.

Why this regulatory behavior in northern France? This chapter offers little by way of evidence to suggest that these unusually active courts were simply seeking to enrich themselves. As we have seen, such a charge has certainly been made. In the fifteenth century, the bishop's court in Troyes faced accusations of aggrandizement and avarice, made by representatives of the French crown who sought to take over a good deal of the business handled by the bishop's court in Troyes.

However, while setting an example by prosecuting bigamists did show the power of the bishop's court in Troyes, it does not seem to have greatly contributed to its coffers. Men and women who attempted to remarry without proof were often fined, as indeed were most offenders in late medieval episcopal justice. Those found guilty of bigamy did not pay fines but instead faced public punishment and imprisonment. Prisoners were expected to pay their own expenses, to be sure, but this would not have served to greatly enrich the bishop. Money alone does not seem a satisfactory explanation. It is far more plausible to argue that the behavior of this court was in some measure a response to the horrors and disorder of the Hundred Years' War. Did not the bishops of Troyes believe that God was punishing the people of the diocese for their sins? Would not the proper response be reform?

What ultimately drove the fifteenth-century bishops of Troyes and their officials to determine that all marriages in the diocese, both marriages newly made and intact marriages, should be subject to scrutiny? I think we must suspect more religious than financial motives, or at the very least a combination of both. More deeply than that, we must acknowledge the power of moral panic in driving social policy. One might expect a society devastated by war to focus on the basic tasks of rebuilding everyday life. Yet we find the bishop of Troyes and his court demanding more of the people of Troyes. They could and should rebuild, but they must also seek to live as better, married Christians. Allowed access to the sacrament of marriage, once admitted to the order of matrimony, spouses could not be permitted acts of bigamy, which violated the core principle of Christian marriage as a singular and indissoluble bond.

To close, I offer a coda on subsequent developments. The events described in this chapter invite reflection on events a century later. Acting in the fifteenth century, the bishop of Troyes's officiality anticipated the widespread prosecution of bigamy found throughout Catholic Europe in the sixteenth and seventeenth centuries.

Indeed, the reformist zeal we see in fifteenth-century Troyes seems to herald the Reformation. A call to reform in the wake of the Hundred Years' War may also have led ecclesiastical officials of Troyes to anticipate the fervor attached to the sixteenth-century identification and prosecution of the crime of bigamy in Catholic countries, a crime that played a central role in the religious controversies of the sixteenth century as Catholic and Protestants fought out a new definition of what it meant to be a Christian and to marry as a Christian. The tale of the regulation of marriage in late medieval Troyes may be, in the end, a tale of the transition from the Hundred Years' War to the Reformation. But I must leave the tale to be explored elsewhere.

Conclusion

Christian Identity at the End of the Middle Ages

Some thirty years ago Natalie Davis first enthralled the world with the story of Martin Guerre; his abandoned wife, Bertrande de Rols; the impostor Arnaud du Tilh, who assumed Martin's identity; and the great Protestant jurist Jean de Coras, who judged the case. For Davis, the story brought to life the central issue of identity in early modern France. The imposture attempted by a man like du Tilh, Davis argued, violated a deeply held belief in the importance of identity, which was intimately bound up with personal status and honor.[1]

There is no gainsaying the brilliance of Davis's work on Martin Guerre, nor of her continuing work on identity in early modern culture.[2] Nevertheless, her ideas about identity have been stretched too far. Identity alone cannot explain all that scholars have subsequently asked it to explain. In particular, identity cannot explain the problem of bigamy as it manifested in northern France in the century before the celebrated trial of Arnaud de Tilh. To speak of identity in analyzing the cases studied in this book without speaking also, and more deeply, of Christianity and Christian identity is to misunderstand the meaning of bigamy in this context.

To be sure, as practiced in late medieval northern France, the crime of bigamy by its very nature involved fraud and identity. Nevertheless, imposture was not the central issue in late medieval understandings of this crime. Distortions of identity undoubtedly mattered to the people of fifteenth-century Troyes. But it is *Christian* identity that mattered most. Whatever notions of honor and status men and women of fifteenth- and even sixteenth-century Troyes cherished, Christianity was no less prized and was intrinsically related to identity. Marriage, like baptism and burial, was a central Christian ritual in many people's lives. How one married, to whom, and the subsequent conduct of married life were all essential acts of Christian identity. The bigamists of this book lived in a world in which Christian identity played a leading role.

Monogamous marriage had supreme importance as the Christian norm, reverenced in late medieval Troyes. Indeed, the ideal of monogamous marriage held such importance that even widows and widowers who remarried faced considerable disapprobation and disapprobation of all kinds. Meanwhile, ecclesiastical courts in northern France implemented rules with such strict requirements for proof of widowed status that one wonders how even a legitimate widow might manage to establish her status without engaging in some bribery or fraud if her husband died anywhere other than in his own bed. As I have shown in this book, widows and widowers both valued marriage enough to engage in considerable lawbreaking. My aim here has been in part to demonstrate how sincere desire for Christian identity, for Christian status and honor as well as Christian benedictions, could drive such people to acts that the Christian church regarded as serious criminal acts.

Drawing on the work of David d'Avray, we can assert that preaching served as an important tool for the dissemination of doctrinal Christian ideas about marriage in the later Middle Ages. Looking to the court records of the Troyes officiality, we find evidence of the dissemination of these ideas not only by preachers but also by priests and judicial officials, whose efforts to uphold Christian norms we read of in the registers. We find evidence for these activities in the records of the efforts of judicial officers to investigate and to prosecute those persons who violated the laws.

We can also find also broad evidence of the presence of Christian marriage norms in the information offered the court by witnesses, suspects, denouncers, and accusers. The world of fifteenth-century Troyes was in many ways a very Christian world. Certainly the notion that marriage norms in late medieval Troyes offer evidence of a failed Christianization is entirely wrong. Christian ideas such as marital chastity or participation in the sacraments were valued and sought after. People forgot the lessons of Christian charity and fought each other, but they fought in church and in cemeteries. They were present and active, for better or worse, in sacred Christian space. Further, they fought largely to defend their sexual honor as upright Christians, married or not.

Also, and what is more revealing, people married more often than they should have according to the law. But it matters that they did so at the doors of a church and with the blessing of the priest. Even if they married less formally, the language they at least subsequently claimed to have used bespoke a heavy Christian ideological current in their society. They may have promised to marry in a tavern, but in so doing they said, "I will join with you in the order of marriage if God and holy church permit."[3] The people of the diocese of Troyes—not all, to be sure, but in manifest numbers—had assimilated a body of Christian norms and had chosen to live out these norms according to principles they established based on their own authority.

These remarrying "widows" and widowers," these wives (and husbands) of Bath, probably knew they could not legally marry without finding proof of death, and that this proof should be legitimate, but like Chaucer's Alison they chose to interpret the laws of marriage in their own way. They had learned to value the Christian institution of marriage and wished to marry again, and at church door. That they violated the law in so doing did not seem as important, or at least seemed worth the risk of exposure and prosecution.

Like the oft-married wife of Bath, these bigamous men and women acted on their own authority. Some men seemed to think that rumors of adultery or the flight of their wives from their homes justified or at least excused their remarriages. Some women thought that many years of absence justified a presumption of death and remarriage. Such thinking, however, challenged the authority of canon law and ecclesiastical courts.

This behavior would not have led to conflict with ecclesiastical authorities had certain authorities themselves not so greatly valued marriage, a strictly monogamous and indissoluble kind of marriage. The officiality of Troyes was provoked by warfare, by dynastic struggle, by religious schism, by plague, and by famine; it was guided by extensive legal and especially theological training that praised marriage as a sacrament and urged that married persons act according to the rules of the order of matrimony. Acting upon such provocations, and in line with the law and theology, the officiality found itself in conflict with its all-too-oft-marrying laity.

Enforcement of these rules broke down along a gendered divide. The court in Troyes found that women and men both entered into potentially bigamous engagements and marriages; both women and men provided false testimony; both men and women perjured themselves in their efforts to remarry. Nevertheless, the court acted most often and most harshly to punish the bigamy of mature adult males. Female bigamists almost always faced fines and the dissolution of suspect marriages at worst. In fifteenth-century Troyes, mature married men were held to high standards of morality and responsibility for their marriages, not only for themselves but also for their wives. Wives, as members of the weaker sex, found that their bad behavior met with a more tolerant attitude from the court.

What is most important to recognize about the crisis of marriage in late medieval Troyes is that it is a two-sided problem. The records reveal not the imposition of norms upon a community by a court nor a cultural sea-change provoked from below. What we discover is an expression of extreme dedication to Christian norms on both sides, above and below, if you will, expressed in different and conflicting ways. Court officials and laity alike valued Christian marriage and Christian identity. Such indeed was the source of their dissension and the source of a growing crisis in the century before the Reformation, a crisis that would spread throughout much of western Europe in the sixteenth century.

Beginning at the close of the fifteenth century, bishops and other religious and also secular officials in some parts of Christian Europe began a more active regulation of the marriage practices of the laity and also of their beliefs concerning marriage. In the final decades of the fifteenth century, Spanish courts in Castile and Aragon, possibly encouraged by the rising Inquisition, began to prosecute bigamy as a form of heresy and as a crime against the sacrament of marriage.[4] Emlyn Eisenach argues that reforming bishops in Verona, particularly Gian Matteo Giberti, began to regulate and reform marriage practice in the 1530s, work that culminated in the 1560s with members of the laity expressing a new and seemingly unprecedented horror of bigamy, once tolerated—especially by lower-status communities—but now a thing of "shame and disgust."[5]

With the Reformation, the Catholic Church, facing calls for reforms from without and within, issued new rules for marriage at the Council of Trent (1545–63). In particular, the Decree Tametsi (1563) radically altered marriage law.[6] No longer could a marriage be validly contracted without the presence of the parish priest and witnesses. Further, banns were required for all marriages, though bishops could provide dispensation in special circumstances.

Clandestine marriages, the Catholic Church still maintained, were true marriages, but they could no longer be allowed. Why? What reasons, if any, were given for such a change? If we take the authors of the decree at their word, the shift in stance on clandestine marriage was not in response to claims that parental consent should be necessary for a marriage, though concerns on that score were certainly voiced in France and in both Lutheran and Reformed doctrine. Nor was clandestine marriage prohibited because a priest's blessing was necessary to make a marriage valid.

Instead, the central issue for the Church was bigamy. Clandestine marriage, the council declared, was outlawed because of "man's disobedience":[7]

> Although it is not to be doubted, that clandestine marriages, made with the free consent of the contracting parties, are valid and true marriages, so long as the Church has not rendered them invalid; . . . nevertheless, the holy Church of God has, for reasons most just,

> at all times detested and prohibited such marriages. *But whereas the holy Synod perceives that those prohibitions, by reason of man's disobedience, are no longer of avail; and whereas it takes into account the grievous sins which arise from the said clandestine marriages, and especially the sins of those parties who live on in a state of damnation, when, having left their former wife, with whom they had contracted marriage secretly, they publicly marry another, and with her live in perpetual adultery; an evil which the Church, which judges not of what is hidden, cannot rectify, unless some more efficacious remedy be applied* [italics my own]; wherefore, treading in the steps of the sacred Council of Lateran celebrated under Innocent III, it ordains that, for the future, before a marriage is contracted, the proper parish priest of the contracting parties shall three times announce publicly in the Church, during the solemnization of mass, on three continuous festival days, between whom marriage is to be celebrated; after which publication of banns, if there be no lawful impediment opposed, the marriage shall be proceeded with in the face of the church; where the parish priest, after having interrogated the man and the woman, and heard their mutual consent, shall either say, "I join you together in matrimony, in the name of the Father, and of the Son, and of the Holy Ghost"; or, he shall use other words, according to the received rite of each province.

We see here that by the time of the Council of Trent, leading officials of the Catholic Church had come to believe that the sacrament of marriage was under worse threat from this hidden bigamy—perpetrated by those who, already married, "publicly marry another, and with her live in perpetual adultery"—than from any other abuse. As important as free consent remained to these officials, the threat of bigamy trumped the primacy once accorded free consent.

Not only were clandestine marriages deemed illegal at Trent; parish priests who married a couple unknown to them, without first receiving permission from the couple's parish priest, were subject to suspension. As we have seen, ecclesiastical officials in northern France had already moved to enforce these rules well before Trent. And the Council of Trent went still further. Perhaps most important for the prevention of bigamy, Trent introduced the new requirement of parish registers, which were to record the names, dates, and places of marriages.[8] Man could no longer be permitted to secretly violate the impediment of prior bonds. Bigamy was not to be tolerated within Christendom:

> Vagrants are to be married with caution. There are many persons who are vagrants, having no settled homes; and, being of a profligate character, they, after abandoning their first wife, marry another, and very often several in different places, during the life-time of the first. The holy Synod, being desirous to obviate this disorder, gives this fatherly admonition to all whom it may concern, not easily to admit this class of vagrants to marriage; and It also exhorts the civil magistrates to punish such persons severely. But It commands parish priests not to be present at the marriages of such persons, unless they have first made a careful inquiry, and, having reported the circumstance to the Ordinary, they shall have obtained permission from him for so doing.[9]

In this new order, marriage had to reflect the sacramental bond of Christ to Church, and this bond, this institution, was more important than population, politics, or even royal succession in England. Polygamy itself, and the belief that polygamy might be a valid form of marriage, were both firmly equated with heresy.[10] Any Christian who said that such a marriage could be appropriate within Christendom was anathema.

The focus on male bigamy throughout these decrees on marriage and bigamy reflects, as we have seen, a concern with male behavior far more than female behavior. Just as the male bigamists of Troyes bore the brunt of punishment in Troyes, and indeed, nearly always when bigamy was prosecuted in the fifteenth and sixteenth centuries,[11] so too here do we find an emphasis on the prevention and punishment of male bigamy.

All these changes found in the Council of Trent's canons postdate the Middle Ages, to be sure. Nevertheless, they cast a revealing backward light on the sources studied in this book. Indeed, this book is about how such doctrines formed. I have examined how Western Christians arrived at the conviction that bigamy should not be tolerated and might even require criminal prosecution. By the sixteenth century, the perception of bigamy as a grave threat to Christendom, already present a century earlier, was a driving force in the reforms of marriage law at the Council of Trent and the explosion of prosecutions and punishments of bigamists in the sixteenth, seventeenth, and eighteenth centuries.[12] Pretending one could get married despite being already married to a living spouse was intolerable behavior. Individual bigamists of the type we have seen in this book faced unprecedented prosecution and even execution. Men were sentenced to row in galleys and women sentenced to whippings and imprisonment or exile. Such active regulation of bigamy would fade over the centuries, yielding to the prosecution of swindlers and deceptive traveling merchants, salesmen, or vagrant muleteers or merchant marines.[13]

Meanwhile, in the sixteenth century and well beyond, Western, Christian rulers also found open polygamy on the model of the patriarchs intolerable. Protestants and Catholics alike massacred the polygamist Anabaptists of Münster.[14] Martin Luther's granting of permission to Philip of Hesse to marry bigamously proved a major source of condemnation.[15] Brief efforts at legalizing polygamy in seventeenth-century England were decisively quashed.[16] In nineteenth-century America, Mormons would also learn that Western society would not tolerate such divisions and duplications of marriage.[17]

Indeed, the problems that plagued Christian Troyes in the later Middle Ages did not end with the Council of Trent. Far from it. In some sense they are still with us today. To be sure, much would change. The values that drove the practice of bigamy and bigamy prosecution in late medieval Troyes are thrown into sharp relief when compared to later centuries. Curiously enough, for example, in its habits of remarriage, at least, marriage practice in fifteenth-century Troyes has its resemblances to nineteenth-century America. As Hendrik Hartog explains in his *Man and Wife in America*, people share a common misconception about marriage in the centuries before the reintroduction of divorce in Western society, before divorce became first a legal and second a commonplace feature of modern Western society.[18] People often assume that when there was no legal divorce, many unhappily or unsatisfactorily married people remained married. As Hartog has argued, they may have remained married in law, but they did not necessarily remain married in fact. If spouses could not seek legal divorce they could and did leave, and they did often remarry. Hartog had no statistics for this phenomenon in nineteenth century America, and I can certainly offer no such numbers for late medieval Europe. Nevertheless, in both times and places married people remarried much more often than the law allowed.

In fifteenth-century Troyes, however, they did so in drastically, and revealingly, different circumstances from those studied by Hartog. Nineteenth-century American culture revered monogamy, disdaining divorce but above all disdaining the polygamy practiced by Mormons.[19] Even so, as Hartog has shown, serial monogamy, abandonment or informal separation followed by remarriage, seems to have been not only fairly common but also largely tolerated both by society and especially by the courts, who preferred to maintain any current grouping that resembled an intact family unit rather than insist on upholding the law and dissolving any potentially bigamous marriages.[20]

Not so in late medieval Troyes, at least, a place where bigamy was treated as an intolerable crime.

In this book I have examined the origins of how bigamy came to face such hostility, the hostility that polygamy still faces in Western society, and indeed much of the non-Muslim world. A great deal has changed, of course. However, while divorce is increasingly acceptable in Western society, the idea of marriage as a singular bond, between one man and one woman, remains a durable notion with a great deal of currency. Such, in no small way, is our medieval, Christian heritage.

APPENDIX: SELECTED TRANSCRIPTIONS FROM A REGISTER OF THE OFFICIALITY OF TROYES

Archives départementales de l'Aube

G4171fols.2r–3r [Thursday, 2 September, 1423]: Eadem die lata fuit presens sententia ad promotionem Nicolay Huyardi. In Dei nomine amen. Auditis confessionibus vestrorum Felisoti dicti Naalot et Colete, relicte defuncti Johannis de Feignis, qui libere et vestris spontaneis voluntatibus confessi fuistis et in jure recognovistis, quod vos decem annis elapsis vel circiter de facto matrimonium in facie ecclesie bannis proclamatis et ceteris rite actis contraxistis vivente prefato Johanne, cui Colete viro et marito, quamvis tu Felisotus ignorares praefatam Coletam esse uxoratam. Et ipsa Coleta verissimiliter credebat dictum virum suum, qui ab istis partibus te relicta extra provinciam abierat et longam moram fecerat, decessisse. Sicque in tali matrimonio de facto, non de jure, cum tu Coleta esses uxorata, contracto per terannum [triennum] vel circiter permansistis et prolem suscepistis. Quo tempore transacto prefatus Johannes Trecensis rediit et per quindecim dies vel amplius ipsum oculata fide cognovistis et cum eodem bibistis et manducavistis, et paulo post idem Johannes iterum recessit et ad aliam regionem se transtulit, vosque predictis non obstantibus et dictum Johannem vivente scientibus vos invicem carnaliter cognovistis, propter que postmodum in jus vocati fuistis, fuitque vobis palam publice et juridice prohibitum sub penis juris et aliis certis penis nec de cetero simul quovismodo in tali matrimonio nec in concubinatu staretis seu cohabitaretis, vosque promisistis mandatis ecclesie humiliter obedire. Istis tamen non obstantibus, vos postmodum claves ecclesie ~~p~~ [crossed out in original] in periculum animarum vestrarum contempnando et multipliciter honorem matrimonii vilipendendo, per quinque annos vel circiter dicto Johanne vivente, simul adultere vivendo et moechando cohabitare cum gravi scandalo ecclesie praesumpsistis, ac etiam dicto Johanne ab hac vice paulo post subtracto in vestro malo praeposito semper perdurastis et simul permansistis in premissis et eorum quolibet multipliciter delinquendo. Et quia talia delicta non debent remanere sine cum digna pugnitione, taliaque connubia seu matrimonia adulterina nullatenus sunt tolleranda, quinymo ut nullus ducat in matrimonium illam quam fide data polluit per adulterium omnia iura clamant. Idcirco per hanc nostram diffinitivam sententiam quam nos, pro tribunali sedentes et Deum solum pre oculis habentes, habita super premissis matura deliberatione cum peritis, ferimus in hiis scriptis, dicimus, declaramus, pronunciamus et decernimus prefatum matrimonium de facto inter vos contractum nullum fuisse vel esse, et inter vos, a tempore quo prefatum Johannem scivistis esse vivum, in adulterio permansisse, inhibentes vobis sub penis excommunicationis et aliis penis iuris nec de cetero quovismodo simul in tali matrimonio vel concubinatu permaneatis vel cohabitetis necnon ne in simul matrimonium de novo contrahatis, necnon ad emendam arbitrariam et penitenciam salutarem pro premissis delictis sic per vos perpetratis peragendam, earum taxatione injunctione seu moderatione penes nos reservata, prolem tam ex predicto matrimonio quamdiu prefatum Johennem vivente ignorastis susceptam legitimam reputantes et decernentes, ac in expensis promotoris condempnantes.

G4171fols.6r–6v [22 January 1423] In Dei Nomine Amen. Audita confessione tui Stepham dicti Languedoc de Mesguil subt. [subiecto?] de Lingonensis diocesis [Mesnil (Haute-Marne) diocese of Langres] qui tua mera et spontanea voluntate confessus fuisti in jure coram nobis et etiam alias sufficienter informati sumus quod a quatuordecim annis citra vel cerciter, matrimonium in facie ecclesie contraxisti in villa de Talant [Chalency, Haute-Marne] dicte Lingonensis diocesis cum Ysabelli [Isabella] filia dicti "le Grant" Nicolas de la Chalou. Et postmodum videlicet a tribus annis citra vel circiter in villa de Bouilleyo [Bouilly] Trecensis diocesis accessisti in qua matrimonium de facto, cum de jure non posses, quia praefata Ysabella tunc vivebat et adhuc vivit, de presenti contraxisti cum Margareta relicta deffuncti Therienini Grisart de dicto Bouilleyo. Absque hoc quod tu fuisses sufficienter informatus de morte dicte Ysabellis nec fecis diligentem inquisicionem de vita vel morte et statu ipsius Ysabellis quamvis ut asseris aliqui falso tibi dixerint et semper [as]severint eamdem [6v] Ysabellim diem suum clausisse extremum. In premissis multipliciter delinquendo, statum matrimonii in paradiso terrestri a domino nostro Jhesu Christo instituti villipendendo, ecclesiam sanctam militantem contempnando populum et potissime praefatam Margaretam dicipiendo periurium et plura alia delicta in detrimentium anime salutis anime [word crossed out] tue publice committendo et jus matrimoniale tue uxoris proprie ab eadem aufferendo et quia talia delicta non debent nec possunt ob honorem nostre sancte matris ecclesie sub dissimulatione celari sed sunt animadversione publica vindicanda et taliter pugnienda [punienda] que aliis cedat in exemplum idcirco per hanc nostram diffinitivam sententiam quam nos pro tribunali sedentes et deum solum pre occulis habentes eius nomine primitus humiliter invocato de peritorum consilio ferimus in hiis scriptis dicimus et declaramus prefatum matrimonium inter te et predictam Margaratam de facto contractum fuisse et esse nullum ac ecclesiam in solemnisacionem dicti matrimonii fuisse deceptam et ulterius ut pena unius sit metus multorum te scalandum fore ante valvas trecensis semel una die dominica vel solemniter Necnon ad Remanendum in prisonaribus Reverendi in Christo patris ac domini domini trecensis episcopi et per semiannum ut ibi in pane doloris et aqua tristitie tua defleas peccata et talia amplius non conmitas Gratia tamen dicti Reverendi patris salua semper et reservata.

G4171fol.17v [21 July 1425]: In Dei nomine amen. Audita confessione tui Casini dicti le Noble de Challey super Maternam, Suessis diocesis [Chailly-en-Brie, Soissons], qui tua mera et spontanea voluntate coram nobis in jure confessus fuisti, quod quamvis tu alias XXV annis vel circiter elapsis sponsalia deinde matrimonium in facie ecclesie solempnisatum cum Johanneta Rouselle de Feritate Bernardi in civitate Carnotensi [Chartres] contraxisses, fuitque dictum matrimonium carnali copula consummatum. Nichilhominus tamen duodecim annis elapsis vel circa, te transtulisti in villa de Nogeto super Sequanam [Nogent-sur-Seine, Aube], Trecensis diocesis, et contraxisti sponsalia cum Melina filia Johannis le Seurre de Conflantio, dicte Trecensis diocesis. Deinde Trecis [Troyes] accesisti et in jure tuo medio juramento false asseruisti te esse solutum ac liberum ad matrimonium contrahendum cum dicta Melina, certis penis et canonibus adhibitis casu quo contrarium verum reperiri. Et sic cum dicta Melina de facto, cum de jure non posses, matrimonium contraxisti, licet de morte prefate Johannete prime uxoris tue, tunc viventis, minime fuisses informatus, stetistique cum dicta Melina secunda, prima vivendi, per spatium novem annorum vel circiter, quequidem Johenneta a tribus annis vel circiter diem suum clausit extremum. Et quia in premissa multipliciter delinquisti, sacramentum matrimoniale vilipendendo, Sanctam Ecclesiam militantem decipiendo, jus uxoris proprie aufferendo, prefatam Melinam decipiendo, adulterium, injurium, et alia delicta committendo, nec debent talia delicta sub dissimulatione transire, nec impugnata remanere, sed taliter vi[n]dicanda sunt publice ut pena unius sit metus multorum, idcirco per hanc nostram diffinitivam sententiam, quam nos pro tribunali sedentes et Deum solum pre oculis habentes, de peritorum consilio super premissa habita deliberatione matura, prefatis consideratis cum aliis amicorum nostrorum moventibus, Christi nomine primitus humiliter invocato, ferimus in hiis scriptis: dicimus, decernimus et declaramus prefatum secundum matrimonium de facto per te cum dicta Melina contractum nullum esse et fuisse, ecclesiamque in solemnisatione dicti matrimonii fuisse et esse deceptam, penasque in praefatis canonibus emissas et commissas. Et ulterius ut ceteris cedat in exemplum, condemnamus te scalandum fore publice inter valvas Trecensis ecclesie, semel una die dominica, necnon ad remandendum in prisonaribus Reverendi in Christo patris ac Domini Domini Trecensis episcopi per tres menses, ut ibi in pane doloris et aqua tristitie tua defleas delicta, et talia amplius non commitas, gratia tamen dicti Reverendi Patris salva semper et reservata.

G4171fol.38v [9 March 1443]: In nomine Domini amen. Audita confessione tui Johannis Pietrequin laici de Sancto Germano Cathalunensis diocesis [St. Germain-la-Ville, Châlons-en-Champagne] oriundi nunc in villa de Chauchigniacum Trecensis diocesis [Chauchigny (Aube), diocese of Troyes] conmorans subditi et justiciabilis nostri, qui tua mera voluntate in judicio coram nobis confessus es, quod sunt decem anni vel circiter, licet Marieta uxor tua legitima viveret, te sciente instigante dyabolo ipsa dimissa quandam dominam Elenam nomine de facto duxisti in uxorem et eam secrete ac clandestine in quadam cappella prope Virdunum [Verdun, Meuse] per verba de presenti per manum cuiusdam cappellani, cui ipsi ii decem [*12*] grossos tradidisti, desponsavisti nullis bannis aut aliis solempnitatibus assuetis precedentibus, ex qua prolem genuisti. Et cum ea usque adhuc in adulterio tue salutis inmemor dampnabiliter permansisti. Ne predicta delicta remaneat impunita, et te, quam [quem] divinus timor a malo non revocavit saltem metus pene temporalis coherceret a peccato Nos Officialis Trecensis pro tribunali sedentes et solum Deum pre oculis habentes ipsius nomine primitus invocato per hanc nostram diffinitivam sententiam quam in hiis scriptis predictum matrimonium clandestine de facto et contra jus contractum decernimus et declaramus fore nullum, teque ad scalandum fore una [fol. 39r] die Dominica aut solemna ante valvas ecclesie Trecensis necnon ad remanendum per unum mensem in carceribus Reverendi in Christo patris et domini nostri domini episcopi Trecensis ut ibi in pane doloris et aqua tristitie peccata tua defleas et amplius talia non commitas. Gratia cum ipsius reverendi patris in omnibus semper salua.

G4171fol.60v–61r [13 January, 1447] In nomine Domini Amen. Quia per confessionem tui Matthei Rucin barberii laici de Vendocino [Vendôme, Loir-et-Cher] Carnotensis [Chartres] diocesis oriundi subditi et justiciabilis nostri, coram nobis judicialiter factam nobis constitit atque constat quod, licet alias matrimonium contraxeris in facie ecclesie cum Johannetta uxore tua legitima, et cum eadem apud Sezannam [Sezanne, Troyes] et alibi per tres annos pacifice permansisti, nichilominus tu eam tempore Quadragesime ultimo preterite apud dictam villam Sezanne dimisisti, et ad civitatem Senonensis [Sens] te transtulisti, ubi cum quadam Johannetta, relicta defuncti Denisoti du Sault de Brayo [Bray-sur-Seine, Yonne] oriunda, per verba de futuro in facie ecclesie instigante dyabolo sponsalia contraxisti, super quibus aliqua banna sunt proclamata, sed cum dicta Johannetta uxor tua legitima illuc causa peregrinacionis, ac devotionis quam habebat ad sanctum Potentianum [St. Potentia] tempore dicte proclamacionis accedit ac predicta didicisset teque redarguendo peteret quare hoc faciebas, tu publice respondisti coram multitudine populi quod dictam Johannetam non cognoscebas nec unquam eam desponsaveras. Et si forte eam aliquando cognoveras ipsam tanquam meretricem aut concubinam cognoveras. Deinde propriam uxorem relinquendo et a civitate Senonensis recedendo ad civitatem Aureliansis [Orléans] cum prefata Johannetta te transtulisti, promittentes ei quod tu [cum] ea matrimonium contraheres in facie ecclesie quod minime fecisti cum per carnalem copulam matrimonium de facto cum de jure non posses saltem presumptum cum dicta Johanneta [fol. 61r] contraxisse eamque de civitate in civitatem et de loco ad locum scilicet Aurelianis, Virdunensis [Verdun], et Parisius [Paris], ipsam esse tuam coniugem mendaciter asserendo necnon in adulterio per spatium quatuor mensium dampnabiliter in anime tue preiudicium perseverando te reduxisti. Ne igitur talia crimina remaneant inpunita et facilitas venie tribuat incentivum delinquendi quodque ceteris cedat in exemplum Nos Officialis Trecensis pro tribunali sedentes ac solum Deum pre oculis habentes ipsius nomine primitus invocato per hanc nostram sententiam diffinitivam quam de peritorum consilio ferimus in hiis scriptis, condemnamus te ad scalandum fore una die Dominica aut solemni ante valvas ecclesie Trecensis, necnon ad remanendum per tres mensis in carceribus Reverendi in Christo patris et domini nostri domini episcopi Trecensis ut ibi in pane doloris et aqua tristiciae, peccata tua defleas et amplius talia non commitas gratia tamen ipsius Reverendi patris in omnibus semper salva.

G4171fols.63r–63v [7 September 1448]: In Nomine Domini Amen. Quia tam per confessionem Johannis dicti le gros Jehan laici de Ancervilla [Ancerville, Aube] Cathalaunensis [Châlons-en-Champagne] diocesis oriundi nunc apud Virdunensis [Verdun, Meuse] Trecensis diocesis commorantis et Perrete eius uxoris de Barbusia [Barbuise] dicte Trecensis diocesis oriunde subditorum et justiciabilium nostrorum coram nobis in iudicio spontanea voluntate factam, quod aliud nobis constitit atque constat, ipsorum adducere matrimonium in facie ecclesie Limone [Les Limons, Marne] sunt xii anni contraxisse et per carnalem copulam consummasse necnon postmodum simul tam in villa de Nogento Supra Secanam [Nogent-sur-Seine, Aube] quam alibi per quadriennium vel circiter tanquam vir et uxor permansisse quodque propter guerras et hostium incursus in illis partibus Brige [Brie] praefatus Johannes predictam uxorem suam relinquendo ad partes Lothoringie [Lorraine] se transtulit et in villa de Bulvilliers [Belleville, Meuthe-et-Moselle] dyabolica sugestione de facto, cum de jure non posset, matrimonium cum Hellinsia relicta defuncti Perreroni Pouel contraxit, cum qua per spatium undecim annorum in adulterio permansit et ex ea prolem suscepit in sue anime detrimentum, cum sciret primam suam uxorem vivere. Predicta vero Perreta ex alia parte matrimonium sibi de facto statuta Sanctorum Patrum contempnendo apud villam de Malle [Mallé, Aisne] Laudinensis [Laon] diocesis cum Felisoto Arnoul dicti loci de Barbuisia [Barbuise, Aube] dampnabiliter contraxit vivente predicto Johanne marito suo, de cuius morte nullam habuerat assertionem, et per spatium vii annorum vel circiter cum dicto Feliseto adulterando in sue salutis praeiudicium cohabitavit. Nos Igitur Officialis Trecensis pro tribunali sedentes et solum Deum pre oculis habentes premissis attente auditisque super hiis predictis Felisoto et Hellinsia et que dicere voluerint per hanc nostram sententiam diffinitivam, quam de peritorum consilio ferimus in hiis scriptis, prefata matrimonia sic, ut premititur, de facto contracta videlicet inter predictos Johannem et Hellensiam ex una parte et inter prefatos Felisetum et Perrotam ex parte altera, decernimus esse nulla et invalida. Insuper cum talia delicta remanere non debeant impunita ne facilitas venie tribuat incentivum delinquendi. Ut ut quo [sic: Et ut quos] divinus timor a malo non revocat saltem metus pene temporalis cohibeat, a primo sepedictum Johannem ad scalandum fore semel die Dominica vel solemni ante valvas ecclesie Trecensis et ad remanendum per sex menses ac praenominatam Perretam per unum annum in carceribus Reverendi in Christo patris et domini nostri comitis domini episcopi Trecensis ad peragendam penitentiam in pane doloris et aqua tristicie condempnamus gratia tamen ipsius Reverendi patris in omnibus semper salva.

G4171fols.82v–83r [26 January, 1454]: Anno Domini M CCCC LIII sabbati post Conversionem Pauli, lata fuit presens sentencia ad promotionem N. Huyart, presentibus Grappin, Joffron, Britonis, N. Henrici, H. Doreti, Sens, Gerry, Coiffardi, cum aliis. Christi Nomine invocato. Audita confessione tui Bartholomii Boulier de Muernis [Les Mineroy, Aube] in villa de Fonvanna

[Fontvanne, Aube] diocesis Trecensis nunc commorantis subdici et justiciabilis nostri, qui tua spontanea voluntate in jure coram nobis confessus es, quod a decem annis citra saltem erant decem anni die Martis post Quasimodo proximo futurum, in facie ecclesie matrimonium contraxisti in dicta villa de Pontaber [Pontoux, Saône-et-Loire] Eduensis [Autun] diocesis cum quadam Pasqueta, filia dicti Gareau, ipsamque matrimonium carnali copula consummasti, et inibi cum ea spatio circiter septem annorum moram traxisti, ex qua genuisti iiii liberos, quorum duo vivus, videlicet filius etatis sex annorum et una filia trium annorum adhuc vivunt, duobus aliis vestris liberis de medio sublatis. Deinde ipsam Pasquetam ad civitatem Aurelianensem [Orléans] etiam moraturam duxisti, in qua eamdem dimittens ad dictam villam de Fonvanna [Fontvanne] eandem Pasquetam tuam uxorem fore mortuam mandaciter [mendaciter] asserendo te transtulisti, inque tui subdoli mandacii [mendacii] testimonium dictam tuam filiam etatis tunc unius anni vel eocirca matre orbatam, ut diversis in locis disseminasti, tecum afferendo, ubi cum quadam Johannetta, relicta defuncti Jaquini Leclerc de dicta Fonvanna, per verba de futuro in facie ecclesie a duobus annis citra, vivente tua legitima uxor prout vivit, te sciente et instigante diabolo sponsalia contraxisti, supra quibus aliqua banna in dicto loco fuerunt proclamata. Et quamquam paratus esses iure iurando affirmare iamdicte tue uxoris mortem, quia tamen dicte mortis testes et cautiones fideiussos Trecensis curie minime dare valuisti, tibi denegata contrahendi licentia, Senonensis [Sens] diocesis adivisti, et in villa de Lorris [Lorris, Loriet] a quodam, ut asseris, capellano litteras fictivas tui curati, tuique boni status et mortis tue sepedicte legitime uxoris testimoniales obtinuisti, mediantes duobus caseis et una pinta vini quos a te recepit capellanus ipse. Quibus quidem litteris tanquam non authenticis, cum perpendisses, officiarios curie Trecensis nolle fidem adhibere, ad diocesis Autisiodorensi [Auxerre] unam cum [unacum] predicta Johannetta te transtulisti, et in quadam cappella dicte diocesis, in villa dicta Arciz [Arcy-sur-Cure, Yonne] prope Cravant [Cravant, Yonne] clandestine dictam Johannettam de facto duxisti in uxore, et eam per verba de presenti per manum cuiusdam capellani, cui propter hoc unum scutum tradidisti, desponsavisti, et cum eadem Johennetta unum annum et amplius amplexibus adulterinis, eadem carnaliter cognoscendo dampnabiliter permansisti. Cumque dicta Pasqueta, uxor tua legitima, per patriam te quereret et premissa didicisset, teque de premissis a Nativitate Domini nuper praeterita redarguendo in suum virum repeteret, tuam coniugem legitimam se esse asserens, tu publice respondisti quod eamdem Pasquetam non cognoscebas nec unquam desponsaveras eamdem, et si aliquid carnaliter cognoveras ipsam, tamquam concubinam et meritricem habueras, clam autem et seorsum eamdem Pasquetam tuam, ut est et erat, legitimam recognoscens et confitens uxorem, quam etiam subornare non es veritus, ne se tuam fateretur et diceret esse et fuisse dumtaxat focariam, promittens quod si id publicaret, a te quamvis receptis bonis et facultatibus dicte Johannette supereminet aut earumdem portione si commode fieri posset, decurso brevi temporis curriculo ad eamdem Pasquetam etiam ut propriam et legitimam tractandam esses reum si[v]eras, omnino eadem Johannetta demissa. In premissis contra Deum et ecclesie ordinationes temere veniendo, periurium et tui ex parte adulterium pluraque alia termina commitens matrimonii sacramento calumpnose [*sic:* calumniose] illudendo praefatam Johannetam decipiendo et ius tue proprie uxoris auferendo. Et quia talia delita et matrimonia de facto contracta non debent impunita remanere nec sub dissimulatione tollerari, sed publice et taliter ob honorem et reverenciam Sancte Matris Ecclesie et ordinis matrimonialis vindicari et puniri, quod ceteris cedat in exemplum et terrorem. Idcirco per hanc nostram sententiam diffinitivam quam nos pro tribunali sedentes et solum Deum pre oculis habentes, ipsius nomine primitus invocato, habita super praemissis et cum peritorum consilio matura deliberacione, dicimus, declaramus, et pronunciamus predictum matrimonium cum dicta Johannetta de facto et contra ius contractum fore nullum, necnon te scalandum fore publice ante valvas ecclesie Trecensis duobus diebus dominicis aut solemnibus et ad remanendum in prisonaribus Reverendi in Christo patris et domini domini episcopus Trecensis per seminannum ut ibi in pane doloris et aqua tristicie tua defleas peccata et talia amplius non commitas, gratia tamen dicti Reverendi patris salua semper et retenta.

G4171fols.85r–v [29 May 1454]: Christi nomine invocato. Audita confessione tui Johannis le Nieps in villa de Rongueil Lingonensis diocesis [Langres] oriundi, qui tua mera et spontanea voluntate coram nobis pro tribunali sedentes in jure confessus fuisti et alias sumus sufficenter informati, quod nunc sunt sex anni vel circiter matrimonium in facie ecclesie contraxisti in villa de Chineyo [Chevigney] dicte Lingonensis diocesis cum quadam Ginota, filia Guillaumi le Roy de dicto Chineyo, ipsumque matrimonium consummasti et cum ea in dicto loco mansisti per spatium xx[ti] mensium et amplius, et ex ea duos liberos sustulisti. Postmodum ab eius consortio quatuor annorum spatio vel circiter te separavisti ab eadem divortendo, et ad diocesis Trecensis te transfferendo mendose cum juramento afferendo eamdem uxorem mortuam [esse]. Deinde de facto, cum de jure non posses dicta Ginota uxore tua vivente, in hac villa cum quadam Perreta, filia Johannis Motian, contraxisti a duobus annis citra solemnizatoque matrimonio ut moris est consummasti, eandem amplexibus adulterinis carnaliter cognoscendo, ac eidem quemdam filium procurando. Cum dicta Perreta spatio sexdecim mensium continuorum remansisti, excepto tamen quod pendente dicto tempore proprie uxoris Ginote apud dictum Chineyum commorantis presentiam admisisti, cum qua carnali etiam subsecuta copula per spatium sex dierum fuisti, et eidem contraxisti quod cum dicta Perreta ut praemititur contraxeras, tandem eadem Ginota iterim demissa ad sepefatam Perretam ut prius eidem cohabitando et ipsam mala fide possidente, tamquam canis ad vomitum reduxisti, non attendens quod crimina tanto graviora sunt quanto diutius infelicem animam detineretur alligatam. In premissis multiplorum delinquendo, statum matrimonium vilipendendo, ecclesiam militantem contempnendo, ipsumque et presertim dictam Ginotam uxorem tuam decipiendo, conjugale debitum ab ea aufferendo, periuriumque dampnabilis incurrendo, et quia talia delicta publice punienda iura canonica determinant ut ceteris cedat in exemplum, huic est per praemissis actentis per hanc nostram sententiam diffinitivam, quam nos pro tribunali sedentes et solum Deum pre oculis habentes eius nomine primitus invocato de peritorum consilio ferimus in hiis scriptis: dicimus et declaramus matrimonium inter te et praefatam Perretam de facto contractum nullum fuisse ecclesiamque in eius solemnisatione fuisse deceptam, et ob hoc te scalandum fore per tres dies dominicos aut solemnes ante valvas ecclesie Trecensis, et ad remanendum in prisonaribus Reverendi in Christo patris et domini nostri domini episcopi Trecensis per semiannum condampnamus, ut ibi in pane doloris et aqua tristicie peccata tua defleas et amplius talia non committas eiusdem Reverendi in Christo patris gratia semper salva.

G4171fols.120v–121r [11 September 1462]: Christi nomine invocato. Audita confessione tui Symonis Lugnet, alias Colier, agricole de Rumilleyo prope Vaudas [Rumilly-les-Vaudas, Aube] Trecensis diocesis oriundi, qui tua mera et spontanea voluntate in jure coram nobis cum juramento ad sancta Dei evangelia a te corporaliter tacta prestito, confessus fuisti et alias sumus sufficienter informati, quod nunc sunt circiter octodecim anni quandam Agnetem, filiam Johannis Marrey de Noulliyo [Neuville sur Seine] dicte Trecensis diocesis, in villa Divionam Lingonensis [Dijon, Langres] diocesis, tunc commorantis in dicta villa Diviona, in facie ecclesie cum ea contraxisti ipsaque matrimonium carnali copula cum ipsa consummasti, et cum ea tam ibidem quam in villa de Bano Supra Albam [Bar-sur-Aube] dicte Lingonensis diocesis morans traxisti continuos spatio septem annorum vel circiter. Quo tempore pendente unus filius nominatus Garnerus, hodiernis diebus vivens, a vobis procreatus existit. Dictaque Agnes, ut asseris, te derelinquit [et] ad civitatem Methensis

[Metz] se transtulit cum quodam custurario [tailor] nuncupato Paseto Galon, cum quo per certum temporem spatium mansit. Postmodum apud dictum Rumilleyum prope Vauds nunc sunt circum septem anni redistis, et ibi te incerto de morte dicte Agnetis tue uxoris, de facto, cum de jure non posses, te ipsum dampnabiliter decipiens et tue carnis unitatem cum dicta Agneta, tua uxore per carnalem copulam contractam, dividere non formidando, attendens quod a vinculo matrimonio solutus eras vivente adhuc iamdicta Agnete legitima tua uxore, sunt nunc circiter septem anni apud villam de Vandis prope dictum Remilleyum te transtulisti, in qua cum Margareta relicta deffuncti Natalis Goubault de dictis Vaudis matrimonium contraxisti, et matrimonio inter te et dictam Margaretam solemnisato [sollemnizato], ut moris est, cum eadem Margareta dicto tempore durante amplexibus adulterinis eandem Margaretam carnaliter cognoscendo remansisti. Quo tempore pendente quattuor liberi, videlicet Margaretam, Johannetam, Petrum, et Nicolam procreati fuerunt, qui omnes decesserint dempto dicto Nicolano. In quibus praemissis non modicum delinquendo militantem ecclesiam populumque, presertim dictam Agnetem uxorem tuam decipiendo debitum coniugale ab ea aufferendo, perjuriumque dampnabile incurrendo, que nimium punienda sunt ut ceteris cedat in exemplum, et ut metus pena sit multorum, huic est quod praemissis actentis aliisque quamplurimis nos juste momentibus per hanc nostram sententiam diffinitivam quam nos pro tribunali sedentes et solum Deum pre oculis habentes eius ut primitus nomine invocato de peritorum consilio ferimus in hiis scriptis: dicimus et declaramus matrimonium inter te et praefatam Margaretam de facto contractum nullum fuisse et esse, ecclesiamque in eius solemnisatione fuisse deceptam. Et ob hoc te scalandum fore per tres dies dominicos aut alios dies solempnes ante valvas ecclesie Trecensis et ad remanendum in carceribus Reverendi in Christo patris ac domini domini Ludovici [Ragvier] misericordia divina Trecensis episcopi per unum annum continuum condemnamus ut ibi in pane doloris et aqua tristicie peccata tua defleas et amplius talia non commitas, eiusdem Reverendi in patris gratia semper salua. J. Johannis.

NOTES

INTRODUCTION

1. See below, Chapter 5.

2. Steven Ozment, *When Fathers Ruled: Family Life in Reformation Europe* (Cambridge, Mass.: Harvard University Press, 1983), 1–49.

3. Canon law mandated that husbands and wives have reached the ages of 14 and 12, respectively.

4. For further discussion see below, Chapter 1.

5. While we have evidence of scattered, seemingly isolated bigamy prosecutions from the fifteenth century, the earliest large-scale bigamy prosecutions generally date to the sixteenth century. For Italy, see Cecilia Cristellon, "L'ufficio del giudice: Mediazione, inquisizione, confessione nei processi matrimoniali veneziani (1420–1532)," *Rivista Storica Italiana* 3 (2003): 851–98, 879–83; idem, "I processi matrimoniali veneziani (420–1545)," *I tribunali del matrimonio (secoli XV–XVIII),* ed. Silvana Seidel Menchi and Diego Quaglioni (Bologna: Il Mulino, 2001), 101–22; 105–7; Daniela Lombardi, *Matrimoni di antico regime* (Bologna: Il Mulino, 2001), 83; Emlyn Eisenach, "Sistemi informali di divorzio e seguenti matrimoni a Verona nella prima metà del cinquecento," trans. Alison A. Smith, *La Donne a Verona: Riconsiderare La Storia Della Città,* ed. Paola Lanaro and Alison A. Smith (Verona: Cierre, 2012); and Pierroberto Scaramella, "Controllo e repressione ecclesiastica della poligamia in età moderna: Dalle cause matrimoniali al crimine di fede (1514–1799)," in *Trasgressioni: Seduzione, concubinato, adulterio, bigamia (XIV–XVIII secolo),* ed. Silvana Seidel Menchi and Diego Quaglioni (Bologna: Il Mulino, 2004), 443–502. For Spain, see Martine Charageat, "Typologie des procès canoniques matrimoniaux à Saragosse (XV–XVI)," in *Sínodos diocesanos y legislación particular: Estudios históricos en honor al Dr. D. Francisco Cantelar,* ed. J. Justo Fernández Rodríguez (Salamanca: Publicaciones de la Universidad Pontifica de Salamanca, 1999), 217–32, 230–31; but compare this to Maria Teresa López Beltrán, "La bigamia y su significación social en Castilla a fines de la Edad Media," *Nuevos enfoques para la enseñanza de la historia* (Madrid: Asociación Cultural Al-Mudayna, 2007), 95–116; María del Carmen García Herrero, "Los matrimonios de Gaspar Eli: Tipología matrimonial en un proceso de 1493," *Aragón en la Edad Media* 7 (1987): 231–44; and Henry Charles Lea, *A History of the Inquisition of Spain,* 4 vols. (New York: Macmillan, 1907), 4:316–27. For Portugal, Isabel M. R. Memdes Drumond Braga, *A Bigamia em Portugal na epoca moderna* (Lisbon: Hugin, 2003).

6. See below.

7. See further, the Conclusion.

8. See further, Sara McDougall, "Bigamy: A Male Crime in Medieval Europe?" *Gender and History* 22:2 (August 2010): 430–46; at 466 nn. 69, 72, 76.

9. Natalie Davis, *The Return of Martin Guerre* (Cambridge: Harvard University Press, 1984); see also her "Les silences des archives, le renom de l'histoire," *Annales du Midi* 120 (2008): 467–83; Jeffrey Ravel, *The Would-Be Commoner: A Tale of Deception, Murder, and Justice in Seventeenth-Century France* (Boston: Houghton Mifflin, 2008).

10. *Oeuvres complètes de Voltaire* (Paris: Aug. Ozanne Rue de Richelieu, 1838), 5:74.

11. Sara McDougall, "Bigamy in Late-Medieval France" (Ph.D. diss., Yale University, May 2009).

12. McDougall, "Bigamy: A Male Crime," 430–46.

13. For a likely example, see Brenda Bolton and Constance M. Rousseau, "Palmerius of Picciati: Innocent III Meets His 'Martin Guerre'," in *Proceedings of the Tenth International Congress of Medieval Canon Law, 1996*, ed. Kenneth Pennington, Stanley Chodorow, and Keith Kendall, Monumenta Iuris Canonici, ser. C: Subsidia, 11 (Vatican City, 2001), 361–85.

CHAPTER 1. MARRIAGE AND REMARRIAGE IN THE LATER MIDDLE AGES

1. For a detailed description of these sources, see below.

2. Charles Donahue, Jr., "Law, Marriage, and Society in the Later Middle Ages: A Look at the English and 'Franco-Belgian' Regions," *Proceedings of the Thirteenth International Congress of Medieval Canon Law*, ed. Anzelm Szuromi and Peter Landau, Esztergom-Budapest, 3–9 August 2008, Monumenta Iuris Canonici, ser. C, subsidia 14 (Vatican City: Biblioteca Apostolica Vaticana, forthcoming); and also his conclusion offered in *Les officialités dans l'Europe médiévale et moderne,* ed. Martine Charageat and Veronique Beaulande (forthcoming, Brepols).

3. Albert Hyma, "Erasmus and the Sacrament of Matrimony," *Archiv für Reformationsgeschichte* 48 (1957): 145–64; H. J. Selderhuis, *Marriage and Divorce in the Thought of Martin Bucer,* trans. John Vriend and Lyle D. Bierma. Sixteenth-Century Essays and Studies 48 (Kirksville, Mo.: Thomas Jefferson University Press, 1999); John Witte and Robert Kingdon, eds., *Sex, Marriage, and Family in John Calvin's Geneva: Courtship, Engagement, and Marriage* (Grand Rapids, Mich. Eerdmans, 2005), 27–61; Ozment, *Fathers.*

4. David Herlihy, "Making Sense of Incest: Women and the Marriage Rules of the Early Middle Ages," in *Women, Family and Society in Medieval Europe*, ed. David Herlihy and Anthony Molho (Providence, R.I.: Berghahn Books, 1995), 96–112; Kathleen Cushing, *Reform and the Papacy in the Eleventh Century* (Manchester: Manchester University Press, 2005), 149; for an excellent summary with some useful explication of the degrees of relationship, see Ruth Karras, *Sexuality in Medieval Europe: Doing Unto Others* (New York: Routledge, 2005), 62–63.

5. Georges Duby, *Medieval Marriage: Two Models from Twelfth-Century France,* trans.

E. Forster, Johns Hopkins Symposia in Comparative History II (Baltimore: Johns Hopkins University Press, 1978); Jack Goody, *The Development of the Family and Marriage in Europe* (Cambridge: Cambridge University Press, 1983).

6. For a more detailed discussion of this, see Charles Donahue, Jr., *Law, Marriage, and Society in the Later Middle Ages: Arguments About Marriage in Five Courts* (Cambridge: Cambridge University Press, 2007), 30–31; see also his "Texts and Commentary" no. 47, available online at http://www.cambridge.org/us/catalogue/catalogue.asp?isbn=9780521877282&ss=res.

7. See especially Georges Duby, *The Knight, the Lady, and The Priest: The Making of Modern Marriage in Medieval France,* trans. Barbara Bracy (New York: Pantheon Books, 1984).

8. Christof Rolker, "Ecclesiastical Marriage Jurisdiction Around 1100," *Studies in Church History* 43, *Discipline and Diversity* (Woodbridge, U.K.: Ecclesiastical History Society, Boydell Press, 2007), 159–68, at 168.

9. Frederick Pollock and Frederic Maitland, *The History of English Law Before the Time of Edward I,* 2nd ed., vol. 2, rev. S. F. C. Milsom (Cambridge: Cambridge University Press, 1968), 389.

10. Charles Donahue, Jr., "Roman Canon Law in the Medieval English Church: Stubbs vs. Maitland Re-Examined After 75 Years in the Light of Some Records from the Church Courts," *Michigan Law Review* 72 (1974) : 647–716; Richard Helmholz, *Marriage Litigation in Medieval England,* Cambridge Studies in English Legal History (Cambridge: Cambridge University Press, 1975; reprint Holmes Beach, 1986), 78–87; Michael Sheehan, "Formation and Stability of Marriage in Fourteenth-Century England: Evidence of an Ely Register," in *Marriage, Family, and Law in Medieval Europe: Collected Studies,* ed. James K. Farge, (Toronto: University of Toronto Press, 1997), 257.

11. Monique Vleeschouwers-Van Melkebeek, "Incestuous Marriages: Formal Rules and Social Practice in the Southern Burgundian Netherlands," in *Love, Marriage, and Family Ties in the Later Middle Ages,* ed. Isabel Davis, Miriam Müller, and Sarah Rees Jones, International Medieval Research 11 (Turnhout: Brepols, 2003), 77–95; David D'Avray, "Lay Kinship Solidarities and Papal Law," in *Law, Laity, and Solidarities: Essays in Honour of Susan Reynolds,* ed. Pauline Stafford, Susan Reynolds, Janet L. Nelson, and Jane Martindale (Manchester: Manchester University Press, 2001), 188–99; Charles Donahue, Jr., "The Monastic Judge: Social Practice, Formal Rule, and the Medieval Canon Law of Incest," in *De Iure Canonico Medii Aevi: Festschrift für Rudolf Weigand,* ed. Peter Laundau and Martin Petzolt, Studia Gratiana 27 (Rome: Libreria Ateneo Salesiano, 1996), 49–69; Vleeschouwers-Van Melkebeek, "Incestuous Marriages," 77–95; see also Donahue, *Law,* 562–97, esp. 577–79. For one example from Troyes see Archives de l'Aube, G4172fol. 27.

12. However, working at the level of the papal penitentiary, Ludwig Schmugge has offered new findings on the subject of incestuous unions. Schmugge calls attention to a large number of German couples seeking dispensations from the papal penitentiary, asking to stay married despite an impediment, most often a consanguine relationship of the third or fourth degree. Based on his study of some six thousand petitions to the papal penitentiary for marital dispensation of an impediment, Schmugge has shown that 55 percent of

these petitions concerned blood relationships and some 30 percent affinity by marriage. He argues that with these numbers, the small role that consanguinity has been found to play in officiality litigation merits reconsideration. However, as the bishop could only dissolve a marriage on these grounds rather than provide a dispensation, and the majority of those who went to the penitentiary sought not an annulment but dispensation to remain married despite the impediment, his findings do not greatly affect the picture presented by Donahue and others. Ludwig Schmugge, *Ehen vor Gericht: Paare der Renaissance vor dem Papst* (Berlin: Berlin University Press, 2008), 59–61.

3. John Noonan, "Power to Choose," *Viator* 4 (1973): 419–34; Charles J Reid, Jr., *Power over the Body, Equality in the Family: Rights and Domestic Relations in Medieval Canon Law* (Grand Rapids, Mich.: Eerdmans, 2004), 37–43.

14. Martin Luther, *On the Estate of Marriage*, vol 45, *Luther's Works,* ed. J. Pelikan and H. Lehman (St. Louis: Concordia; Philadelphia: Fortress Press, 1957–), 44; idem, *Tischreden* 1:229–30, in *Sämmtliche Werke,* ed. Ernst Ludwig Enders and Johann Conrad Irmischer, 2nd. ed., vol. 28 (Frankfurt am Main: Berlad von Sender and Zimmer, 1832–81), 62.

15. 4 Lateran (1215) c. 51, in *Decrees of the Ecumenical Councils*, ed. Ginseppe Alberigo, trans. Norman P. Tanner (London: Sheed and Ward, 1990), 1:258.

16. Étienne Diebold, "L'application en France du canon 51 du IVe concile du Latran d'après les anciens statuts synodaux," *L'Année Canonique* 2 (1953): 187–95.

17. Carole Avignon, "L'église et les infractions au lien matrimonial: Mariages clandestins et clandestinité, théories, pratiques, et discours, France du nord-ouest (XIIe–milieu XVI siècle)," Ph.D. diss. Université Paris-Est, 2008, 160–63; Donahue, *Law*, 388–89; Léon Pommeray, *L'officialité archidiaconale de Paris aux XVe–XVIe siècles* (Paris: Sirey, 1933) 320; Statutes of Eudes de Sully, bishop of Paris (1196–1208), in *Les statuts synodaux français du XIII siècle* vol. 1, ed. Odette Pontal (Paris, 1971), 89; Troyes: Charles Lalore, ed., *Ancienne et nouvelle discipline du diocése de Troyes jusqu'en 1788,* vol. 2, *Statuts synodaux et Ordonnances épiscopales* (1374) (Troyes, 1882), 74–75, Locus 15: "Prohibemus sub pena excommunicationis et emende arbitrarie, licitis usibus applicande, ne alique persone inter se ad invicem matrimonium contrahant per verba de presenti, donec sint in valvis ecclesie in qua debebunt ad benedictionem admitti nuptialem; possunt tamen inter se dare fidem de matrimonio inter eos contrahendo, si sancta Ecclesia in hoc consenserit, et hoc fiat in facie Ecclesie et per manum sacerdotis. Illi vero qui contra fecerint, sive sint persone matrimonium contrahentes, sive sint illi qui associando interfuerint, et qui hoc fieri procuraverint, se per Nos noverint graviter puniendos"; Lalore, *Ancienne discipline* 2:185–86: "Statuta synodalia, 1 julii 1427, VII Aliud preceptum de Matrimonio. Cum matrimonia clandestina de jure sub magnis penis prohibeantur fieri, Nos, quorundam predecessorum nostrorum vestigiis inherendo, curatis et ecclesiarum presbyteris precipimus quod de cetero suis parrochianis, ex parte Nostri, precipiant quod, si quis sciat clandestina matrimonia, que scilicet non fuerint contracta vel celebrata in facie Ecclesie, hoc referat curato suo, qui infra unum mensem habebit notificare nomina sic contrahentium nostre dicte curie; et hoc precipimus observari sub pena quadraginta solidorum in pius usus convertendorum."

18. Statutes of Eudes de Sully, bishop of Paris (1196–1208), c. [98], in *Statuts synodaux français* 1: 89; Donahue, *Law*, chap.1; Pommeray, *L'officialité,* 320.

19. Avignon, "L'église," 266.

20. The Troyes statutes compiled and issued in 1374 included statutes from as far back as 1270 and probably earlier.

21. Shannon McSheffrey, *Marriage, Sex, and Civic Culture in Late-Medieval London* (Philadelphia: University of Pennsylvania Press, 2006), 121–36.

22. Shannon McSheffrey, "Place, Space, and Situation: Public and Private in the Making of Marriage in Late-Medieval London," *Speculum* 79 (2004): 960–90.

23. Donahue, *Law*, 46–296.

24. Silvana Seidel Menchi and Diego Quaglioni, eds., *Matrimoni in dubbio: Unioni controverse e nozze clandestine in Italia dal XIV al XVIII secolo* (Bologna: Societa editrice il Mulino, 2001); *I tribunali,* 360; Christiane Klapisch-Zuber, "Le complexe de Griselda: Dot et dons de mariage au Quattrocento," *Mélanges de l'école française de Rome* 94 (1982): 7–43; David D'Avray, "Marriage Ceremonies and the Church After 1215," in *Marriage in Italy, 1300–1650,* ed. Trevor Dean and Kate Lowe (Cambridge: Cambridge University Press, 1998), 107–15.

25. Federico R. Aznar Gil, "Penas y sanciones contra los matrimonios clandestinos en la península Ibérica durante la baja edad media," *Revista de estudios históricos-jurídicos* 25 (2003): 189–214.

26. Mia Korpiola, *Between Betrothal and Bedding: Marriage Formation in Sweden, 1200–1600* (Leiden: Brill, 2009), 179–81.

27. There is some reason to think that at least some local courts in fourteenth- to sixteenth-century England made a practice of inspecting and investigating suspicious couplings and marriages. See, for example, L. R. Poos, "The Heavy-Handed Marriage Counsellor: Regulating Marriage in Some Later Medieval English Local Ecclesiastical-Court Jurisdictions," *American Journal of Legal History* 39 (1995: 291–309; and also Lindsay Bryan, "Marriage and Morals in the Fourteenth Century: The Evidence of Bishop Hamo's Register," *English Historical Review* 491 (April 2006): 467–86.

28. Avignon, "L'église."

29. Jean-Baptiste Molin and Protais Mutembe, *Le rituel du mariage en France du XIIème au XVI siècle*, Théologie Historique 26 (Paris: Éditions Beauchesne, 1974); Juliette Turlan, "Recherches sur le mariage dans la pratique coutumière (XIIe–XVIe s.)," *Revue historique de droit français et étranger* 35 (1957): 477–528.

30. Beatrice Gottlieb, "Getting Married in Pre-Reformation Europe: The Doctrine of Clandestine Marriage and Court Cases in Fifteenth-Century Champagne" (Ph.D. diss., Columbia University, 1974), 193–287, esp. 270–89.

31. Jean-Louis Flandrin, *Le sexe et l'Occident* (Paris: Seuil, 1981), 34; Valérie Lamon Zuchuat, "Mariages clandestins dans le diocèse de Sion à la fin du Moyen Âge," *Annales valaisannes: Bulletin trimestriel de la Société d'histoire du Valais romand* (2004) : 7–25, at 11; Prisca Lehmann, *La répression des délits sexuels dans les Etats savoyards,* Cahiers Lausannois d'Histoire Médiévale 39 (Lausanne: Université de Lausanne, Section d'histoire, Faculté des lettres, 2006), 40–46.

32. Avignon, "L'église": see esp. 84–86, 319–20; Jean Gaudemet, *Le mariage en Occident: Les moeurs et le droit* (Paris: Cerf, 1987), 60–61.

33. Examples from the Troyes register comply with the notion of "affidare" as a future-tense engagement in two cases, A. D. de l'Aube G4174fol.23v and G4172fol.134r. In each case the woman is described as "affidatam," and the alleged offense was an engagement in the future tense "sponsalia contraxerunt per verba de futuro in facie ecclesie" (for a transcription and discussion of one of these cases see below, Chapter 3 n. 21). However, in G4174fol.7r a future-tense engagement "sponsalia contraxit per verba de futuro" is described not as "affidare" but as "desponsare" (see below, Chapter 3, n. 24).

34. *Canons and Decrees of the Council of Trent*, ed. and trans. H. J. Schroeder (Rockford, Ill.: Tan Books and Publishers, 1978), 180–85. For further discussion of this topic, see the Conclusion.

35. Gottlieb, "Getting Married," 226–27.

36. David D'Avray, *Medieval Marriage: Symbolism and Society* (Oxford: Oxford University Press, 2005).

37. Genesis 2:24; Laurent Mayali, " 'Duo erunt in carne una' and the Medieval Canonists," in *Iuris Historia: Liber amicorum Gero Dolezalek*, ed. Vincenzo Colli and Emmanuele Conte (Berkeley: Robbins Collection, 2008), 161–76.

38. Ephesians 5:22–33.

39. Philip Reynolds, *Marriage in the Western Church: The Christianization of Marriage During the Patristic and Early Medieval Periods* (Leiden: E. J. Brill, 1994).

40. Letter 123, "To Ageruchia," in *Jerome: Letters and Select Works*, trans. W. H. Fremantle, G. Lewis, and W. G. Martley. Select Library of the Nicene and Post-Nicene Fathers of the Christian Church, 2nd ser., vol. 6, ed. Philip Schaff and Henry Wace (Grand Rapids, Mich.: Eerdmans, 1892), 230–32.

41. *St. Justin Martyr: Dialogue with Typho*, trans. Thomas B. Falls (Washington, D.C.: Catholic University of America Press, 2003), chap. 134: "The marriages of Jacob were types of that which Christ was about to accomplish. For it was not lawful for Jacob to marry two sisters at once. And he serves Laban for [one of] the daughters; and being deceived in [the obtaining of] the younger, he again served seven years. Now Leah is your people and synagogue; but Rachel is our Church. And for these, and for the servants in both, Christ even now serves."

42. Suzanne Fonay Wemple, *Women in Frankish Society: Marriage and the Cloister, 500 to 900* (Philadelphia: University of Pennsylvania Press, 1981), 75–96.

43. X 4.19.8. "Quia vero tam patriarchae quam alii iusti viri ante legem pariter et post legem multas uxores insimul habuisse leguntur, nec contrarium apparet in evangelio vel lege praeceptum, neque pagani subiiciuntur canonicis institutis post inventis, quemadmodum est praemissum: videtur, quod nunc etiam iuxta ritum suum licite contrahant cum diversis, quorum coniunctiones legitimas unda sacri baptismatis non dissolvit, et ita patriarcharum exemplo ad fidem Christi conversi pagani coniugiorum pluralitate gaudebunt. Verum absonum hoc videtur et inimicum fidei Christianae, quum ab initio una costa in unam feminam sit conversa, et scriptura divina testetur, quod propter hoc relinquet homo patrem et matrem, et adhaerebit uxori suae, et erunt duo in carne una; non dixit: 'tres vel plures,' sed: 'duo,' nec dixit: 'adhaerebit uxoribus,' sed: 'uxori.' Unde Lamech, qui plures simul uxores legitur habuisse, reprehenditur in scripturis eo, quod ipse primus reprobandam bigamiae

speciem introduxit. Licet autem de his non quaesieris, volentes tamen tam te quam alios super his etiam reddere certiores, et quod veritas praevaleat falsitati, sine dubitatione qualibet protestamur, quod Nec ulli unquam licuit insimul plures uxores habere, nisi cui fuit divina revelatione concessum . . ."

44. Hostiensis, *Summa aurea in titulos decretalum* (Venice: Iacobus Italis, 1574), lib. 1 tit. De bigamis §3, fols. 40va–b. Hostiensis describes here six different kinds of bigamy. Whatever they may have called it, canonists and theologians unanimously rejected as completely illegal what Hostiensis described as true bigamy. James A. Brundage, *Law, Sex, and Christian Society in Medieval Europe* (Chicago: University of Chicago Press, 1987), 478.

45. Giuliano Marchetto, " 'Primus fuit Lamech': La bigamia tra ittegolarità e delitto nella dottrina di diritto commune," in *Trasgressioni:* Menchi and Quaglioni, 43–105.

46. Burkhard Roberg, *Das zweite Konzil von Lyon (1274)* (Paderborn: Ferdinand Schoningh, 1990), 319–21.

47. See also d'Avray, *Marriage*, 252 and 134. Innocent IV (pope), *Apparatus super libros Decretalium,* ed. Franciscus Moneliensis (Venice, 1481) fol.45

48. "Large vero et improprie dicitur bigamus, qui eodem tempore duas habet uxores, licet cum altera non possit matrimonium, nisi de facto." D 34 c.5, C 31 q.1 c.10, X 4.19.4. Raymond of Peñafort, *Summa Sancti Raymundi de Pennafort,* Liber III, Tit. III De Bigamis (Verona, 1744), 240.

49. Luigi Sandirocco, "Binae nuptiae et bina sponsalia," *Studia et Documenta historiae et iuris* 70 (2004), 165–216.

50. D'Avray, *Marriage*, 252.

51. Sandra Cavallo and Lyndan Warner, eds., *Widowhood in Medieval and Early Modern Europe: Women and Men in History* (New York: Longman, 1999); Sue Sheridan Walker, *Wife and Widow in Medieval England* (Ann Arbor: University of Michigan Press, 1993); M. Parisse, ed., *Veuves et veuvage dans le haut Moyen Âge* (Paris: Picard, 1993).

52. Katherine Clark, "Purgatory, Punishment, and the Discourse of Holy Widowhood in the High and Later Middle Ages," *Journal of the History of Sexuality* 16:2 (2007): 169–203, at 169.

53. Ibid., 196–97; "The Gast of Gy," ed. and trans. Mona L. Logarbo, in *Cultures of Piety: Middle English Devotional Literature in Translation*, ed. Anne Clark Bartlett and Thomas H. Bestul (Ithaca, N.Y.: Cornell University Press, 1999), 64–65.

54. See, for example, Patricia Skinner, "The Widow's Options in Medieval Southern Italy," in *Widowhood,* ed. S. Cavallo and L. Warner (London: Longman, 1999); Barbara A. Hanawalt, ed., *Women and Work in Pre-Industrial Europe* (Bloomington: Indiana University Press, 1986); Barbara A. Hanawalt, "Remarriage as an Option for Urban and Rural Widows in Late Medieval England," in *Wife and Widow in Medieval England*, ed. Sue Sheridan Walker (Ann Arbor: University of Michigan Press, 1993), 141–64; Martha C. Howell, *The Marriage Exchange: Property, Social Place, and Gender in Cities of the Low Countries, 1300–1550* (Chicago: University of Chicago Press, 1998), 109–22, 146, 151–52, 171–72.

55. André Rosambert, *La veuve en droit canonique jusqu'au XIVe siècle* (Paris, 1923), 145. The Paris coutumier of 1510 placed restrictions on women who remarried that were intended to protect the inheritance of the children of the first marriage.

56. As Christiane Klapisch-Zuber explains, in late medieval Florence, a widow could take her dowry away with her when she remarried, but not her children: *Women, Family, and Ritual in Renaissance Italy* (Chicago: University of Chicago Press, 1985), 125.

57. *Le charivari: Actes de la table ronde organisée à Paris (25–27avril 1977)*, ed. J. Le Goff and J. C. Shmitt (Paris: Mouton, 1981).

58. Roger Vaultier, *Le folklore pendant la Guerre de Cent Ans d'après les lettres de rémission du Trésor des Chartes* (Paris: Librairie Guénégaud 1965), 30–35; P. Fortier-Beaulieu, "Le charivari dans le Roman de Fauvel," *Revue de folklore français et de folklore colonial* 11 (1940): 1–16; Lucien Barou, "Le charivari en Forez," *Patois Vivant*, 10 (May 1982): 1–12.

59. Arnold Van Gennep, *Manuel de folklore français* (Paris: Editions Augusta Picard 1943–49), 1: 247, 614; André Varagnac, *Civilisation traditionnelle et genres de vie* (Paris: Albin Michel, 1948), 196–99.

60. Natalie Zemon Davis, *Society and Culture in Early Modern France* (Stanford: Stanford University Press, 1975), 101–7.

61. Claude Gauvard and Alton Gokalp, "Les conduites du bruit et leur signification à la fin du Moyen Âge: le charivari." *Annales. Économies, sociétiés, civilisations* (1974) 693–704: 699." 699; Claude Gauvard, *De grâce especial: Crime, état, et société en France à la fin du Moyen Âge*, 2 vols. (Paris: Publications de la Sorbonne, 1991), 1:591; Claude Karnoouh, "Le charivari ou l'hypothèse de la monogamie," *Le charivari,* 33–44.

62. See further below.

63. Davis, *Society and Culture*, 307–8. Davis, in n. 90, compiling the work of various scholars, identifies Church prohibitions against charivari for second marriages in the council of Anger (1269); the synod of Avignon (1337); the council of Tours (1445); fourteenth-century councils in Meaux, Bourges, Tréguier, Reims, and Troyes; and fifteenth-century prohibitions in Langres; Lyons by Archbishop Charles de Bourbon in 1466; and Nevers. See also Jean Dauviller, *Le mariage dans le droit classique de l'Église, depuis le Décret de Gratien (1140) jusqu'à la mort de Clément V (1314)* (Paris: Recueil Sirey, 1933), 119.

64. Lalore, *Ancienne discipline*, 2:79 Locus 19, "Cum sit damnabile primas aut secondas nuptias damnare aut vituperare, ut sacri canones declarant, ac etiam Novi et Veteris Testamenti documenta, ludum igitur turpem et nocivum, bonis moribus contrarium, ac specialiter contra dictum Apostoli veniendo, per quem nuptiis potissime secundis detrahitur non modicum, que nuptiae (quas Dominus noster Jesus Christus honoravit et honorari precepit) vertunt in derisum, qui ludus vulgo nuncupatur Charivary, qui ludus efficitur cum horridis et blasphemis vociferationibus et obscena loquacitate, sub turpi transfiguratione larvarum injuriosarum, contumeliosisque clamoribus dictarum binarum nuptiarum confutando, reprobamus ad instar libellorum vel carminum famosorum, et inhibimus de cetero fieri qualitercumque in dictis civitate et diocesi Trecensi, precipientes omnibus presbyteris et rectoribus parrochialium ecclesiarum ut hoc publicent in suis ecclesiis, taliter quod nullus contra ipsam inhibitionem ignorantiam valeat pretendere, et inhibeant ex parte dicti Reverendi Patris fieri dictum ludum sub pena excommunicationis et decem librarum, piis usibus applicandarum, tam contra actores ipsius ludi quam contra dantes in eo auxilium, consilium et juvamen."

65. Ibid, 2:79. A close companion to this is found in an edition of the synodal statutes

of Langres: "Liber sinodalis lingonensis ecclesie auctoritate reverendissimi in christo patris ac domini domini Ludivici cardinalis Barren perpetio . . . Anno domini millesimo quadrinigentesimio quarto," BN lat. ms. 1596 fol.195r.

66. Archives de l'Aube G246fol.3r.

67. Lalore, *Ancienne discipline* 2:69: "Matrimonium cum reverentia et honore celebretur et in facie ecclesie, non jocose et cum risu, ne hujusmodi sacramentum contemnatur."

68. X 4.21.3: "Si unus ex coniugibus fuit alias benedictus, non debent coniuges de novo benedici."

69. X 4.21.3: "Urbanus III. Vigiliensi Episcopo. Vir autem vel mulier, ad bigamiam transiens, non debet a presbytero benedici, quia, quum alia vice benedicti sint, eorum benedictio iterari non debet."

70. X 4.21.1: "Capellanum nihilominus, quem benedictionem cum secunda tibi constiterit celebrasse, ab officio beneficioque suspensum cum literarum tuarum testimonio appellatione cessante ad sedem apostolicam nullatenus destinare postponas. [Dat. Laterani.]"

71. C. 32 q. 2 c. 1

72. Reynolds, *Marriage*, 384.

73. James A. Brundage, "The Merry Widow's Serious Sister: Remarriage in Classical Canon Law," in *Matrons and Marginal Women in Medieval Society*, ed. Robet Edwards and Vickie L. Ziegler (Boydell and Brewer, 1985), 43; G. Mollat, "La benediction des secondes noces," *Etudes d'histoire de droit canonique dediees à Gabriel Le Bras*, 2 vols. (Paris: Sirey, 1965), 2:1337–39.

74. Molin and Mutembe, *Rituel du mariage*, 243–44.

75. Anders Winroth, *The Making of Gratian's Decretum* (Cambridge: Cambridge University Press, 2000); idem, "Recent Work on the Making of Gratian's Decretum," *Bulletin of Medieval Canon Law* 26 (2008): 1–29; *Corpus Iuris Canonici*, ed. Emil Friedberg, 2 vols. (Graz: Akademische Druck, 1959) vi.

76. "C. 34, q. 1 and 2."

77. Alexander III allowed remarriage after ten years with no news. See Walther Holtzmann, *Decretales ineditae saeculi 12*, Monumenta iuris canonici 4 (1982), ed. Stanley Chodorow and Charles Duggan, p. 55, no. 32. Cited in Brundage, *Law*, 374.

78. X 4.21.2.

79. X 4.21.2. In Raymond's edition, the text read: "Dominus ac redemptor noster. Sane, super matrimoniis, quae quidam ex vobis nondum habita obeuntis coniugis certitudine contraxerunt, id vobis respondemus, ut nullus amodo ad secundas nuptias migrare praesumat, donec ei constet, quod ab hac vita migraverit coniux eius. Si vero aliquis vel aliqua id hactenus non servavit, et de morte prioris coniugis adhuc sibi existimat dubitandum: ei, quae sibi nupsit, debitum non deneget postulanti, quod a se tamen noverit nullatenus exigendum. Quodsi post hoc de prioris coniugis vita constiterit, relictis adulterinis complexibus ad priorem coniugem revertatur."

80. X 4.1.19.

81. Peñafort, *Summa Sti. Raymund* . . . (Rome: Joamis Tollini, 1603) 554. Peñafort. Extra de sponsalibus, "In praesentia," X 4.1.19.

82. *Las Siete Partidas*, trans., Samuel Parsons Scott, ed. Robert Burns, 5 vols.

(Philadelphia: University of Pennsylvania Press, 2001), 3: 661 (pt. 3, title 14, law 13); see also Marjorie Ratcliffe, " 'Matris et munium . . .' Marriage and Marriage Law in Medieval Spanish Legislation," *Revista Canadiense de Estudios Hispánicos* 13:1 (1988): 93–109, at 106. Prosecution of bigamists in Spain may well have been considered largely a secular affair. See below.

83. Philippe de Beaumanoir, *Coutumes de Beauvaisis*, ed. Amédée Salmon 2 vols. (Paris: Alphonse Picard, 1899) 2:331.

84. Clarence Gallegar, S.J., *Canon Law and the Christian Community: The Role of Law in the Church,* Analecta Gregoriana 208, ser. Facultatis Iuris Canonici sec. A, no. 8 (Rome: Università Gregoriana Editrice, 1978), 130–35.

85. Hostiensis, *Summa aurea* 4.5.6, tit. de sponsa duorum (Lyons, 1537; reprint Aalen, 1962), fol. 203ra: "Non ergo requiritur probatio, sed verisimilis presumptio . . . vel dic quid refert utrum presens velit matrimonium accusare et canonicum probare impedimentum et tunc sufficit verisimilis presumptio puta fama communis sine testibus, et sic loquitur proximus. § vel velit contrahere simpliciter contra matrimonium nihil opponens et tunc requiritur probatio certi nuncii coram episcopo facta . . . sed quod prius dixi verius est, nam et unicus testis non probationem sed presumptionem inducit . . ."

86. Hostiensis, *Lectura* to X 4.1.19 (Venice, 1581; reprint Turin: Bottega d'Erasmo 1965), pt. 4, fol. 6.

87. *Abbatis Panormitani Commentaria . . . in primum [Quartum et Quintum] Decretalium librum,* 7 vols. (Venice: Guerraeos fratres and socios, 1578), vol. 7, fol. 10r.

88. Lalore, *Ancienne discipline* 2:76 ; Locus 17: "Periculis curatorum et parrochialium ecclesiarum rectorum, damnisque et litibus ac controversiis futuris obviare cupientes, inhibemus eisdem tam in civitate quam in diocesi Trecensi constitutis, ne alienis parrochianis ad ipsos et eorum parrochias venientibus, sive pro parrochiatum acquirendo, sive pro aliter morando, sive jam acquisierint parrochiatum per tempus legitimum de jure vel loci consuetudine, sive non, sacramenta ecclesiastica quecumque, solo casu necessitatis excepto, nisi prius a curato priori litteris receptis super bono statu parrochiani predicti, ministrare presumat; et quod etiam super sponsalibus et matrimonio fiant utrobique banna. Sed ne precedentes curati gravamen inferre valeant nubere volentibus occasione litterarum super hoc habendarum, statuimus et ordinamus in hunc modum, videlicet: quod si precedens curatus parrochianum suum cum se dimittat et alteri curato liberet et cedat, vel etiam suus parrochianus ante parrochiatum acquisitum in altera parrochia velit nubere, circa salarium vel precium litterarum expeditionis sue a precedente curato conservetur loci consuetudo. Si vero parrochianus absque licentia sui curati recedat et alibi parrochiatum acquisierit, cum fient banna in precedente ecclesia parrochiali, pro litteris super hoc ultimo curato mittendis capiet dictus curatus duos solidos turonenses tantummodo. Pro litteris quoquo de relatione boni status parrochiani sui sic recedentis curato novissimo dirigendis super facto matrimonii (que littere continebunt quod ipse precedens curatus nullum scit impedimentum propter quod tali parrochiano debent refutari ecclesiastica sacramenta, sive ante parrochiatum acquisitum, sive post) solum exigat ipse precedens curatus XII denarios turonenses."

For Rouen and northern France more broadly, see Avignon, "L'église," 295–304. For Cambrai, T. Gousset, ed. *Les actes de la province ecclésiastique de Reims,* 2 vols. (Reims: L.

Jocquet, 1843) 2:490 (VI). For Paris, the synodal statutes of Étienne Poncher, issued in 1514 or 1515, required a "certificata de morte" of those married to distant or long-absent spouses prior to remarriage "per duos aut tres testes de visu, non de visu sed juramentis ipsorum sub quibus militaverunt si in expeditione belli necati fuerint et amplius a nemine visi" (Pommeray, *L'officialité*, 351). In 1560, the Estates General asked that spouses be required to marry in their home parish with banns announced beforehand. Barbara Diefendorf, *Paris City Councillors in the Sixteenth Century: The Politics of Patrimony* (Princeton, N.J.: Princeton University Press, 1983), 162–63.

89. Lalore, *Ancienne discipline* 2:71, Locus 10: "Nullus sacerdos presumat mulierem cujus vir est absens, alteri viro matrimonialiter copulare, donec de morte viri, per testes idoneos, certissime sibi constet. Et illud observandum est circa virum, cujus uxor est absens."

90. For the use of fines in Rouen, Chartres, and Pointoise, see Avignon, "L'église," 435–41.

91. Christina Deutsch, "Zwischen Leben und Tod. Die Verschollenen und ihre Hinterbliebenen im Spätmittelalter," in *Trajekte: Zeitschrift des Zentrums für Literatur und Kulturforschung Berlin* 14 (2007): 12–16.

92. For a potentially suggestive exception to this rule, see Poos, "Heavy-Handed," 295–96.

93. See above, n. 5.

94. Emmanuël Falzone, " 'Ad secunda vota rite convolare posse': Le remariage des personnes veuves à la fin du moyen âge dans les registres de sentences de l'officialité de Cambrai (1438–1453)," *Revue d'histoire ecclesiastique* 102 (2007): 815-36; 823–24.

95. Avignon, "L'église," 548.

96. Gautier d'Arras, *Ille et Galeron,* ed. and trans. Penny Ele, (London: Kings College London Centre for Late Antique and Medieval Studies, 1996).

97. Paris AN Z/10/21fol.188v.

98. See above, n. 96.

99. Bruce Frier and Thomas McGinn, *A Casebook on Roman Family Law* (Oxford: Oxford University Press, 2003), 38; Sandirocco, "Binae," 166; Inst. 1.10.6; Dig. 3.2.1. par. 8; Dig. 40. 2.15.

100. Joseph Avril, *Les conciles de la province de Tours (XIIIe–XV siècles).* Sources d'Histoire Médiévale publiées par l'Institut de Recherche et d'Histoire des Textes (Paris: CNRS, 1987), 162: 10: "De hiis qui binas nuptias contrahunt. Statuimus quod singulis diebus dominicis in parrochialibus ecclesiis inhibeatur per sacerdotes, ne quis binas nuptias vel bina sponsalia eodem tempore presumat contrahere et expressim adjiciant quod si contra aliqui fecerint, infames ipso facto effecti, a testimoniis et aliis legitimis actibus excludantur, firmiter injungentes quod si qui reperiantur talia perpetrasse, nominatim denuntientur infames et in scala ponantur; postea publice fustigentur, nisi pecunialiter penam illam redimant arbitrio et judicio judicantis, que pena fabrice majoris ecclesie publice conferatur, parentibus et consanguineis et aliis eidem pene subdendis, quorum consilio talia fuerint perpetrata, cui pene subjacere censemus eum qui scienter duxerit alterius conjugatam."

101. Charles du Cange, *Glossarium mediae et infimae latinitatis*, 7 vols. (Niort: L. Favre, 1883–87), 7:326c. "Scala . . . quippe pro criminum quorumdam aut malefactorum

punitione ergitur intra dominorum, qui jus gladii habent, jurisdictionem aut districtum, quam ascendere coguntur rei, qui ejusmodi poena quae Scalatio infra dicitur, mulctantur, ut universae plebi expositi, infamiae notam subire cogantur." First, he cites the example of the ladder and whipping being used against bigamists in Tours 1236; second, against witchcraft, 1256 Aresta Regesto Parlam fol. 13; then perjury, 1331, then Troyes 1427: "Si quis vero Deum negaverit vel despitaverit, pro prima vice duos dies; pro secunda quatuor in pane et aqua jejunare compelletur; pro tertia autem in Scala, ut moris est, reponetur."

102. Barbara Morel, *Une iconographie de la répression judiciaire* (Paris: Éditions du Comité des travaux historiques et scientifiques, 2007), 101–2, 105–6, 108. Morel's images of *échelles* are consistently of this ladder up to a raised platform. We find, however, other descriptions of *échelles* from the eighteenth century that also included a stocks or pillory. Célestin Louis Tanon, *Histoire des justices des anciennes églises et communautés monastiques de Paris* (Paris: Larose et Forcel, 1883), 42, citing one Abbé Lebeuf, offers an idea of what the échelle of the Abbey of Chelles consisted of: "Elle était détachée de tout édifice, et très élevée, et les échelons étaient en forme d'escaliers. Dans le haut, se trouvait une plate forme, au-dessus de laquelle étaient dressées deux planches, maintenues, sans doute, dans les rainures de deux montants en bois. Ces deux planches, disposées verticalement entre les montants, et mobiles à la façon d'une trappe, étaient échancrées dans le milieu et sur les côtés. On plaçait la tête et les mains du condamné dans les échancrures de la planche inférieure, et on rabattait la planche supérieure, dans les ouvertures. Certaines échelles avaient un double système de planches, pour exposer à la fois, la tête, les mains et les pieds du condamné."

103. For Paris, Donahue, *Law*, 373–75; see also "Ex officio cases at Paris," in *Mélanges Anne Lefebvre* ed. Bernard d'Alteroche et al. (Paris: Éditions Panthéon Assas, 2010) 393–412; Pommeray, *L'officialité*, 356–68. For Senlis, A. Hardel, "Suicide et polygamie," *Mémoires de l'académie nationale des sciences arts et belles-lettres de Caen* (Académie nationale des sciences arts et belles lettres de Caen, 1883), 12: 431–38. For Rouen, Avignon, "L'église," 340–41 ADSM Rouen G 246 fol.83v (1424–25): an Englishman is condemned to one day on the ladder, six weeks' imprisonment on bread and water, and two gold *écus*; another case is mentioned in the *Inventaire sommaire des Archives Départmentales de la Seine Maritime*, 7 vols. (Rouen: Lecerf Fils, 1905), 7: L'officialité de Rouen G256 (1439–40). For Malines, L. Th. Maes, "Les délits de moeurs dans le droit pénal coutumier de Malines," *Revue du Nord* 30 (1948): 5–25. For Pamiers, Leah Otis-Cour, 355. "Lo pecat de la carn: La repression des délits sexuels à Pamiers à la fin du Moyen Âge." *Studi di Storia del diritto* 1 (1996) 335–66 ;355.

104. *Inventaire sommaire des Archives Départmentales Bouches-du-Rhône* (Marseilles: Typographie et Lithographie Cayer et C, 1897), 2: 243 (1341–42).

105. For Châlons, Véronique Beaulande found six bigamy cases in a Châlons register dated 1493–94. See her "Rompre le lien conjugal en Champagne à la fin du moyen âge," in *Répudiation, séparation, divorce dans l'Occident médiévale*, ed. Emmanuelle Santinelli, Recherches Valenciennoises 25 (Le Mont-Huy: Presses Universitaires de Valenciennes, 2007), 211–13. For Cambrai, *Registres de sentences de l'officialité de Cambrai (1438–1453)*, ed. Cyriel Vleeschouwers and Monique Vleeschouwers-van Melkebeek, (Brussels: Ministère de la Justice, 1998), 567–68. For Bourges, Anne Lefebvre-Teillard, "Règle et réalité: Les nullités

de mariage à la fin du moyen âge," *Revue de droit canonique* 32 (1982): 145–55, at 149. For Paris, Donahue, *Law*: 289–90, 371–75. Ruth Karras has found roughly twenty allegations of bigamy in the fifteenth- and sixteenth-century records of the Paris archdeacon's officiality. My thanks to Professor Karras for sharing digital images of many of these cases with me. For Brussels, *Liber sentenciarum van de Officialiteit van Brussel, 1448–1459*, ed. Cyriel Vleeschouwers and Monique van Melkebeek, Verzameling van de oude rechtspraak in België, 7th ser., 2 vols. (Brussels: Ministerie van Justitie, 1982–83), vol. 2, 241, 667.

106. *Inventaire sommaire des Archives départementales de la Côte d'Or*, ser. B (Dijon: Imprimerie Darantiere, 1876), 4:185.

107. *Inventaire sommaire des Archives départementales de l'Yonne*, ser. G (Auxerre: Imprimerie, Librairie et Lithographie de Ch. Gallot, 1873), 2:70.

108. Schmugge, *Ehen*, 108–18.

109. This would be a dispensation for incurring the impediment of crime. For more on this impediment see below, Chap 3, "Abandoned Wives."

110. As discussed earlier, the only clear exception to this insistence on the primacy of prior marriage bonds is found in the officiality of Regensburg, which recognized as valid remarriages made without first providing proof that a first spouse had died.

111. Martine Charageat, "Les sentences de l'official à Saragosse au XV siècle," *Cahiers de Fanjeaux* 42 (Privat: Toulouse, 2007), 317–42, at 331–32.

112. Ibid., 332.

113. Christine Meek, "Liti matrimoniali nel Tribunale Ecclesiastico Lucchese sotto il vescovo Nicolao Guinigi (1394–1435)," *Quaderni Lucchesi di Studi sul Medioevo e sul Rinascimento* 1:1 (2000), 105–42; Corinne Weiben, "A Kind of Marriage: Marriage in Dispute in Medieval Lucca (1341–1361)" (Ph.D. diss., University of California at Santa Barbara, 2010); Cecilia Cristellon, "I processi matrimoniali veneziani (1450–1545)," in *I tribunali del matrimonio,* ed. Silvana Seidel Menchi and Diego Quaglioni (Bologna: Il Mulino, 2006), 101–22; Gero Dolezalek, *Das Imbreviaturbuch des Erzbischöflichen Gerichtsnotars Hubaldus aus Pisa, Mai bis August 1230, Forschungen zur neueren Privatrechtsgeschichte* 13 (Cologne: Böhlau, 1969); Charageat, "Typologie," 217–32.

114. For Barcelona, Yolanda Serrano Seoane, "El sistema penal del Tribunal Eclesiástico de la Diócesis de Barcelona en la Baja Edad Media," *Clio & Crimen* 3 (2006): 334–429; 430–508; for Saragossa, Charageat, "Typologie," 217; for Lucca, Wieben, "Kind," 5; for Venice, Cristellon, "Charitas versus eros: Il matrimonio, la Chiesa, e i suoi guidici nella Venezia del Rinascimento 1420–1545" (Ph.D. diss., European University Institute, 2005), for Pisa, Dolezalek, *Imbreviaturbuch.*

115. Medieval courts are not known for concerns over double jeopardy, except when it met their interests to be so concerned. That an individual might have been prosecuted in a secular court for bigamy does not mean that the same individual, or at any rate other individuals, would not have been prosecuted in ecclesiastical courts.

116. Henry Charles Lea described the penalty for bigamy in Aragon as imprisonment and confiscation of property, offering two examples from 1488. Lea, *History* (New York: AMS Press, 1988) 4:316.

117. Beltrán "Bigamia" 99; Enrique Gacto Fernández, "El delito de bigamia y la

Inquisición españolà," *Anuario de historia del derecho español* 57 (1987): 465–92, at 479. The Cortes de Briviesca of 1387 stated that bigamists should be punished with infamous branding, on the forehead, of a q. There is, evidently, much scholarly debate about the significance of a q. Scholars have suggested that the scribe who copied out the text made a mistake and that it should, in fact, have been either a b for bigamia, or a 10 for the Ten Commandments, or a cross, or two parallel bars that signified two marriages.

118. Beltrán, "Bigamia," 99. Beltrán describes the Canary Islands as the "frequent" destination for exiles. Beginning in the sixteenth century, North Africa served as the destination for noble or privileged exiles. Beltrán also describes a case from 1490 in which a viticulturalist of some means was condemned to branding on the forehead, confiscation of his property, and perpetual banishment to an island.

119. Christian Schwab, *Augsburger offizialatsregister (1348–1352): Ein Dokument geistlicher Diözesangerichtsbarkeit: Edition und Untersuchung,* Forschungen zur kirchlichen Rechtsgeschichte und zum Kirchinrecht, 25 (Cologne: Böhlan Verlag, 2001), 717.

120. See above.

121. I have certainly written in support of this view.

122. Poos, "Heavy-Handed," 291–309; Richard Wunderli, *London Church Courts and Society on the Eve of the Reformation* (Cambridge, Mass.: Medieval Academy of America, 1981).

123. Donahue describes a whipping for incest in thirteenth-century Canterbury: Donahue, *Law*, 568. For further examples, see the work of Helmholz and Sheehan, cited below.

124. This is the abjuration "sub pena nubendi": Helmholz, *Marriage*, 174. See also Helmholz, "Abjuration sub pena nubendi in the Church Courts of Medieval England," *Jurist* 32 (1972): 80–90; and "Mariage consenti et mariage contraint: L'abjuration sub pena nubendi à l'officialité de Cerisy (1314–1346)," *Médiévales* 20 (2001): 101–11.

125. Helmholz, *Marriage*, 182; Poos, "Heavy-Handed," passim.

126. Helmholz, *Marriage*, 182, 185.

127. McSheffrey, *Marriage*, 162, 209, 229, 249; Wunderli, *London*, 51–52.

128. Poos, "Heavy-Handed," 294–96.

129. Sheehan, *Marriage*, 51.

130. Wunderli, *London,* 51–53.

131. Johnson, *Registrum*, xxiv. But see also Bryan, "Marriage," 484–85.

132. Bryan, "Evidence," 472–73.

133. Ibid, "Evidence."

134. Margaret M. Harvey, *Religious Life in Late Medieval Durham* (Rochester, N.Y.: Boydell Press, 2006), 50–51. Harvey describes the cases as bigamy, but there is no claim of two marriages in the accusations that I can find.

135. Charles Donahue assumes that the Paris court included flogging in its punishments because the synodal statutes from Tours describe such punishment, but no Paris officiality records describe the use of whipping. Donahue, *Law*, 373.

136. Ibid., 135.

137. Ibid., 246.

138. Ibid., 255, another penance for a chaplain, 274.

139. Ibid., 280. Donahue also gives an example of penance for adultery on 294.

140. Charles Johnson, ed., *Registrum Hamonis Hethe, Diocesis Roffensis,* vols 48–49 Canterbury and York Society 2 vols. (Oxford: Oxford University Press, 1948–), 956, 984, 985, 990.

141. Ibid., 49: 924–25. Johnson suggests that the whippings were around the church, but the court record does not specify.

142. Ibid., 998.

143. Philippa Maddern, "Moving Households: Geographical Mobility and Serial Monogamy in England, 1350–1500," *Parergon* 24:2 (2007): 73, 82–83, 86–87.

144. For further discussion of Maddern's and Butler's work on bigamy see below, chapter 4.

145. Sara M. Butler, "Runaway Wives: Husband Desertion in Medieval England," *Journal of Social History* (winter 2006): 351, 345.

146. J. Michael Hayden and Malcolm Greenshields, *600 Years of Reform: Bishops and the French Church, 1190–1789* (Montreal: McGill Press, 2005), 228.

147. "Inserting his official into purely temporal and secular matters." Théophile Boutiot, *Histoire de la ville de Troyes et de la Champagne méridionale*, 4 vols. (Paris: Dumoulin, 1870), 2: 229; see also chapter 5.

148. Boutiot, *Histoire*, 281.

149. For a list of some of the very few cases known to be brought "ex officio promoto" in York, see Donahue *Law,* texts and commentary, no. 98.

150. About England, see Donahue, *Law*, 599–600. However, the border between regions in which officialities made active use of promotors and regions in which courts made scant or no use of promotors is drawn with some difficulty. We know of active promotors throughout northern France and in Cambrai, Brussels, and Tournai. We hear of an active (and evidently unsavory) promotor in mid-fifteenth-century Strasbourg, but nothing similar has emerged from other court records. For some discussion of the impact of active promotors on determining the kinds of cases more likely to be brought to court *ex officio*, see 614–15.

151. M. H. d'Arbois de Jubainville, *Inventaire sommaire des Archives départementales antérieures à 1790: Aube, Archives ecclésiastiques, série G (Clergé séculier),* 3 vols. (Troyes, 1873–1930): vol. 2.

152. Gottlieb, "Getting Married," 226–27.

153. Ibid., 399–404; idem, "The Meaning of Clandestine Marriage," in *Family and Sexuality in French History*, ed. Robert Wheaton and Tamara K. Hareven (Philadelphia: University of Pennsylvania Press, 1980), 49–83.

154. A.D. de l'Aube G4171fol.6r [*1423*]. See Appendix for transcription.

155. For more on this language, see below pages 127–28.

156. John Baldwin, *The Language of Sex: Five Voices from Northern France Around 1200* (Chicago: University of Chicago Press, 1994), 6.

157. For further discussion of this topic see Chapter 4, "Why Commit Bigamy?"

CHAPTER 2. BIGAMOUS HUSBANDS

1. John Arnold, *Inquisition and Power: Catharism and the Confessing Subject* (Philadelphia: University of Pennsylvania Press, 2001).

2. A. D. Aube G4172fols.49v–50r (hereafter, simply G . . .).

3. For examples of the behavior and treatment of those who fled religious life in medieval England, see F. Donald Logan, *Runaway Religious in Medieval England, c. 1240–1540* (Cambridge: Cambridge University Press, 2002).

4. E. Coüard-Luys, "Variétés. 1. Suicide et polygamie," *Mémoires de la Société d'Archéologie, Sciences, et Arts du Département de l'Oise* 12:2 (1884): 431–38; Pommeray, *L'officialité*, 355, 563.

5. Nicole Gonthier, *Le châtiment du crime au moyen âge* (Rennes: Presses Universitaires de Rennes, 1998); Patricia Turing, "The Right to Punish: Jurisdictional Disputes Between Royal and Municipal Officials in Medieval Toulouse," *French History* 24:1 (2010) : 1–19, at 3; Gauvard, *Grace*, 2: 299–346.

6. An English soldier accused of bigamy in Rouen is included in the cases studied by Carole Avignon, "L'église," 340–41.

7. See Chapter 1.

8. G4172fol.11v. [16 March 1427]: "In Dei nomine amen. Audita confessione tui Petri de Louay alias Galey de Praeria [Preize, Aube] prope Trecas [Troyes] qui tua mera et spontanea voluntate confessus fuisti in jure coram nobis et alias sumus sufficienter informati quod a decem annis citra vel circiter matrimonium in facie ecclesie contraxisti in villa de Prunino [Prunoy?] Senonensis [Sens] diocesis cum quadam Coleta et ipsum matrimonium consumasti et postmodum ipsam in dictam praeviam moraturam tecum adduxisti mansistique in dicta Praeria cum dicta Coleta per spatium duorum mensium et amplius et deinde dicta Coleta a consortio tuo ut asseris recessit et te dimisit tandem de facto cum de jure non posses dicta Coleta vivente matrimonium contraxisti cum Johenneta relicta defunctis R[emi?] de dicta Praeria, licet dicta Coleta non fuisset mortua ac quae de morte ipsiusque Colete non fuisses sufficienter informatus, quamvis ut asseris aliqui falso [folsi] testes dixerunt eandem Coletam dicere suum clausisse extremum . . ."

9. G4171fols.124v–125r [16 April 1463]: "In nomine Domini Amen. Audita confessione tui Renaudi des Maraulx barberii clerici coniugati ac justiciabilis nostri filii Thome des Maraulx de villa Molisinensis diocesi Lingonensis prisonarii nostri . . . Quod nunc sunt circiter decem anni quandam Dyonisiam filiam Jacquini Jolyet in villa de Muxeyo . . . in facie ecclesie in dicta villa de Muxeyo cum ea matrimonium contraxisti ipsam que matrimonium carnali copula inde subsecuta cum ipsa consummasti et cum ea continue . . . apud villam de Courtisot Cathalanensis diocesi te ipsam damnabiliter decipiendo et tue carnis unitatem cum tua uxore per carnalem copulam contractam de facto cum de jure non posses dividere non formidando, dolose actestante quod a vinculo matrimonii solutus eras vivente iamdicta Dyonisia tua uxore que adhuc vivit circiter festum nativitatis Beati Johannis Bapstite fuit annus elapsus in ipso festo ultimo preterito inibi te transtulisti in quo loco malitiose nomen tuum mutasti et Johannem Juignet te nominari fecisti, et in facie ecclesie Beati Marie de Spina parrochie de dicto Courtisot circiter festum Beati Johannis Baptiste

cum quadam Maria filia defuncti Columinii Coulon contraxisti et sollemnizavisti, et ipso sollemnizato cum dicta Maria consummasti, et cum ipsa mansisti spatio quatuor mensium vel circiter amplexibus adulteris eandam carnalis cognoscens deflorando . . ."

10. Margaret Pelling, "Appearance and Reality: Barber-Surgeons, the Body, and Disease," in *London, 1500–1700,* ed. A. L. Beier and Robert Finlay (London: Longman, 1985), 82–112, at 94–95.

11. Bronislaw Geremek, "The Marginal Man," in *Medieval Callings,* ed. Jacques Le-Goff, trans. Lydia G. Cochrane, (Chicago: University of Chicago Press, 1995), 347–74, at 362.

12. Canon 18, Fourth Lateran Council, in Norman P. Tanner, ed., *Decrees of the Ecumenical Councils,* 2 vols. (London: Sheed and Ward, 1990), 1: 244.

13. G4171fol.60v [13 January 1447]: See Appendix.

14. Email communication with Sharon Farmer.

15. David Herlihy, "Women's Work in the Towns of Traditional Europe," in *Women, Family, and Society in Medieval Europe, Historical Essays, 1978–1991* (Providence, R.I.: Berghahn Books, 1995), 69–95, at 74–75; Martha Howell, *Women, Production, and Patriarchy in Late Medieval Cities* (Chicago: University of Chicago Press, 1988), 136–37.

16. G4171fols.106r–v [19 August 1458]: "Christi nomine invocato. Audita confessione tui Petri Chenalier textoris telarum de Trecensis oriundi, qui tua mera et spontanea voluntate in jure coram nobis cum juramento ad sancta dei evangelia a te prestito confessus fuisti et aliis fuimus sufficientes informati. Quod nunc sunt circiter sex anni et a dicto tempore citra quandam Ysabellem filiam Johannis le Maulvaix de Chemino prope Motam [Graffigny-Chemin, Meurthe-et-Meuselle] in Burgondia Tullensis [Toul] diocesis commorantis apud villam de Graffigny dicte diocesis in matrimonium in facie ecclesie contractum duxisti, et cum ea contraxisti ipsumque matrimonium carnali copula consummasti et cum ipsa ibidem fere spatio quatuor annorum moram traxisti, quo tempore pendente filius unus unaque filia a vobis procreati fuerunt. Postmodum aut aliquo dilapso temporis curriculo de facto cum de jure non posses te ipsum damnabiliter decipiendo, et tue carnis unitatem cum tua uxore per carnalem copulam contractam dividere non formidando, dolose attestando quod a vinculo matrimoniale solutus eras, vivente adhuc tua iamdicta legitima uxore, circiter festum Nativitatis Beati Johannis Baptiste anni domini millesimi quadrigentesimo quinquagesimi septimi te transtulisti apud villam de Fontvanne [Fontvannes] diocesis Trecensis in qua cum Jaquota filia deffuncti Jehannoti Jehanart contraxisti solemnizatoque matrimonio ut moris est cum eadem Jacota dimidii anni vel circiter spatio amplexibus adulterinis eandam carnaliter cognoscendo remansisti."

17. There are at least three towns in the diocese of Toul called Dommartin (Dommartin-le-Franc, Dommartin-le-Saint-Père, and Dommartin-lès-Toul . . .). I cannot claim to know which Dommartin Jean Freppier was born in.

18. G4171fols.125v–126r [18 June 1463]: "In nomine domini amen Audita confessione tui Johannis Freppier textoris telarum de Dommomartinis [*Dommartin*]Tullensis diocesis oriundi prisonarii nostri qui tua mera et spontanta voluntate in jure coram nobis cum juramento ad sancta dei evangelia a te corporaliter tacta prestito confessus fuisti quod nunc sunt circiter viginti septem anni quandam Margaretam filiam Johannes Gigny de Villeyo ad

Juratum [sic; Bois de Juré] dicte Tullensis diocesis tunc commorantes in facie ecclesie in villa Beate Marie de Doulevant le Chastel dicte Tullensi diocesi cum ea matrimonio contraxisti et carnali copula inde subsecuta ipsam matrimonium cum eadem Margareta consummasti et cum ea continue mansiste usque ad festum beate Marie Magdalenes ultimo preteritum quo tempore pendentes decem liberi a vobis procreati fuerunt quorum hodiernis diebus sex videlicet: Jacobus, Johannes, Symonneta, Petrus, Aubricus et Katherina fuerunt viventes postmodum dicto Margareta, cum predictis liberis per te inibi dimissis ut asseris recessisti juistique et te transtulisti apud Prisseyum Beate Marie Trecensis diocesi te ipsum damnabiliter decipiens et tue carnis unitatem cum tua uxore per carnalem copulam contractis de facto cum de jure non posses dividere non formidando dolose actestante quod a vinculo matrimonio solutus eras vivente iamdicta Margareta tua uxore qua vivens sciebas que adhuc vivit circiter festum purificationis Beate Marie Virginis ultimo preteritum in facie ecclesie de dicto Prisseyo Beate Marie cum quadam Johanna Relicta defuncti Jacobi Girardini de dicto Prisseyo . . ."

19. Auguste Siméon Luce, *Jeanne d'Arc à Domremy, recherches critiques sur les origines de la mission de la Pucelle* (Paris: Librairie Hachette et Cie, 1887).

20. G4171fols.120v–121r [11 September 1462]: See Appendix for transcription.

21. G4171fols.63r–v [7 September 1448]: See Appendix for transcription.

22. John Hajnal, "European Marriage Patterns in Perspective," in *Population in History: Essays in Historical Demography*, ed. D. V. Glass and D. E. C. Eversley (London: Aldine, 1965), 101–43; Mary S. Hartman, *The Household and the Making of History: A Subversive View of the Western Past* (Cambridge: Cambridge University Press, 2004).

23. Lalore, ed. *Ancienne discipline*, Ordonnances de 1455, 2: 262–63.

24. G4171fol.17v [21 July 1425]: See Appendix for transcription.

25. G4171fols.85r–v [29 May 1454]: See Appendix for transcription.

26. For a related argument on the avoidance of perjuring oneself, see James Whitman, *The Origins of Reasonable Doubt: Theological Roots of the Criminal Trial* (New Haven, Conn.: Yale University Press, 2008), 78; see also Ruth Karras, "Telling the Truth About Sex in Medieval Paris," forthcoming.

27. G4172fol. 11v [16 March 1427] : ". . . de facto cum de jure non posses dicta Coleta vivente, matrimonium contraxisti cum Johenneta relicta defuncti Ramon de dicta Praevia [Preize], licet dicta Coleta non fuisset mortua atque de morte ipsiusque Colete non fuisses sufficienter informatus quamvis, ut asseris, aliqui falso testes dixerunt eandem Coletam diem suum clausisse extremum . . ."

28. G4171fols.6r–6v. See Appendix for full transcription.

29. G4171fols.6r–6v. ". . . nec feris diligentem inquisicionem de vita vel morte et statu ipsius Ysabellis [Ysabelle] quamvis, ut asseris, aliqui falso tibi dixerint et sumpserint eandem Ysabellim diem summum clausisse extremum."

30. G4171fols.124v–125r: "In nomine Domini Amen. Audita confessione tui Renaudi des Maraulx barberii clerici coniugati ac justiciabilis nostri filii Thome des Maraulx de villa Molisinensis diocesi Lingonensis prisonarii nostri . . . Quod nunc sunt circiter decem anni quandam Dyonisiam filiam Jacquini Jolyet in villa de Muxeyo ... in facie ecclesie in dicta villa die Muxeyo cum ea matrimonium contraxisti ipsam que matrimonium carnali copula inde subsecuta cum ipsa consummasti et cum ea continue . . . apud villam de Courtisot

Cathalanensis diocesi te ipsam damnabiliter decipiendo et tue carnis unitatem cum tua uxore per carnalem copular contractam de facto cum de jure non posses dividere non formidando, dolose actestantes quod a vinculo matrimonii solutus eras vivente iamdicta Dyonisia tua uxore que adhuc vivit circiter festum nativitatis Beati Johannis Bapstite fuit annualis elapsus in ipso festo ultimo preterito inibi te transtulisti in quo loco malitiose nomen tuum mutasti et Johannem Juignet te nominari fecisti, et in facie ecclesie Beati Marie de Spina parrochie de dicto Courtisot circiter festum Beati Johannis Baptiste cum quadam Maria filia defuncti Columinii Coulon contraxisti et sollemnizavisti, et ipso sollemnizato cum dicta Maria consummasti, et cum ipsa mansisti spatio quatuor mensium vel circiter amplexibus adulteris eandam carnalis cognoscens deflorando."

31. G4171fols.149r–v. ". . . Postmodum sunt tres anni vel circiter apud Sanctum Leonardum Trecensis diocesis mansum venisti et te inibi transtulisti mendose asserendo dictam Jaquettam esse mortuam saltim nobis cum juramento assecuristi quod nunquam fueras coniugatus prout nec pro tunc eras ut dicebas et quod deterius est, non contentus te ipsum sic dampnabiliter decipere et unitatem carnis cum tua Jaquetta dicta uxore per carnalem copulam contractam dividere non formidando, dolose ac fraudulenter tuum nomen mutasti et quia prius vocabaris Anthonius Bonnari te nominare fecisti Johannem Bourdon de ~~de~~ Blaigineau gallice incolas dicte Sancti Leonardi [parrochie] . . . "

32. G4171fols.82v–83r: See Appendix.

33. See above, the case of Casini, G4171fol.17, p. 78–79.

34. G4172fol.16r [13 April 1426]: "In Dei Nomine Amen. Audita confessione tui Bertrandi dicti Bourroche tonnelarii in villa de Molismo lingonensis diocesis conmorantis qui tua mera et spontanea voluntate in jure coram nobis confessus fuisti et alias sumus sufficienter infomati quod a sexdecim annis citra vel circiter matrimonium in facie ecclesie constraxisti in hac villa Trecensi cum Alisonna relicta defincti Colini de Boyges ipsamque matrimonium carnali copula consummasti et cum ea in hac villa seu spatio quatuordecim annorum moram traxisti. Deinde ipsam moraturam apud civitatem Virdunensem [Verdun] tecum duxisti ibique moram . . . et ab infirmitate qua spacio trium mensium vel eocirca in grabato detentus fuisti, reconvalescente, eandem uxorem tuam in grabato jacentem dimictendo ad hanc villam te transferando mendose afferendo ipsam esse mortuam . . ."

35. Sara McDougall, "The Punishment of Bigamy in Late-Medieval Troyes," *Imago Temporis: Medium Aevum* 3 (2009): 189–204.

36. Shannon McSheffrey, "Men and Masculinity in Late Medieval London Civic Culture: Governance, Patriarchy, and Reputation," in *Conflicting Identities: Men in the Middle Ages* ed. Jacqueline Murray (New York: Garland Press, 1999), 243–78, at 245, 261.

37. McSheffrey, *Marriage*, 142.

38. Ibid., 180–81.

39. Leah Otis-Cour, "De jure novo: Dealing with Adultery in the Fifteenth-Century Toulousain," *Speculum* 84:2 (April 2009): 347–92.

40. Gauvard, *Grace*, 2:875–76.

41. Rosalind Brown-Grant, "Learning to Be a Good Husband: Competing Masculine Identities in the Roman du Comte d'Artois," *Cahiers de recherches médiévales et humanistes* 9 (2002): n.p.; http://crm.revues.org//index62.html.

42. Rosalind Brown-Grant, *French Romance of the Later Middle Ages: Gender, Morality, and Desire* (Oxford: Oxford University Press, 2008), 129–42.

43. Jean Gerson, "Considérations sur Saint Joseph," in Gerson, *Oeuvres complètes,* ed. Palémon Glorieux, 8 vols. (Paris: Desclée and Cie, 1971), 1:63–99; Paul Payan, "Pour retrouver un père . . . La promotion du culte de saint Joseph au temps de Gerson," *Cahiers de recherches médiévales et humanistes* 4 (1997): n.p.; http://crm.revues.org// index959.html.

44. David Herlihy, "The Making of the Medieval Family: Symmetry, Structure, and Sentiment," *Journal of Family History* 8 (1983): 116–30, at 127–28; Susan Mosher Stuard, "Burdens of Matrimony: Husbanding and Gender in Medieval Italy," in *Medieval Masculinities: Regarding Men in the Middle Ages*, ed. Clare Lees, Thelma Fenster, and Jo Ann McNamara (Minneapolis: University of Minnesota Press, 1994), 61.

45. Stuard, "Burdens," 64.

46. Brian Patrick McGuire, *Jean Gerson and the Last Medieval Reformation* (University Park, Pa.: Pennsylvania State University Press, 2005), 235–39.

47. Gerson, *Oeuvres*, 7:14: "avoir telle amour, telle foy et loyaulte envers leurs epouses, et les amer, les nourrir et garder"; see also Brown-Grant, *French,* 139.

48. Jérome Baschet, *Le sein du père: Abraham et la paternité dans l'occident médiéval* (Paris: Gallimard, 2000).

CHAPTER 3. ABANDONED WIVES

1. G4171fols.63r–63v [7 September 1448]: See Appendix for transcription.

2. See further, McDougall, "Bigamy: A Male Crime."

3. The hundred cases are found in the following registers: G4171 (1423–75), G4172 (1426–47), G4173 (1455), G4174 (1456), G245 (1411–13), G246 (1414–16), and G247 (1450–72). I made use of G4175–G4177 only to follow up on cases that initiated in the earlier registers and the registers of sentences but did not add any new cases of bigamy from those later registers to the first hundred cases.

4. Richard M. Fraher, "The Theoretical Justification for the New Criminal Law of the High Middle Ages: 'Rei Publicae Interest, Ne Crimina Remaneant Impunita,' " *University of Illinois Law Review* (1984): 577–99, at 577. See further below, Chapter 5, "Why Prosecute Bigamy?"

5. See further below, Chapter 5.

6. G4171fols.143r–v; see also Christelle Walravens, "L'officialité episcopale de Troyes à la fin du Moyen Âge" (Ph.D. diss., École des Chartes, 1995), 110, and a transcription of the case in her appendix, n. 47. This woman, one Jeanne, claimed to worship a god she called "Rex Paradisi," a deity living in her hip who would save humanity. She also claimed that despite twenty years of marriage and seven children, she was still a virgin. Her refusal to recant these beliefs resulted in her remission to the secular arm and burning at the stake.

7. We also do not know, or at any rate I do not know, how to resolve the contradictory

time spans offered throughout this account. Clearly they do not add up, but the officiality does not seem to have minded. See further Chapter 2, "Bigamous Husbands," 73–74.

8. G4171fols.63r–v: "Predicta vero Perreta ex alia parte matrimonium sibi de facto statuta Sanctorum Patrum contempnendo apud villam de Malle [Mallé, Aisne] Laudinensis [Laon] diocesis cum Felisoto Arnoul dicti loci de Barbuisia [Barbuise, Aube] dampnabiliter contraxit vivente predicto Johanne marito suo, de cuius morte nullam habuerat assertionem, et per spatium vii annorum vel circiter cum dicto Feliseto adulterando in sue salutis praeiudicium cohabitavit."

9. "Matimonium cum duobus" or "matrimonium cum primo [*marito*] vivente."

10. G245v.3fol.1v, G246v.2fol.11v.

11. For an example, see the case of Isabelle, "widow" of Jean Pot.

12. G246v.1,fol.3v [6 October 1414]: "Johanetta filia defuncti Feliseti Auberi nunc uxor Johannis Vallet de Longosolido pro eo quod ante contraxerat per verba matrimonii de presenti cum Symono Jacqueto de Monteygonis dictum Symonum affidabat ante contractum dicti Johannis Vallet sui mariti. Emendavit Casini [the promotor in this case] lx s.t.," "Dominus Jacobus curatus de Longosolido eos desponsavit et non sunt nisi duo banna proclamata prout confessus fuit emendavit Casini praedicta die et tax. xlv. s.t."

13. Pommeray, "L'officialité," 352. See further Chapter 4, "Why Commit Bigamy?"

14. See above, Chapter 1, for a detailed discussion.

15. G4171fols.2v–3r: See Appendix.

16. Lalore, *Ancienne discipline* 2:71, Locus 10. "Nullus sacerdos presumat mulierem cujus vir est absens, alteri viro matrimonialiter copulare, donec de morte viri, per testes idoneos, certissime sibi constet. Et illud observandum est circa virum, cujus uxor est absens."

17. G4171fol.3r: "Nullus ducat in matrimonium illam quam fide data polluit per adulterium." See further C.4 q.10; X4.7. "De eo qui duxit in matrimonium, quam polluit per adulterium."

18. G4171fols.2v–3r [Thursday, 2 September 1423]: See Appendix for full transcription.

19. See further the beginning of Chapter 4.

20. G4174fol.14r [16 May 1456]: "Stephanus bon Chevaul de Rameruco et Philippa de Beaufort eius uxor promissunt stare juri et comparere ad omnes assignationes eiusdem in presenti causa s [?] eidem ad poenam excommunicationem et decem librarum turonensium promissunt."

21. G4174fol.23v [3 June 1456]: "De promotore contra Stephanum bon Cheval de Ramerumpt [Ramerupt] et Philipam eius affidatam emendaverunt eo quod sponsalia contraxerunt per verba de futuro in facie ecclesie et consummaverunt licet non constaret de morte mariti [Phillipe] et [dominus officialis] inhibuit [eos] ne simul conversantur. tax xx s. pro quolibet."

22. G4171fol.94v [3 June 1456]: "Dominus officialis monuit in scriptis Stephanum bon Cheval et Philippam uxorem Johannis Asselini de Ramerupt ne ipsos de cetero scilicet conversantur in adulterium et scandalum sub penis excommunicationis et decem librarum turonensium."

23. Butler, "Runaway," 340–41.

24. G4174fols.7r, 10v, 23v, G247fol.20r.

G4174fol.7r [12 May 1456]: "Item contra Guillelmum Vincent de capella Lapsonis confitetur quod sponsalia contraxit per verba de futuro cum Isabella relicta defuncti Bastardi sancti Pauli ab anno uno in mense septemberis et apost [postea] cum ipsa frequentavit et ipsam carnaliter cognovit. Item confessus [est] quod dixit in aliquibus locis quod ipsam desponsaverat et etiam confessus quod illam promisit ducere in uxore casu quo sibi constaret de morte dicti sui mariti. Constituitur prisionaria: Dicta Isabella confessa consimiliter . . ."

G4174fol.10v [13 May 1456]: "Taxatur pro quolibet unum scutum auri quod promisit quilibet insolidum solvere domino episcopo. Item contra Guillelmum Vincent de capella Lapsonis. Item contra Isabellam relictam defuncti Johannis Pot alias le Bastart de Saint Pol. Dominus officialis inhibuit eis sub penis decem marcharum argenti ne ulterius procedant ad eorumdem matrimonium donec constet de morte dicti Johannis Pot et etiam quod non conversantur simul nisi prius matrimonio solemnizato sub eisdem penis et emendaverunt consummationem matrimonii."

G247fol.20r [11 November 1456]: "G. Vincent de capella Lapsonis unum scutum, item pro Ysabella eius pedisecca unum scutum [solvit]."

25. G4171fol.40v [28 December 1442]: "Veneris post Cantate. Dominus officialis inhibuit Johannem de Sermiselles [Sermizelles, Yonne] quondam Vig[or]is Franquelance et Glandinam eius affidatam sub pena excommunicationis et decem librarum tournensium ne de cetero scilicet cohabitent donec constituit de morte mariti dicte Glandine ac etiam ne alter a priori nubet cum alio donec fuerit aliter ordinatum."

26. G4174fol.12r [1456] : "Item contra Colinetum Cardun de Fontvana et Perretam relictam defuncti Floreti de Lemire, confitentur quod circiter festum Purificationis Beate Virginis Marie ultimo preteritum sponsalia contraxerint per verba de futuro in facie ecclesie et consummaverint matrimonium inter ipsos licet non constatum [est] de morte dicti Floreti; dominus officialis inhibuit eis sub penis excommunicationis et viginti librarum turonensium ne simul conversari presumant et etiam quod dictus Colinetus eam carnaliter [cognoverat]."

27. G4174fol.23v: "Martis post Sacramentum [1 June 1456] in margin: tax. xl soldi tournenses. Item contra Johannem le Mercerat presbiterum curatum de Barbarsia emendavit eo quod dedit licentiam Guillelmo Vincent de capella Lapsonis ad matrimonium contrahendum cum Isabella relicta defuncti Johannis Ponart eius parrochiana licet sibi non constaret de morte sui mariti."

28. G4173fol.64v [25 August 1455] continues throughout G4173, beginning with fol.64v, throughout G4174, G4175, and G4171fol.90r.

29. G4173fol.67r [26 August 1455]: "Dominus Dyonisius Larguel, presbiter Trec[ens]is [Troyes] commorans, deponit quod quadam die sunt circiter tres menses, ipso existente in domo a la Fourniere, predictus Manchinus venit ad dictam domum et etiam dicta actrix. Ipsa deponens petiit [a] reo an iret ad ordines, qui respondit quod bene credebat quod ita faceret, et actrix sibi dixit: tu m'as promis que tu n'auras autre femme que moy, et reus respondit quod non poterat habere aliam uxorem, et ipse actrix respondit quod erat contenta, et dederunt ad bibendum ad nucem [nuncium], presentibus partibus predictis et quodam Johanne Barbier."

30. G4173fol.67r. [26 August 1455]: "Nicola uxor Johannis de Souleines, cognoscens partes, non fuit praesens ubi se creantaverunt, deponit quod quadam die reus erat in sua domo et querebat ad emendandam quandam culcitram pictam et misit quaesita unam quartam vini de qua bibererunt et ibi erat. Supervenit actrix [Isabelle] et tunc actrix dixit reo 'vous savez que vous estez mon creante, et ne pouvez avoir aultre femme que moy.' Cui actrici reus [Manchin] respondit: 'Je suis bien contant mais que vous vous gouvernez bien.' Et hoc tempore Quadragesime. Et a quindecim diebus citra vidit actricem et reum simul cubitos sub eodem coopertorio et in eodem lecto tanquam conjuges, si nudi essent nescit ipsa deponens, et ibat constitutum son seriz gallice [evening] in domo actricis."

31. G4173fols.96v–97r [Tuesday, September 23 1455]: "Item contra Manchin le Jon. Gerardus de Prasses filius Gileti de Prasses custurarii Trecensis commorans etatis quindecim annorum, deponit quod die Mercurii ultimo preterita hora octava de nocte vel circiter vidit dictum reum [Manchin] exeuntem a domo dicte denunciatricis [Isabelle] et eandem extrahendem [extrahentem] a predicta sua domo usque ad finem et descensum fuit bassum certorum graduum existentium ante domo prostratam et eandem detrahendo emissit reus a zona de denunciatricis unam bursam argento ferratam boutonnis argenteis albis qui reus cum teneat dictam bursam dixit alta voce or ey ce qui est mien et tunc extincta per ipsum reum candela tunc accensa et prostrata ad terram . . . abiit et fugit eundo ad ecclesiam Beati Remigii Trecensis . . ."

32. G4171fol.90r [26 November 1455].

33. G4173fols.111r–v [24 September 1455].

34. G4173fol.121v [20 December 1455].

35. G4175fol.51r [4 November 1458]: The court does not use the word "marriage"; the record reads "contraxit clandestine extra ecclesiam et consumavit."

36. G4179fol.14r [1464]: "Magister Johannis Pinette proposuit quod rea est uxorata et dimisit suum maritum spatio duorum mensium, ivit per patriam cum bastardo de Castro Villano. Confitetur rea et ordinatur, ad penas excommunicationis et 10 lb. t., quod revertatur cum suo marito et obediat suo marito. Tax 60 s.t. reductum ad 20 s.t."

37. G4173fol.114v [11 March 1454] : "De promotore contra Johannem le Cherisat de Chineyo. Dominus officialis inhibuit le Clerisat sub penis excommunicationis et decem lb. t. ne indebite verberet eius uxorem et quod sibi ministret alimenta necessaria et predicta uxor ordinavit ut obediat suo marito."

38. "En sa bonne pais avec son epous": Gerson, *Oeuvres*, 7: 12; Brown-Grant, *French*, 132–43; Yelena Mazour-Matusevich, "La position de Jean Gerson (1363–1429) envers les femmes," *Le Moyen Âge* 2 (2006): 337–53; Dorothy Catherine Brown, *Pastor and Laity in the Theology of Jean Gerson* (Cambridge: Cambridge University Press, 1987), 216–20.

39. Silvana Vecchio, "La Bonne Épouse," in *Histoire des femmes en Occident 2 Le Moyen Âge*, dir. Christiane Klapisch-Zuber, ed. Georges Duby and Michelle Perrot (Paris: Perrin, 2002), 143–80.

40. Gerson, *Oeuvres*, 2:861.

41. Sharon Farmer, "Persuasive Voices: Clerical Images of Medieval Wives," *Speculum* 61:3 (1986): 517–43.

42. Elizabeth Makowski, "The Conjugal Debt and Medieval Canon Law," in *Equally*

in God's Image: Women in the Middle Ages, ed. Julia Bolton Holloway, Constance S. Wright, and John Bechtold (New York: Peter Lang, 1990), 129–43; James Brundage, *Sex, Law and Marriage in the Middle Ages* (Brookfield, Vt.: Variorum, 1993), 241; Reid, *Power*, esp. 120–26.

43. Karras, *Sexuality,* 89–90.

44. Gerson, *Oeuvres,* 7:542–46.

45. Ton Brandenbarg, "Saint Anne: A Holy Grandmother and Her Children," in *Sanctity and Motherhood: Essays on Holy Mothers in the Middle Ages*, ed. Anneke B. Multer-Bakker (New York: Taylor and Francis, 1995), 31–65, at 46.

46. Jacobus de Voragine, "The Birth of the Blessed Virgin Mary," in *The Golden Legend: Readings on the Saints*, trans. William Granger Ryan, 2 vols. (Princeton, N.J.: Princeton University Press, 1993), 2:149–58; Ton Brandenbarg, "St. Anne and Her Family: The Veneration of Saint Anne in Connection with Concepts of Marriage and the Family in the Early Modern Period," in *Saints and She-Devils: Images of Women in the Fifteenth and Sixteenth Centuries*, ed. Lene Dresen-Coeders (London: Rubicon Press, 1987), 101–27; at 102–3.

47. Angeliki Laiou, "The Evolution of the Status of Women in Marriage and in Family Law," in *Mütter Nonne Diakonin: Frauenbilder im Recht der Ostkirchen*, *Kanon* 16 (2000) 71–86; 75–77.

48. James Brundage, "The Crusader's Wife: A Canonistic Quandary," *Studia Gratiana* 12 (1967): 425–42; idem, "The Crusader's Wife Revisited," *Studia Gratiana* 14 (1967): 241–52.

49. See also Brundage, *Law*, 453 n. 188.

50. Anne Lefebvre-Teillard, *Les officialités à la veille du concile de Trente,* Bibliothèque d'histoire du droit et droit romain, 19 (Paris: Sirey, 1973), 112.

51. G4179fol.67v [1464] "Larrecier proposuit quod loquendo cum Theobauldo Salmon dixit et publicavit in vineis de Sandoya quod eius uxor et uxor Jaqueti Broart erant ribalde. Confitetur dixisse, remonstrando dicto Theobaldo quod dicta filia Theobaldi aliquando dimittebat suum maritum et quod dum una mulier dimittebat suam domum per unam diem, dicebatur quod erat ribalda."

52. Nicole Gonthier, *Sanglant coupaul, orde ribaude: Les injures au moyen âge* (Rennes: Presses Universitaires de Rennes, 2007); Thelma S. Fenster and Daniel Lord Smail, eds., *Fama: The Politics of Talk and Reputation in Medieval Europe* (Ithaca, N.Y.: Cornell University Press, 2005).

53. G4173fol.148v: "Va, larronnesse, paillarde, ribaude, gendarmesse, tu as este a plus de IIII homes."

54. Daniel Lord Smail, *The Consumption of Justice* (Ithaca, N.Y.: Cornell University Press, 2003).

55. Claude Gauvard, "Honneur de femme et femme d'honneur en France à la fin du Moyen Age," *Francis* 28 (2001) 159–191.

56. Gerson, *Oeuvres,* "Sermon contre la luxure," 7:819.

CHAPTER 4. WHY COMMIT BIGAMY?

1. For bigamy cases from England, see Helmholz, *Marriage*, 64–65; Donahue, *Law*, 289–90; Michael Sheehan, "The Formation and Stability of Marriage in Fourteenth-Century England: Evidence of an Ely Register," *Mediaeval Studies* 33 (1971): 228–63, in idem, *Marriage, Family, and Law in Medieval Europe: Collected Studies*, ed. James K. Farge, (Toronto: University of Toronto Press, 1996), 38–76, at 74–76; L.R. Poos, "Heavy-Handed," 291–309; Butler, "Runaway," 337–59; Shannon McSheffrey, "Detective Fiction in the Archives: Court Records and the Uses of Law in Late Medieval England," *History Workshop Journal* 65 (spring 2008): 65–78; Maddern, "Moving Households."

For France: Anne Lefebvre-Teillard, "Règle"; Pommeray, "L'officialité, " 351–61, appendix; Donahue, *Law*, 371–76; idem, "Ex officio," passim; Jean-Philippe Lévy, "L'officialité de Paris et les questions familiales à la fin du XIVe siècle," in *Études de droit canonique dédiées à Gabriel le Bras* (Paris: Sirey, 1965), 2:1265–94.

For Belgium: Monique Vleeschouwers Van Melkebeek, "Bina matrimonia: Matrimonium praesumptum vs. matrimonium manifestum. Hoe passen de officialiteiten van Kamerijk en Brussel in de Vijftiende eeuw canoniek recht en doctrine terzake toe?" *Juris Scripta Historica* 13 (1997):245–55; idem, "Aspects du lien matrimonial dans le *Liber sententiarum* de Bruxelles," *Tijdschrift voor Rechtsgeschiedenis* 53 (1985): 43–97; "Self-Divorce in Fifteenth-Century Flanders: The Consistory Court Accounts of the Diocese of Tournai," *Tijdschrift voor Rechtsgeschiedenis* 68 (2000): 83–98.

For Geneva, Portugal, and Italy: Marie-Ange Tricarico Valazza, "L'officialité de Genève et quelques cas de bigamie à la fin du moyen âge: L'empêchement de lien," *Zeitschrift für schweizerische Kirchengeschichte* (1995), 89: 99–118; Braga, *A Bigamia;* idem, "Para o estudo da bigamia em Portugal no século XV," in *Os Reinos ibéricos na Idade Média: Livro de homenagem ao professor doutor Humberto Carlos Baquero Moreno*, ed. Luís Adão da Fonseca, Luís Carlos Amaral, and Maria Fernanda Ferreira Santos (2003), 2:519–27; Christine Meek, "Women, the Church, and the Law: Matrimonial Litigation in Lucca Under Bishop Nicolao Guinigi (1394–1435)," in *Chattel, Servant, or Citizen: Women's Status in Church, State, and Society*, ed. Mary O'Dowd and Sabine Wichert, Institute of Irish Studies, Queen's University, Belfast, Historical Studies, 19 (Belfast, 1995), 82–90; see also Pierroberto Scaramella, "Controllo e repressione ecclesiastica della poligamia a Napoli in età moderna: Dalle cause matrimonial al crime di Fede (1514–1799)," in Seidel Menchi and Quaglione, *Trasgressioni*, 443–501; 443–502.

2. Helmholz, *Marriage*, 76; Donahue, *Law*, 68.

3. Donahue, *Law*, 109, 128; Helmholz, *Marriage*, 65, 162–63; Corinne Weiban, "In the Year of Mortality: Plague and Marriage in the Fourteenth-Century Diocese of Lucca," paper presented at the American Historical Association, January 2010.

4. McSheffrey, "Detective Fiction"; see also Donahue and Helmholz, cited above. For one case from Augsburg, see Schwab, *Augsburger*, 765 n. 1822.

5. Annulments on the grounds of incest remained common in France in the fifteenth century. See Ludwig Schmugge, "Female Petitioners in the Papal Penitentary," *Gender and History* 12:3 November 2000): 585–703, 695; for earlier examples, see Martin Aurell, *Les*

noces du comte: Mariage et pouvoir en Catalogne, 785–1213, Histoire Ancienne et Médiévale 32 (Paris: Publications de la Sorbonne, 1995), 440–46.

6. AI 1347 Episcopi Rofensis, 925, *Registrum Hamonis Hethe, Diocesis Roffensis,* ed. Charles Johnson (Oxford: Oxford University Press, 1948), 2:33; Susan L'Engle, "Justice in the Margins: Punishment in Medieval Toulouse," *Viator* 33 (2002): 133–65.

7. Cristellon, "L'ufficio," 879–83, at 855 and n.14; idem, "Marriage and Consent in Pre-Trentine Venice: Between Lay Conception and Ecclesiastical Conception, 1420–1545," *Sixteenth Century Journal* 39:2 (2008): 390–418, at 399.

8. Pommeray, "L'officialité," 352.

9. Ibid., 351–58.

10. Ibid., 542.

11. See above, n. 1.

12. For further scholarship that links bigamy to geographical mobility, see Scaramella, "Controllo," 443–501; Trevor Dean, "Fathers and Daughters: Marriage Laws and Marriage Disputes in Bologna and Italy, 1200–1550," in *Marriage in Italy, 1300–1650*, ed.Trevor Dean and Kate Lowe (Cambridge: Cambridge University Press, 1998), 102; and Alexandra Parma Cook and Noble David Cook, *Good Faith and Truthful Ignorance: A Case of Transatlantic Bigamy* (Durham, N.C.: Duke University Press, 1991).

13. Maddern, "Moving," 69.

14. Sheehan, "Formation," 62.

15. Laura Betzig, "Medieval Monogamy," *Journal of Family History* 20.2 (1995): 181–216.

16. Butler, "Runaway," 351–52.

17. Duby, *Knight:* see above, Chapter 1. n. 7.

18. D'Avray, *Marriage*, passim.

19. G4171fols.6v–7r [1423]: "In Dei nomine amen. Audita confessione tui Huguenimi dicti Chenilloy de Joyaux Eudensenis [Autun] diocesis qui tua mera et spontanea voluntate confessus fuisti in jure coram nobis—et etiam alias sufficienter informati fuimus—quod a quindecim annis citra vel circiter matrimonium in facie ecclesie contraxisti in dicta villa de Joyaux cum Margareta relicta defuncti Petri dicti le Coquat fuitque dictum matrimonium solemnisatum et per carnis copulam consumatum, et paulo post prefatam Margaretam propter rancores inter te et ipsam Margaretam, ut asseris, exortos absque tamen autoritate ecclesie sed tua ipsa et temeraria voluntate dimisisti et ad adversas alias partes te transtulisti, dumque moram in villa de Latiginiacum [Lagny] Meldenses [Meaux] diocesis moram traxisti . . ."

20. G4171fols.120v–121r [11 September 1462]: See Appendix for transcription.

21. G4171fol.68r: "Sed circiter festum Beati Michaelis anni domini millesimo quadracesimo xlvii dictam Jacotam, uxorem tuam in dicta villa de Valerailles viventem, dimisisti occasione accepta quod ipsa in legem matrimonii adulterando peccaverat prout ab aliquibus audiveras."

22. Otis-Cour, "Dealing," 352–53 focusing on southern France, describes a general transition in the handling of adultery by secular courts, moving from harsh, even capital, punishments in the thirteenth century toward fines by the fifteenth century. She describes general practice for much of western Europe in the fifteenth century as involving

prosecution in a secular court, usually punished by a short term of imprisonment, banishment for several months or years, or a fine. For an overview of adultery prosecutions in Northern France see Vincent Tabbagh, "Recherches sur l'adultère et sa repression par les officialités de France septentrionale à la fin du Moyen Âge," *La petite délinquance du Moyen Âge à l'époque moderne*, ed. Benoit Garnot (Dijon: Editions Universitaires de Dijon, 1998), 393–402.

23. Cristellon, "Marriage and Consent," 394–95.

24. G4171fol.60v [13 January 1447] "In nomine Domini Amen. Quia per confessionem tui Mathei Rucin barberii laici de Vendocino [Vendôme, Loir-et-Cher] Carnotensis [Chartres] diocesis oriundi subditi et justiciabilis nostri, coram nobis judicialiter factam nobis constitit atque constat quod, licet alias matrimonium contraxeris in facie ecclesie cum Johannetta uxore tua legitima, et cum eadem apud Sezannam [Sezanne, Aube] et alibi per tres annos pacifice permansisti, nichilominus tu eam tempore Quadragesime ultimo praeterite apud dictam villam Sezanne dimisisti et ad civitatem Senonensis [Sens] te transtulisti, ubi cum quadam Johannetta relicta defuncti Denisoti du Sault de Brayo [Bray-sur-Seine, Yonne] oriunda per verba de futuro in facie ecclesie instigante dyobolo sponsalia contraxisti, super quibus aliqua banna sunt proclamata, sed cum dicta Johannetta uxor tua legitima illuc causa peregrinacionis, ac devotionis quam habebat ad sanctum Potentianum, tempore dicte proclamacionis accedit ac predicta didicisset teque redarguendo peteret quare hoc faciebas."

25. G4171fol.63r : "propter guerras et hostium incursus in illis partibus . . ."

26. For an example, see above, Chapter 3.

27. X 4.17.6; Reid, *Power,* 195–207; Bernhard Schimmelpfennig, "Ex fornicatione nati: studies on the Position of Priests' Sons from the Twelfth to the Fourteenth Century," *Studies in Medieval and Renaissance History* 2:2 (1979): 3–50, at 41; John Russell, *The Sanatio in Radice Before the Council of Trent,* Analecta Gregoriana 138 (Rome: Gregorian University Press, 1964), 27–30; Laurent Mayali, "Note on the Legitimization by Subsequent Marriage from Alexander III to Innocent III," in *The Two Laws: Studies in Medieval Legal History Dedicated to Stephan Kuttner*, ed. Laurent Mayali and Stephanie A. J. Tibbetts (Washington, D.C.: Catholic University Press, 1990), 56–72.

28. All cases from G4171 unless designated as "2fol.": those are taken from G4172. The appreviation fac. ecc. is for marriage made "in facie ecclesie"; acc.: according to custom; "de presenti": a present-tense marriage, with no further information given.

29. Caesar of Heisterbach, Dist. VIII, Cap. LIX, *Anecdotes Historiques, Légendes, et Apologues tirés du recueil inédit d'Etienne de Bourbon, dominicain du xiiie siècle*, publiés pour la Société de l'Histoire de France (Paris: A. Lecoy de la Marche, 1877), 2:131.

30. Giovanni Boccaccio, *The Decameron*, trans. G. H. McWilliam, (London: Penguin Classics, 1972), 794–812.

31. Brown-Grant, *French*, 155–80; see also above.

32. *Histoire de Gilion de Trasignyes et de Dame Marie, sa femme,* ed. O. L. B. Wolff, (Paris: Brockhaus; Leipzig, J. J. Weber, 1839).

33. Philippe de Vigneulles, *Les cent nouvelles nouvelles*, ed. Charles H. Livingston, (Geneva: Drox, 1972).

34. *Riverside Chaucer*, 5th ed. (New York: Oxford University Press, 1987), "Wife of Bath's Prologue" 3 (Group D); Alistair Minnis, *Fallible Authors: Chaucer's Pardoner and the Wife of Bath* (Philadelphia: University of Pennsylvania Press, 2007), 290.

35. Peggy A. Knapp, "Alisoun of Bath and the Reappropriation of Tradition," *Chaucer Review* 24:1 (summer 1989): 45–52; Robert Longsworth, "The Wife of Bath and the Samaritan Woman," *Chaucer Review* 34:4 (2000): 372–87; Warren S. Smith, "The Wife of Bath Debates Jerome," *Chaucer Review* 32:2 (1997): 129–45.

36. Betzig, "Medieval," 181–216.

CHAPTER 5. WHY PROSECUTE BIGAMY?

1. G4171fols.63r–v; G4171fols.64r–v.

2. Millard Meiss, *Painting in Florence and Siena After the Black Death: The Arts, Religion and Society in the Mid-Fourteenth Century* (Princeton, N.J.: Princeton University Press, 1951).

3. Gauvard, *Grâce,* chap. 1.

4. Vincent Tabbagh, "Rouen 1438: De l'extension du champ de la répression judiciare en situation de crise," *De la déviance à la délinquance, XVe–XXe siècle,* ed. Benoît Garnot, (Dijon: Éditions universitaires de Dijon, 1999), 13–39.

5. Ibid., 17; Pierette Paravy, *De la chrétienté romaine à la Réforme en Dauphiné. Évêques, fidèles, et déviantes (vers 1340–vers 1530),* 2 vols. (Paris: De Boccard, 1993).

6. See above, Chapter 1.

7. Emmanuel LeRoy Ladurie, *Montaillou, village occitan, de 1294 à 1324* (Paris: Gallimard, 1975).

8. Lefebvre-Teillard, *Officialités*, 45.

9. G4171fol.31v; Lalore, *Ancienne discipline* 2:174–75.

10. Walravens, "Officialité," 80–83.

11. Ibid., 85: "On trouve de véritables dynasties exerçant à l'officialité parmi les nonprêtres: les La Viezville sont à ce titre exemplaires. Jaquinet en 1420 et Gui en 1473 occupent la fonction de garde des registres, Nicolas est promoteur à la fin du XVe siècle. Au début du siècle, les Baudet, Jean et Gilet, sont tabellions et notaires apostoliques. La fille de Jean épouse Guillaume Sarraud, un notaire de la cour. Les Huyart constituent une lignée toujours bien représentée à la cour ecclésiastique. Jean le Jay lègue a son filleul Jean Guerry 20 livres pour 'luy aidier a tenier aux escolles' nous retrouvons par la suite ledit Guerry comme tabellion."

12. Nathalie Gorochov, *Le Collège de Navarre de sa fondation (1305) au début du XVe siècle (1418): Histoire de l'institution, de sa vie intellectuelle, et de son recrutement* (Paris: Honoré Champion, 1997).

13. Walravens, "Officialité," 82.

14. See, for example, Jean Raulin, *Itinerarium Paradisi Johannis Raulin complectes Sermones* (Paris: Jean Petit, 1518), 135.

15. Françoise Bibolet, "Deux canons et un évêque à Troyes au XV siècle: Guillaume

Galeret, Etienne Grappin, Jean Leguise," *Mémoires de la société académique de l'Aube* 126 (2002): 137–47, at 144–46.

16. A. Prevost, *Le Diocèse de Troyes* (Dijon: Domois, 1924), 2:33.

17. Edouard Fournier, "L'enseignement des Décrétales à l'université de Paris au Moyen Âge," *Revue d'histoire de l'Église de France* 26:110 (1940): 58–62 at 62.

18. Bibliothèque municipale de Troyes, MS. 604, *Tabula juris civilis et canonici secundum ordinem alphabeti,* edita a domino Berengario, cardinali et episcopo Tusculano (13th century).

19. Bibolet, "Deux canons," 142.

20. Ibid., 143–44.

21. *Répertoire des statuts synodaux des diocèses de l'ancienne France du XIIIe à la fin du XVIIIe siècle,* ed. André Artonne, Louis Guizard et Odette Pontal (Paris: CNRS, 1969).

22. Herve Martin, *Le Metier de predicateur en France septentrionale à la fin du moyen âge, 1300–1520* (Paris: Cerf, 1988), 150–54, 166. Troyes hired a number of these preachers, which, including Jean Cleree, numbered 13 Dominicans, 13 Franciscans, 1 Augustinian, and 1 of an unknown order, who were hired to preach in Troyes between 1400 and 1520.

23. See, for example, G4179fol.83v.

24. Cristellon, "Marriage," 396.

25. See beginning of Chapter 4, "Why Commit Bigamy?"

26. Silvana Seidel Menchi, "Introduction," *Les officialités dans l'Europe médiévale et moderne: Des tribunaux pour une société chrétienne* (forthcoming, Brill Press).

27. Théophile Boutiot, "Recherches sur la juridiction du roi sur celle de l'evêque dans le Bailliage de Troyes et sur les coutumes de ce bailliage," in *Mémoires de la Société académique d'agriculture, des sciences, arts et belles-lettres de l'Aube* 36 (Troyes: Dufour Bouquot, 1872), 6–74:8–12. 57:14: "Item et combien que de toute ancienneté ne feussent ou ayent esté que deux promoteurs, en tout ledit évesché, ce néantmoins lesdits monsr. levesque et son official, pour tourjours vexer et travailler les povres subgetz du Roy et pour tirer amende et argent en plus grant affluance et habondance, ont comiz et de nouvel créez et mis sus jusques au nombre de six promoteurs, les aucums desquels, combien qu'ilz aient procuré la pugnicion et correction des vices sur leurs subgetz, sont gens de petit et povre gouvernement, quant aux meurs, dissoluz et déordonnez, qui est malsént et de piteuse exemple tous lesquelz promotteurs prengnent et exigent, chascun jour, grans despens sur les povres parties et n'en rendent nulz, qui est contre droit et raison et contre ce que anciennement se faisait et doit faire." The designation of two to three promotors in a few given years can be found here: G247fols.14, 32, 33.

28. Ibid., 8–12.

29. Ibid., 20–22.

30. Donahue, *Law,* 615: "The sentences suggest, however, that some, perhaps all, of the judges thought that there was something seriously wrong with marriage in that diocese in this period, that the institution was, in some sense, spinning out of control. The rhetoric, at least, of many of the sentences suggests an urgency that is not found in the sentences of York and Ely."

31. Meiss, *Painting,* esp. 67–73.

32. Avignon, "L'église," passim.

33. Julien Havet, "L'hérésie et le bras séculier au moyen âge jusqu'au XIII siècle," *Bibliothèque de l'École des Chartres* 41 (1880): 488–517, 570–670.

34. Fraher, "Theoretical," 577, 587.

35. For more on public punishment of heretics, see esp. Arnold, *Inquisition,* 58–63.

36. Morel, *Iconographie,* 101–02, 105–06, 108.

37. See further above n. 93.

38. Morel, *Iconographie,* 101–02.

39. Nicole Gonthier, "Prison et prisonniers à Lyon," *Mémoires de la Société pour l'Histoire du Droit et des Institutions des Anciens Pays Bourguignons, Comtois et Romands* 39 (1982), 15–30, at 16; Guy Geltner, "Detrusio: Penal Cloistering in the Middle Ages," *Revue Benedictine* 118 (June 2008): 89–108, discusses lay incarceration for "detrusio," a form of confinement normally used to punish monks.

40. See above, Chapters 2 and 3.

41. Donahue, *Law*, 385.

42. Ibid.

43. "Farce des femmes qui demandent arréages," *Ancien théâtre français*, vol. 1. ed. Viollet-le-Duc (Paris, 1854); see also Howard Graham Harvey, *The Theatre of the Basoche: The Contribution of the Law Societies to French Mediaeval Comedy* (Cambridge, Mass.: Harvard University Press, 1941), 120–21: "Ilz ont une guise, / Autant au soir comme au matin, / Qu'il ne parlent rien que Latin, / Ou je n'entendz pas une goute."

44. Donahue, *Law,* 386.

45. Ibid., 386–87. "We will see, for example, that it is characteristic of cases that seem to involve very serious offenses, such as bigamy, for a heightened rhetoric to be employed."

46. G4171fols.6r–6v. [1423]: See Appendix.

47. In what follows I will examine four references to marriage as instituted in the Garden of Eden taken from two of the Troyes officiality registers (G4171fols.6r–6v, fols.6v-7r, 11v; G4172fol.11v). These three examples are not exactly theologically sound, in that they seem to describe Christ rather than God as instituting marriage in the Garden of Eden. While it is certainly possible that these scribes meant that marriage had been instituted in the Garden of Eden (by God) *and* instituted by Jesus Christ (at Cana), I decided to leave the passages unaltered.

48. Martin, *Métier*, 150.

49. Ibid., 701. Cleree is known to have preached in Troyes, Paris, Châlons-en-Champagne, Metz, and Lyons.

50. Larissa Taylor, "French Preaching, 1215–1535," in *The Sermon,* ed. Beverly Kienzle, Typologie des sources du moyen âge occidental (Brepols: Turnhout-Belgium, 2000), 711–58.

51. "Matrimonium est status dignissimus, quia in paradiso terrestri a Deo institutus est, et priusquam alii ordines instituerentur . . ." St. Bonaventure, *Opera omnia (*Quaracchi: Collegi S. Bonaventurace, 1882–1902), 14, 155.

52. Johannes Cleree, *Sermones quadragesimales* (Paris, 1525), ccxvi, De Sacramento Matrimonii: "et a domino ordinatum et in paradiso terrestri factum in principio veteris testamenti et a domino confirmatum in primo miraculo quod fecit tempore novi testamenti."

53. G4171fols.6r–6v, 6v–7r.

54. G4171fols.6v–7r [1423] : "In Dei nomine amen. Audita confessione tui Huguenimi dicti Chenilloy de Joyaux Eudensenis [Autun] diocesis qui tua mera et spontanea voluntate confessus fuisti in jure coram nobis—et etiam alias sufficienter informati fuimus—quod a quindecim annis citra vel circiter matrimonium in facie ecclesie contraxisti in dicta villa de Joyaux cum Margareta relicta defuncti Petri dicti le Coquat fuitque dictum matrimonium solemnisatum et per carnis copulam consumatum, et paulo post prefatam Margaretam propter rancores inter te et ipsam Margaretam, ut asseris, exortos absque tamen autoritate ecclesie sed tua ipsa et temeraria voluntate dimisisti et ad adversas alias partes te transtulisti, dumque moram in villa de Latiginiacum [Lagny] Meldenses [Meaux] diocesis moram traxisti et postmodum videlicet ad sex annis [sic: annos] citra vel circiter in hac [word crossed out] civitate accessisti in qua matrimonium de facto cum de jure non posses, quia prefata Margareta tunc vivebat et adhuc vivit, de presenti contraxisti cum Robina relicta defuncti Johannis de Bellomonte trecensis dum vivebat commorantis absque hoc quod tu fuisses sufficienter informatus de morte dicte Margarete nec feris deligentem [diligentem] inquisicionem de vita vel morte et statu ipsius Margarete quamvis ut asseris aliqui falso [word crossed out] dixerint et semper [as]severint eandem Margaretam diem suum clausisse extremum. In premissis ~~cum sanctam militantem~~ multipliciter delinquendo statum matrimonii in paradiso terrestri a domino nostro Jhesu Christi instituti vilipendendo ecclesiam sanctam militantem contempnando populum et potissime praefatam Robinam decipiendo periurium et plura alia delicta in detrimentum salutis anime tue publice commitendo et jus matrimoniale tue uxoris proprie ab eadem aufferendo, et quia talia delicta non debent nec possumus ob honorem nostre sancte matris ecclesie sub dissimulacione celari sed sunt animadversione publice vindicanda et taliter punienda quod aliis cedat in exemplum. Idcirco per hanc nostram sententiam difinitivam quam nos pro tribunali sedentes et Deum solum pre oculis habentes eius nomine primitus humiliter invocato, de peratorum [peritorum] consilio ferimus in hiis scriptis dicimus, decernimus, et declaramus praefatum matrimonium inter te et predictam Robinam de facto contractum fuisse et ecce nullum ac ecclesiam in solemnisatione dicti matrimonii fuisse deceptam Teque incurisse penam appositam in canone [in hac] parte emisso cum dictum matrimonium ausus fuisti contrahendum cum dicta Robina et ulterius ut pena unius sit metus multorum te scalandum fore ante valvas Trecensis ecclesie semel una die dominica vel solemni necnon ad remanendum in prisonibus Reverendi in Christo patris ac domini domini Trecensis episcopi per dimidium annum ut ibi in pane doloris et aqua tristicie tua defleas peccata et talia amplius non committas, gratia tamen dicti reverendi patris salva semper et reservata."

55. G4171fols.7–rv. ". . . In premissis ~~cum sanctam militantem~~ [crossed out in original] multipliciter delinquendo statum matrimonii in paradiso terrestri a domino nostro Jhesu Christi instituti vilipendendo ecclesiam sanctam militantem contempnando populum et potissime praefatam Robinam decipiendo periurium et plura alia delicta in detrimentum salutis anime tue publice commitendo . . ."

56. G4171fol.11r: ". . . in premissis contra Deum et ordinationem ecclesie veniendo, periurium et ex parte tui stuprum, adulterium, pluraque alia crimina conmittendo, sacramento matrimonii quod a dicto nostro Jhesu Christo in terrestri paradiso primitus sit constitum calumpniose illudendo, praefatam Johannetam decipiendo et ius uxoris tue proprie

auferendo. Et quia matrimonium sic de facto non de jure contracta [contractum] non deberet sub dissimulatione et in certitudine tollerari nec talia delicta superius declarata impugnita remanere sed taliter et publice ob honorem sancte matris ecclesie et ordinis matrimonialis vindicare . . ."

57. G4172fol.11v. ". . . tandem de facto cum de jure non posses dicta Coleta vivente matrimonium contraxisti cum Johanneta relicta defuncti Ramon de dicta Praeria, licet dicta Coleta non fuisset mortua ac quia de morte ipsius Colete non fuisses sufficienter informatus, quamvis ut asseris aliqui falso [falsi] testes dixerunt eandem Coletam diem suum clausisse extremum . . . In premissis multiplicer delinquens statum matrimonii in paradiso terrestri a domino nostro Jesu Christo instituti villipendentes ecclesiam militantem contempnens populum et potissime praefatam Johannetam decipiens periurium et plura alia delicta in detrimentum salutis anime tue publice conmittens et jus matrimoniale tue uxoris ab eadem auferens . . ."

58. G4171fols.63r–v: ". . . statuta Sanctorum Patrum contempnendo . . ."

59. G4171fol.17v [21 July 1425] ". . . Et quia in premissis multipliciter deliquisti, sacramentum matrimoniale vilipendendo, Sanctam Ecclesiam militantem decipiendo, jus uxoris proprie aufferendo, prefatam Melinam decipiendo, adulterium, injuriam, et alia delicta committendo, nec debent talia delicta sub dissimulatione transire, nec impugnita remanere, sed taliter vindicanda sunt publice ut pena unius sit metus multorum, idcirco per hanc nostram diffinitivam sententiam . . ."

60. G4171fol.17v: ". . . in jure tuo medio juramento false asseruisti te esse solutum ac liberum ad matrimonium contrahendum cum dicta Melina, certis penis et canonibus adhibitis casu quo contrarium verum reperiri."

61. Nothing was said about perjury or that his crime was public and thus deserving of public punishment. However, he still was sentenced to one day on the ladder and one month of confinement. As suggested in the last chapter, it seems his crimes were considered less serious than any overt and explicit perjury. Perjury was in his case circumvented by a clandestine marriage in a chapel with a chaplain bribed to skip both the banns and any investigation. Bad enough, certainly, but not a fully public celebration of an illegal marriage, made after swearing a false oath or providing false proof as found in the other cases described above and in what follows.

62. Nicole Bériou and David d'Avray, "Henry of Provins, O.P.'s Comparison of the Dominican and Franciscan Orders with the 'Order' of Matrimony," *Archivum Fratrum Praedicatorum* 49 (1979): 513–17.

63. G4171fols.82v–83r [26 January 1454]: ". . . Et quia talia delicta et matrimonia de facto contracta non debent impunita remanere nec sub dissimulatione tollerari, sed publice et taliter ob honorem et reverenciam Sancte Matris Ecclesie et ordinis matrimonialis vindicari et puniri, quod ceteris cedat in exemplum et terrorem."

64. Bériou and D'Avray, "Henry of Provins," 513–17; see also Albert Lecoy de la Marche, *La chaire française au Moyen Âge* (Geneva: Slatkine Reprints, 1974), 429.

65. Bériou and D'Avray, 516.

66. G4171fols.85r –v [29 May 1454]: "In premissis multipliciter delinquendo, statum matrimonium vilipendendo, ecclesiam militantem contempnendo, ipsumque et presertim

dictam Ginotam uxorem tuam decipiendo, conjugale debitum ab ea aufferendo, periuriumque dampnabile incurrendo, et quia talia delicta publice punienda iura canonica determinant ut ceteris cedat in exemplum."

67. G4171fol.6r : ". . . ecclesiam militantem delusisti, divinam et inenerrabilem maiestatem offendisti, sacrum sacerdotale misterium vilipendisti, claves ecclesie contempsisti, ac crimina et delicta indicibilia perpetrasti . . ."

68. G4171fol.24v: ". . . Existimans in tua mala simplicitate quod populus hoc non perciperet et quod tantum dum sibi valeret et illas pluribus personis credentibus corpus Christi recipere tradidisti solemniter et honorifice sanctificari solet in administracione corporis Christi. In hoc multipliciter et enormiter delinquendo . . ."

69. G4171fols.130r –131v : ". . . Non considerans aut attendens preceptum decalogi quo dominus praecepit hominem non occidere Quinymo dyabolo suadente tu dictum Denisetum dicto actu repente interfecisti . . ."

70. G4171fol.136v : ". . . excessivo calore ac dyabolica suggestione . . . non considerans aut attendens preceptum decalogi quo dominus precepit hominem non occidere quinymo tu dyabolo suadente . . . temeriter homicidum perpetrasti . . ."

71. G4171fol.96r: ". . . In tuo dampnabili proposito perseverando ac contra preceptum decalogi quo cavetur non furtum facies . . ."

72. G4171fol.35v. ". . . tanquam canis reddiens ad vomitum et tanquam incorrigibilis, immemor tue salutis in pristina mala dampnabiliter recidivisti . . ."

73. G4171fols.85r –v [29 May 1454] See Appendix for a transcription of this case.

74. First Council of Nicea (318), Canon 12, *Nicene and Post-Nicene Fathers,* 2nd ser., vol. 14, ed. Philip Schaff, (Buffalo, N.Y.: Christian Literature Publishing Co., 1900), 27.

75. Augustine, *Sermons: The Works of Augustine, a Translation for the Twenty-First Century*, ed. and trans. Edmund Hill (Hyde Park, N.Y.: New City Press, 1995),154; Arnold, *Inquisition*, 55, 84.

76. G4171fol.150r: "Sed nec unquam presens in morte dicti Jaqueti Passe tuque tue salutis inmemor et subjestionibus [subjectionibus] iniquis ymo dyabolicis subornationibus praedictis perversus in tuo et animorum subornatione detrimentum non modicum acquievisti et deierasti [?], pariuriumque [periuriumque] publicum detestabile crimen coram nobis incurrere non erubescens et etiam quod supra [word crossed out] deposuisti hoc solum fuit ad prescriptum subornationem . . ."

77. G4171fol.60r : ". . . et illud scires esse cadaver mortuum, nichilominus instigante dyabolo abutendo sancto sacramento baptisimatis . . ."

78. G4171fol.16r : ". . . Te Hugonem palam et publice protulisse verba hereticalia et contra honorem intemerate virginis . . ."

79. G4171fol.122r : ". . . Necnon abusione sacramentorum ecclesie presertim preciosissimi corporis christi quia nobis per tui coram nobis spontaneam in jure factam confessionem et processum super hoc licite factum plene constitit de praemissis per te conmissis et in anime tue grave preiudicum totiusque populi christiani scandalum non modicum . . ."

CONCLUSION: CHRISTIAN IDENTITY AT THE END OF THE MIDDLE AGES

1. Davis, *Return.*

2. Davis, *Society and Culture*; Davis, *Women on the Margins: Three Seventeenth-Century Lives* (Cambridge, Mass.: Harvard University Press, 1995); Davis, *Trickster Travels: A Sixteenth-Century Muslim Between Worlds* (New York: Hill and Wang, 2006).

3. G4173fol.129r.

4. Charageat, "Sentences," 331–32; Beltrán, "Bigamia," 99.

5. Emlyn Eisenach, *Husbands, Wives, and Concubines* (Kirksville, Mo.: Truman State University Press, 2004), 13–17, 27–30, 37; see also her forthcoming chapter "Sistemi."

6. Unhappy with some of the reforms made at the Council of Trent and eager to assert their own national powers, the French refused to promulgate Tametsi. Nevertheless, the *ordonnance* of Blois of 1579 threatened children who married without parental consent with disinheritance, if it did not invalidate clandestine marriages. Barbara Diefendorf, *Paris*, 157–63.

7. *Canons and Decrees*, 180–85. See also Eugene Hillman, "Polygamy and the Council of Trent," *Jurist* 33 (1973): 358–76; and Jean Bernhard, "Le décret Tametsi du Concile de Trente: Triomphe de consensualisme matrimonial ou institution de la forme solennelle du mariage?" *Revue de droit canonique* 30 (1980): 209–34.

8. Some bishops, notably the bishop of Nantes, had called for this sort of recordkeeping as early as 1406, but the Catholic Church did not formally require such registers for all parishes until the Council of Trent.

9. *Canons and Decrees*, 187.

10. *Canons and Decrees*, 175: On the Sacrament of Matrimony, Canon 2: "If any one saith that it is lawful for Christians to have several wives at the same time, and that this is not prohibited by any divine law; let him be anathema."

11. McDougall, "Bigamy: A Male Crime," passim.

12. Solange Alberro, "El discurso inquisitorial sobre los delitos de bigamia, poligamia, y de solicitación," in *Seis ensayos sobre el discurso colonial relativo a la comunidad doméstica: Matrimonio, familia, y sexualidad a través de los cronistas del siglo XVI, el Nuevo Testamento y el Santo Oficio de la Inquisición*, ed. Solange Alberro (Mexico City: INAH, 1980), 215–26; idem, *La actividad del Santo Oficio de la Inquisición en Nueva España, 1571–1700* (Mexico City: INAH, 1981).

13. Richard Boyer, *Lives of the Bigamists: Marriage, Family, and Community in Colonial Mexico* (Albuquerque: University of New Mexico Press, 1995); Lawrence M. Friedman, "Crimes of Mobility," *Stanford Law Review* 43:3 (February 1991): 637–58.

14. Ronald Po-Chia Hsia, "Münster and the Anabaptists," in Ronald Po-Chia Hsia, ed., *German People and the Reformation* (Ithaca, N.Y.: Cornell University Press, 1988), 51–70.

15. John Alfred Faulkner, "Luther and the Bigamous Marriage of Philip of Hesse," *American Journal of Theology* 17:2 (April 1913): 206–31.

16. A. Owen Aldridge, "Polygamy in Early Fiction: Henry Neville and Denis Verias," *PMLA* 65:4 (June 1950): 464–72.

17. See, for example, Sarah Gordon, *The Mormon Question: Polygamy and Constitutional*

Conflict in Nineteenth-Century America (Philadelphia: University of Pennsylvania Press, 2001).

18. Hendrik Hartog, *Man and Wife in America: A History* (Cambridge, Mass.: Harvard University Press, 2002), esp. 1–3. See also Beverly Schwartzberg, " 'Lots of Them Did That': Desertion, Bigamy, and Marital Fluidity in Late-Nineteenth-Century America," *Journal of Social History* 37:3 (spring 2004): 573–600; Schwartzberg, "Grass Widows, Barbarians, and Bigamists: Fluid Marriage in Late Nineteenth-Century America" Ph.D. diss., University of California, Santa Barbara, 2001.

19. Gordon, *Mormon*. For a study on modern Western perceptions of bigamy (and polygamy), see Mélanie Méthot, "Bigamists Meet Polygamists: Confronting the Popular Image of Bigamists in Canadian Society," *History of the Family* 12 (2007): 169–77.

20. Hartog, *Man and Wife*, 87–90, 249–58, 261–79.

BIBLIOGRAPHY

ARCHIVAL SOURCES

Troyes, Archives départementales de l'Aube

Account book of fines for the diocesan officiality (1400–1474): G243–47.
Case Registers (1390–96, 1427–1504): G4170, G4172–79, 4188.
Register of sentences (1423–75): G4171.
Synodal Statutes (1373–1450): G28.
Ordinances (1427–1713) G 29.
Proceedings with two lords and the bishop concerning the officiality (1441–86) G136.
Jurisdictional disputes (1448–1650) G136.
Les concordats d'entre le roi et l'évêque (1458) G944.
Investigation and division of king's and bishop's serfs: (1458–61): G472–480.

Troyes, Médiathèque de l'Aube

Speculum judiciale Guillelmo Durandi. Clairvaux (fifteenth century) MS 118.
Summa Goffridi de Trano super titulos Decretalium (fouteenth century) MS 456.
Tabula Juris Civilis et Canonici Secundum Ordinem Alphabeti (thirteenth century) MS 604.
Summa summarum (fourteenth century) MS 747.
Tancred. *de Ordine Judicario*; Anon. *Summa de Matrimonio* MS 936.
Magistri Johannis Abbatisville. *Sermones de festis et Sanctis* (thirteenth century) MS 1237.
Synodal Statutes of Louis de Bar (Langres, 1404) BM 2329.

Paris, Archives nationales de France

Grands Jours de Troyes (1398, 1402, 1406, 1411) x1a9182, x1a9184–85.
Officiality of Paris z1018–z1024.

Paris, Bibliothèque Nationale de France

BN lat. 1560: Synodal Statutes of the Diocese of Troyes.
BN lat. 3468: Synodal Statutes of the Diocese of Troyes.

Paris, Bibliothèque Sainte-Geneviève

Statuta synodalia Langres, Cardinalis Barensis (1404) OE 739.

Châlons-en-Champagne, Archives Départementales de la Marne

Registers of the Officiality of Châlons-sur-Marne (1441–1503): G897–923.

PRINTED PRIMARY SOURCES

Les actes de la province écclésiastique de Reims. Ed. Gousset. 2 vols. Reims: L. Jacquet, 1843.

L'ancien coutumier de Champagne (XIII siècle). Ed. Paulette Portejoie. Poitiers, 1956.

Ancien theatre français, Vol. 1. Ed. Viollet-le-Duc. Paris, 1854.

Ancienne et nouvelle discipline du diocèse de Troyes jusqu'en 1788. Vol. 2. Statuts synodaux et Ordonnances épiscopales. Ed.Charles Lalore. Troyes, 1882.

Giovanni d'Andrea. *Novella Joannis Andree super Decretalibus*. Turin: Johannis de Ferrariis, 1512.

Aquinas, Thomas. *Summa contra gentiles. Opera omnia iussu Leonis XIII edita*. 48 vols. Rome: Ex typographia polyglotta S.C. de Propaganda Fide, 1882–.

———. *Summa theologica*. Trans. Fathers of the English Dominican Province, New York: Benziger Bros., 1948.

———. *Super Epistolam B. Pauli ad Galatas lectura*. Ed. R. Cai. 8th ed. Turin-Rome: Marietti, 1953.

Annales du Comité flamand de France. Comité flamand de France, Société d'ethnographie française. Vol. 3, 1857. Lille, 1856–57.

Anon. *Summa sententiarum septem tractatibus distincta* "De coniugio." PL 176.

Augustine, St. *De civitate Dei*. Ed. Bernhard Dombart and Alfons Kalb. CCL, vols. 47–48. Turnhout: Brepols, 1955.

Avril, Joseph. *Les conciles de la province de Tours (XIIIe–XV siècles)*. Sources d'Histoire Médiévale publiées par l'Institut de Recherche et d'Histoire des Textes. Paris: CNRS, 1987.

Bernard of Pavia. *Summa de matrimonio*. In idem., *Summa decretalium*, ed. Theodor Laspeyres. Regensburg, 1860.

Boccaccio, Giovanni. *The Decameron*. Trans. G. H. McWilliam. London: Penguin Classics, 1972.

Bonaventure, St. *Opera omnia.* Quaracchi: Collegi S. Bonaventurae, 1882–1902.

———. *Sermo XV in Hexameron, Opera Omnia.* Ed. A. C. Peltier. Paris: L. Vives, 1864.

Burchard of Worms, *Decretorum libri XX.* Ed. Gérard Fransen and Theo Kölzer. Aalen: Scientia Verlag, 1992.

Caesar of Heisterbach. *Caesarii Heisterbacensis monachi ordinis Cisterciensis Dialogus Miraculorum.* Ed. 2 vols., Joseph Strange. Cologne: H. Lemperta and Co., 1851.

Canons and Decrees of the Council of Trent. Ed. and trans. H. J. Schroeder. Rockford, Ill.: Tan Book and Publishers, 1978.

Cleree, Johannes. *Sermones quadragesimales.* Paris, 1525.

———. *Sermones quadragesimales declamati Parisius apud sanctum Severinum.* Paris: Engleberto Marnesio, 1526.

Compotus sigilliferi curie Tornacensis (1429–1481). Ed. Monique Vleeschouwers-van Melkebeek, 3 vols. Brussels: Paleis der Academiën, 1995.

Concilios visigoticos e hispano-romanos. Ed. José Vives, Tomás Martín Martínez, and Gonzalo Martínez Diez. Barcelona: Consejo Superior de Investigaciones Cientificas, Instituto Enrique Florez, 1963.

Corpus Iuris Canonici. Ed. Emil Friedberg. 2 vols. Leipzig: B. Tauchnitz, 1879. Reprint Graz: Akademische Druck, 1959.

Decrees of the Ecumenical Councils. Ed. Giuseppe Alberigo. Trans. Norman P. Tanner, 2 vols. London: Sheed and Ward, 1990.

Le diocèse de Troyes: Histoire et documents. Ed. Arthur Prévost. 3 vols. Dijon, 1923–24.

Durand, William. *Speculum iudiciale.* Basel, 1574. Reprint Aalen: Scientia, 1975.

Établissements de Saint Louis. Ed. Paul Viollet. Société de l'histoire de France. Paris: Renouard, 1881–86.

Froissart, Jean. *Chronicles.* Ed. and trans. Geoffrey Brereton. London: Penguin Classics, 1978.

"The Gast of Gy." Ed. and trans. Mona L. Logarbo. In *Cultures of Piety: Middle English Devotional Literature in Translation,* ed. Anne Clark Bartlett and Thomas H. Bestul, 64–65. Ithaca, N.Y.: Cornell University Press, 1999.

Gautier d'Arras. *Ille et Galeron.* Ed. and trans. Penny Eley. London: Kings College London Centre for Late Antique and Medieval Studies, 1996.

Gerson, Jean. *Oeuvres complètes,* Ed. Palémon Glorieux, 8 vols. Paris: Desclée and Cie, 1971.

———. *Opera omnia.* Ed. Louis Ellies Du Pin. Hildesheim: Georg Olms Verlag, 1987.

Haymo Halberstatensis. *Historiae sacrae epitome.* PL 118, 823–24.

Histoire d'Abbeville et du Comte de Ponthieu jusqu'en 1789. Francois Cesar Louandre, 3rd ed. Vol. 2. Abbeville: Libraire-Éditeur, 1884.

Histoire des conciles mérovingiens. Ed. Odette Pontal, Paris: Cerf, 1989.

Histoire de Gilion de Trasignyes et de Dame Marie, sa femme. Ed. O. L. B. Wolff. Paris: Brockhaus; Leipzig, J. J. Weber, 1839.

Hostiensis. *Lectura in Decretales (In primum* [etc.] *librum decretalium commentaria).* Venice: Iuntas, 1581. Reprint Turin, 1965.

———. *Summa aurea d. Henrici Cardinalis Hostiensis.* London: Haeredes Iacobi Iuntae, 1548.

———. *Summa aurea in titulos decretalium.* Venice: Iacobus Vitalis, 1574.

———. *Summa super titulis Decretalium.* Speier: Georgius de Spira, 1478.

Hugh of St Victor. *De sacramentis Christiane fidei.* In PL 176:173–616.

———. *Hugh of Saint Victor on the Sacraments of the Christian Faith.* trans. Roy J. Deferrari. Cambridge, Mass.: Medieval Academy of America, 1976.

———. *Opera omnia Hugonis de S. Victore.* IV in Epistolam ad Galatas. In PL 175.

Innocent IV. *Apparatus super libros Deretaliam,* ed. Franciscus Moneliensis Venice, 1481.

Ivo of Chartres. *Decretum.* Provisional edition by Martin Brett and Bruce Brasington. http://project.knowledgeforge.net/ivo/decretum.html.

———. *Panormia.* Provisional edition by Martin Brett and Bruce Brasington. http://wt faculty.wtamu.edu/bbrasington/panormia.html.

Jacobus a Voragine. *Legenda aurea vulgo historia Lombardica dicta.* Ed. Johann Georg Theodor Graesse. Impensis Librarie Arnoldianae, 1846 Reprint Osnabrück: Zeller, 1969.

Jerome, St. *Comment. in Matt.* CCL, vol. 77. Turnhout: Brepols, 1955.

———. *Letters and Select Works,* Trans. W. H. Fremantle, G. Lewis, and W. G. Martley. Select Library of the Nicene and Post-Nicene Fathers of the Christian Church. 2nd ser. Ed. Philip Schaff and Henry Wace. Grand Rapids, Mich.: Eerdmans, 1892.

Johannes Andreae. *In* (*primum* [etc.]) *librum decretalium novella commentaria.* Venice: Franciscus Franciscius, 1581.

St. Justin Martyr: Dialogue with Typho. Trans. Thomas B. Falls. Washington, D.C.: Catholic University of America Press, 2003.

Liber sentenciarum van de Officialiteit van Brussel, 1448–1459. Ed. Cyriel Vleeschouwers and Monique van Melkebeek. Verzameling van de oude rechtspraak in België, 7th ser. 2 vols. Brussels, 1982–83.

Lombard, Peter. *Collectaneorum in Epistolas S. Pauli. In Epistolam ad Galatas.* PL 192.

———. *Sententiae in IV libris distinctae* 2. 18. 5. Ed. Collegium S. Bonaventurae. 3rd ed. 2 vols. *Spicilegium Bonaventurianum* 4–5, Grottaferrata, 1971–81.

Luther, Martin. *Sämmtliche Werke.* Ed. Ernst Ludwig Enders and Johann Conrad Irmischer. 2nd ed. 67 vols. Frankfurt am Main: Berlad von Sender and Zimmer, 1832–81.

———. *Vom Ehelichen Leben und Andere Schriften Über die Ehe.* Ed. Dagmar C. G. Lorenz. Ditzigen: Reclam, 1978.

———. *Luther's Works.* Ed. J. Pelikan and H. Lehman. St. Louis: Concordia Publishing; Philadelphia: Fortress Press, 1957–.

Marguerite de Navarre. *Heptameron.* Paris: Éditions Garnier Frères, 1862.

Marie de France. *Les lais de Marie de France.* Ed. Jean Rychner. Paris: Champion, 1969.

Nider, Johannes. *Sermones aurei de tempore et de sanctis.* Reutlingen: Michel Greyff, not after 1480.

Pepin, Guillaume. *Sermones dominicales totius anni.* Paris: J. Parvus, 1523.

———. *Sermones quadraginta de destructione Niniue, hoc est vis generis vitiorum, authore fratre Guillermo Pepin.* Paris: Claude Chevallon, 1527.

Peter of Vaux. Vita of Charlotte of Corbie. *Acta sanctorum.* 539–89. 6 March *Acta Sanctorum,* 62 vols. (Antwerp, Tongedoo, and Brussels 1643–1902) March 1: 539–89.

Petrus Cantor. *Summa de sacramentis et animae consiliis.* Ed. Jean Albert Dugauquier. 3 vols. in 5. Analecta mediaevalia namurcensia, 4, 7, 11, 16, 21. Louvain, 1954– .

Philippe de Vigneulles. *Les cent nouvelles nouvelles.* Ed. Charles H. Livingston. Geneva: Drox, 1972.

Pithou, Pierre. *Coustumes du bailliage de Troyes en Champaigne.* Troyes: Imprimeur du Roy, 1609.

Quinque Compilationes antiquae. Ed. Emil Friedberg. Leipzig, 1882.

Raymond of Peñafort (Raimundus de Pennaforte). *Summa de poenitentia et matrimonio cum glossis Johannis de Friburgo.* Rome: Ioannes Tallini, 1603. Reprint Farnborough, 1967.

———. *Summa Sancti Raymundi de Pennafort.* Verona, 1744.

Registre de l'Officialité de Cericy, 1314–1457. Ed. G. Dupont. *Mémoires de la Société des antiquaires de Normandie*. Ser. 3, 10. Caen, 1880.

Registre de l'Officialité épiscopale de Troyes, 1389–1396. Ed. Jean Breban. LL.D. diss. Typescript. Paris, 1954.

Registre des causes civiles de l'Officialité épiscopale de Paris, 1384–1387. Ed. Joseph Petit. Collection de documents inédits sur l'histoire de France. Paris: Picard, 1919.

Registres de sentences de l'officialité de Cambrai (*1438–1453*). Ed. Cyriel Vleeschouwers and Monique van Melkebeek. Recueil de l'ancienne jurisprudence de la Belgique. 7th ser. 2 vols. Brussels: Ministère de la Justice, 1998.

Registrum Hamonis Hethe, Diocesis Roffensis. Ed. Charles Johnson. 2 vols. Oxford: Oxford University Press, 1948.

Repertorium poenitentiariae Germanicum. Ed. Ludwig Schmugge et al. 5 vols. Tübingen: Niemeyer, 1998–.

Riverside Chaucer. 5th ed. New York: Oxford University Press, 1987.

Le Roman de Gilion de Trazegnies. Ed. A. Bayot. Louvain: Université Catholique de Louvain. Librairie Peeters, 1903.

Las Siete Partidas. Trans. Samuel Parsons Scott. Ed. Robert Burns. 5 vols. Philadelphia: University of Pennsylvania Press, 2001.

Statuta antiquissima diocesis Cameracensis. Ed. Edmond H. J. Reusens. Analectes pour servir à l'histoire ecclésiastique de la Belgique. 2d sec. fasc. 6. Louvain, 1903.

Les statuts synodaux français du xiiie *siècle. I: Les statuts de Paris et le synodal de l'Ouest* (*xiii*[e] *siècle*). Ed. Odette Pontal. Collection de documents inédits sur l'histoire de France, ser. in 8°, 9. Paris, 1971; *II: Les statuts de 1230 à 1260*. Ed. idem, Idem, 15. idem. 1983; *III: Les statuts synodaux de la seconde moitié du xiii*[e] *siècle*. Ed. Joseph Avril. Idem. 19. Idem. 1988; *IV: Les statuts synodaux de l'ancienne province de Reims* (*Cambrai, Arras, Noyon, Soissons, et Tournai*). Ed. idem., idem., 23. Idem. 1988; *V: Les statuts synodaux des anciennes provinces de Bordeaux, Auch, Sens et Rouen* (*fin XIIIe siècle*). Ed. idem., idem., 28bis, idem. 2001.

Tancred of Bologna. *Ordo iudiciarius*. Ed. Friedrich C. Bergmann. In *Pilii, Tancredi, Gratie, Libri de iudiciorum ordine, 87–316.* Göttingen, 1842. Reprint Aalen, 1965.

———. *Summa de matrimonio.* Ed. Agathon Wunderlich. Göttingen: Vandenhoeck and Ruprecht, 1841.

Tertullian. "On Exhortation to Chastity." In *The Ante-Nicene Fathers,* ed. Alexander Roberts and James Donaldson, trans. Rev. S. Thewall. Vol. 4, 54. Buffalo, N.Y.: Christian Literature Publishing Co, 1885.

———. *Treatises on Marriage and Remarriage.* Ed. T. C. Lawler, Walter J. Burghardt, and William P. Le Saint, Trans.William P. Le Saint. Westminster, Md.: Newman Press, 1951.

Trithemius, Johannes. *De laudibus S. Annae.* Leipzig: Melchior Lotter, ca. 1500.

SECONDARY LITERATURE

Alberro, Solange. *La actividad del Santo Oficio de la Inquisición en Nueva España, 1571–1700.* Mexico City, Mexico: Instituto Nacional de Antropología e Historia, 1981.

d'Albiousse, Lionel. "De la suppression du crime de bigamie." *Annales de la Société littéraire, scientifique, et artistique d'Apt*, 1863–65, 234–39.

———."El discurso inquisitorial sobre los delitos de bigamia, poligamia, y de solicitación." In *Seis ensayos sobre el discurso colonial relativo a la comunidad doméstica: Matrimonio, familia, y sexualidad a través de los cronistas del siglo XVI, el Nuevo Testamento y el Santo Oficio de la Inquisición.* Solange Alberro, ed. 215–26. México: Instituto Nacional de Antropología e Historia, 1980.

Arnold, John. *Inquisition and Power: Cathariam and the Confessing Subject.* Philadelphia: University of Pennsylvania Press, 2001.

Avignon, Carole. "L'église et les infractions au lien matrimonial: Mariages clandestins et clandestinité, théories, pratiques, et discours, France du nord-ouest (XIIe–millieu XVI siècle)." Ph.D. diss, Université Paris-Est, 2008.

Baldwin, John. *The Language of Sex: Five Voices from Northern France Around 1200.* Chicago: University of Chicago Press, 1994.

Barou, Lucien. "Le charivari en Forez." *Patois Vivant* 10 (May 1982) 1–12.

Baschet, Jérome *Le sein du père: Abraham et la paternité dans l'Occident médiéval.* Paris: Gallimard, 2000.

Bautier, Robert-Henri. "Les Foires de Champagne: Recherches sur une évolution historique." In *Recueils de la Société Jean Bodin,* 97–147. Société Jean Bodin pour l'histoire comparative des institutions. Brussels: Éditions de la librairie encyclopédique, 1953.

Beaulande, Veronique. "Le blasphème et les blasphémateurs au XVe siècle d'après les registres de l'officialité épiscopale de Châlons-en-Champagne." *Société d'Agriculture, commerce, sciences, et arts de la Marne* 114 (1999): 55–73.

———. "Excommunication et pratiques eucharistiques à la fin du Moyen Âge en Champagne méridonale." *Revue d'histoire de l'église de France* 90:225 (2004): 411–26.

———. *Le Malheur d'être exclu? Excommunication, réconciliation, et société à la fin du moyen âge.* Paris: Publications de la Sorbonne, 2006.

———. "Rompre le lien conjugal en Champagne à la fin du moyen âge." In *Répudiation, séparation, divorce dans l'occident médiévale*, ed. Emmanuelle Santinelli, 211–13. Recherches Valenciennoises 25. Le Mont-Huy: Presses Universitaires de Valenciennes, 2007.

Beltrán, Maria Teresa López. "La bigamia y su significación social en Castilla a fines de la Edad Media." In *Nuevos enfoques para la enseñanza de la historia,* 95–116. Madrid: Asociación Cultural Al-Mudayna, 2007.

Bériou, Nicole, and David D'Avray. "Henry of Provins, O.P.'s Comparison of the Dominican and Franciscan Orders with the 'Order' of Matrimony" *Archivum Fratrum Praedicatorum* 49 (1979) 513–17.

Bernhard, Jean. "Le décret Tametsi du Concile de Trente: Triomphe de consensualisme matrimonial ou institution de la forme solennelle du mariage?" *Revue de droit canonique* 30 (1980) 209–34.

Betzig, Laura. "Medieval Monogamy," *Journal of Family History* 20:2 (1995) 181–216.

Bibolet, Françoise. "Deux canons et un évêque à Troyes au XV siècle: Guillaume Galeret, Etienne Grappin, Jean Leguise" *Mémoires de la Société académique de l'Aube.* 126 (2002): 137–47.

———. "Les métiers à Troyes aux XIV et XV siècles." *Actes du 95e Congres National des Sociétés Savantes Reims 1970: Champagne et pays de la Meuse.* Questions d'Histoire et de Philologie. Vol.2, Philosophie et Histoire jusqu'à 1610. Paris, 1975, 113–32.

———. "La participation du clergé aux affaires municipales de la ville de Troyes aux XIV et XV siècles." *Mémoires de la Société académique d'agriculture, des sciences, arts, et belles-lettres du département de l'Aube* 100 (1943–45):51–65.

Bolton, Brenda, and Constance M. Rousseau. "Palmerius of Picciati: Innocent III meets his 'Martin Guerre.' " In *Proceedings of the Tenth International Congress of Medieval Canon Law, 1996,* ed. Kenneth Pennington, Stanley Chodorow, and Keith Kendall, 361–85. Monumenta Iuris Canonici, ser. C: Subsidia, 11. Vatican City, 2001.

Boutiot, Théophile. *Histoire de la ville de Troyes et de la Champagne meridionale*, 4 vols. Paris: Dumoulin, 1870.

———. "Recherches sur la juridiction du roi sur celle de l'évêque dans le bailliage de Troyes et sur les coutumes de ce bailliage." *Mémoires de la Société d'agriculture, sciences, et arts du département de l'Aube.* 36, 6–74. Troyes: Dufour-Bouquot, 1873.

Boyer, Richard. *Lives of the Bigamists: Marriage, Family, and Community in Colonial Mexico.* Albuquerque, University of New Mexico Press, 1995.

Braga, Isabel M. R. Memdes Drumond. *A Bigamia em Portugal na epoca moderna.* Lisbon: Hugin, 2003.

———. "Para o estudo da bigamia em Portugal no século XV." In *Os Reinos ibéricos na Idade Média: Livro de homenagem ao professor doutor Humberto Carlos Baquero Moreno,* eds. Luís Adão da Fonseca, Luís Carlos Amaral, and Maria Fernanda Ferreira Santos, 2:519–27. 3 vols. 2003.

Brandenbarg, Ton. "St. Anne and Her Family: The Veneration of Saint Anne in Connection with Concepts of Marriage and the Family in the Early Modern Period." In *Saints and She-Devils: Images of Women in the Fifteenth and Sixteenth Centuries*, ed. Lene Dresen-Coeders, 101–27. London: Rubicon Press, 1987.

Le Bras, Gabriel. "La doctrine du marriage." In *Dictionnaire de théologie catholique,* 9:2201–11. Paris: H. Welter, 1927.

Brown, Dorothy Catherine. *Pastor and Laity in the Theology of Jean Gerson.* Cambridge: Cambridge University Press, 1987.

Brown-Grant, Rosalind. *French Romance of the Later Middle Ages: Gender, Morality, and Desire.* Oxford: Oxford University Press, 2008.

———. "Learning to Be a Good Husband: Competing Masculine Identities in the Roman du Comte d'Artois." *Cahiers de recherches médiévales et humanistes* 9 (2002) n.p. http://crm.revues.org//index62.html.

Brundage, James A. "The Crusader's Wife: A Canonistic Quandary." *Studia Gratiana* 12 (1967): 425–42.

———. "The Crusader's Wife Revisited." *Studia Gratiana* 14 (1967): 241–52.

———. *Law, Sex, and Christian Society in Medieval Europe.* Chicago: University of Chicago Press, 1987.

———. *Medieval Canon Law.* London: Longman, 1995.

———. "The Merry Widow's Serious Sister: Remarriage in Classical Canon Law" In *Matrons and Marginal Women in Medieval Society,* Robert Edwards and Vickie L. Ziegler. Woodbridge, U.K.: Boydell and Brewer, 1985.

———. "The Problem of Impotence." In *Sexual Practices and the Medieval Church,* ed. Vern Bullough and James Brundage. Buffalo, N.Y.: Prometheus Books, 1982.

———. *Sex, Law, and Marriage in the Middle Ages.* Variorum Reprints CS397. Brookfield, Vt.: Variorum. 1993.

———. "Widows and Remarriage: Moral Conflicts and Their Resolution in Classical Canon Law." In *Wife and Widow*, in Medieval England, ed. Sue Sheridan Walker, 17–31. Ann Arbor; University of Michigan Press, 1993.

Bryan, Lindsay. "Marriage and Morals in the Fourteenth Century: The Evidence of Bishop Hamo's Register." *English Historical Review* 491 (April 2006): 467–86.

Butler, Sara M. " 'I will never consent to be wedded with you!': Coerced Marriage in the Courts of Medieval England." *Canadian Journal of History* 39:2 (2004): 247–70.

———. "The Law as a Weapon in Marital Disputes: Evidence from the Late Medieval Court of Chancery, 1424–1529." *Journal of British Studies* 43 (2004): 291–316.

———. "Runaway Wives: Husband Desertion in Medieval England." *Journal of Social History* (Winter 2006): 337–59.

Cavallo, Sandra, and Lyndan Warner, eds. *Widowhood in Medieval and Early Modern Europe.* Women and Men in History. New York: Longman, 1999.

Chapin, Elizabeth. *Les villes de foires de Champagne des origines au début du XIVe siècle.* Paris: Champion, 1937.

Charageat, Martine. "Les sentences de l'official à Saragosse au XV siècle." In *Cahiers de Fanjeaux* 42, 317–42. Toulouse: Privat, 2007.

———. "Typologie des procès canoniques matrimoniaux à Saragosse (XV–XVI)." In *Sínodos diocesanos y legislación particular. Estudios históricos en honor al Dr. D. Francisco Cantelar Rodríguez,* ed. J. Justo Fernández, 217–32. Salamanca: Publicaciones de la Universidad Pontifica de Salamanca, 1999.

Le charivari. Actes de la table ronde organisée par l'EHESS et le CNRS. Ed. J. Le Goff and J. C. Shmitt. Paris, 1977; Paris-The Hague, 1981.

Clark, Katherine. "Purgatory, Punishment, and the Discourse of Holy Widowhood in the High and Later Middle Ages." *Journal of the History of Sexuality* 16:2 (2007): 169–203.

Colish, Marcia L. *Peter Lombard.* Vol. 1. Leiden: Brill, 1994.

Coüard-Luys, E. "Variétés. 1. Suicide et polygamie." *Mémoires de la Société d'archéologie, sciences, et arts du département de l'Oise* 12:2 (1884) : 431–38.

Cristellon, Cecilia. "Charitas versus eros: Il matrimonio, la Chiesa, e i suoi giudici nella Venezia del Rinascimento (1420–1545)." Ph.D. diss., European University Institute, 2005.

———. "Marriage and Consent in Pre-Trentine Venice: Between Law Conception and Ecclesiastical Conception, 1420–1545." *Sixteenth Century Journal* 39:2 (2008) 390–418.

———. "L'ufficio del giudice: Mediazione, inquisizione, confessione nei processi matrimoniali veneziani (1420–1532)" *Rivista Storica Italiana* 3 (2003) 851–98.

Crozet, René. *Histoire de Champagne*. Paris: Ancienne Librarie Furne Boivin et cie, 1933.

Cushing, Kathleen. *Reform and the Papacy in the Eleventh Century*. Manchester: Manchester University Press, 2005.

Dauviller, Jean. *Le mariage dans le droit classique de l'Église, depuis le Décret de Gratien (1140) jusqu'à la mort de Clément V (1314)*. Paris: Recueil Sirey, 1933.

Davis, Natalie Zemon. "On the Lame." AHR Forum: The Return of Martin Guerre. *American Historical Review* 93 (June 1988) 572–603.

———. *The Return of Martin Guerre*. Cambridge, Mass.: Harvard University Press, 1983.

———. "Les silences des archives, le renom de l'histoire." *Annales du Midi* 120 (2008). 467–83.

———. *Society and Culture in Early Modern France*. Stanford, Calif.: Stanford University Press, 1975.

D'Avray, David. "Lay Kinship Solidarities and Papal Law." In *Law, Laity, and Solidarities: Essays in Honour of Susan Reynolds*, ed. Pauline Stafford, Susan Reynolds, Janet L. Nelson, and Jane Martindale, 188–99. Manchester: Manchester University Press, 2001.

———. "Marriage Ceremonies and the Church After 1215." In *Marriage in Italy, 1300–1650*, ed. Trevor Dean and Kate Lowe, 107–15. Cambridge: Cambridge University Press, 1998.

———. *Medieval Marriage Sermons: Mass Communication in a Culture Without Print*. Oxford: Oxford University Press, 2001.

———. *Medieval Marriage: Symbolism and Society*. Oxford: Oxford University Press, 2005.

———. *Modern Questions About Medieval Sermons: Essays on Marriage, Death, History, and Sexuality*. Ed. Nicole Beriou and David D'Avray. Spoleto, Italy: Centro Italiano di Studi sul'Alto Medioevo, 1994.

D'Avray, David, and M. Tausche. "Marriage Sermons in Ad Status Collections of the Central Middle Ages." *Archives d'histoire doctrinale et litteraire du moyen âge* 47 (1981) 71–119.

Dean, Trevor. "Fathers and Daughters: Marriage Laws and Marriage Disputes in Bologna and Italy, 1200–1500." In Trevor Dean and Kate Lowe, eds., *Marriage in Italy*, 85–106. Cambridge: Cambridge University Press, 1998.

Deutsch, Christina. *Ehegerichtsbarkeit im Bistum Regensburg (1480–1538)*. Forschungen zur kirchlichen Rechtsgeschichte und zum Kirchenrecht, 29. Cologne: Böhlau, 2005.

———. "Zwischen Leben und Tod: Die Verschollenen und ihre Hinterbliebenen im Spätmittelalter." *Trajekte: Zeitschrift des Zentrums für Literatur- und Kulturforschung Berlin* 14 (2007) 12–16.

Diebold, Étienne. "L'application en France du canon 51 du IVe concile du Latran d'après les anciens statuts synodaux." *L'Année Canonique* 2 (1953) 187–95.

Diefendorf, Barbara B. *Paris City Councillors in the Sixteenth Century: The Politics of Patrimony.* Princeton, N.J.: Princeton University Press, 1983.

Dillard, Heath. *Daughters of the Reconquest: Women in Castilian Town Society, 1100–1300.* Cambridge: Cambridge University Press, 1984.

Dörfler-Dierken, Angelika. *Die Verehrung der heiligen Anna in Spätmittelalter und früher Neuzeit.* Göttingen: Vandenhoek and Ruprecht, 1992.

Doherty, Denis. *The Sexual Doctrine of Cardinal Cajetan.* Regensburg: Pustet, 1966.

Dolezalek, Gero. *Das Imbreviaturbuch des Erzbischöflichen Gerichtsnotars Hubaldus aus Pisa, Mai bis August 1230.* In Forschungen zur neueren Privatrechtsgeschichte 13. Cologne: Böhlau, 1969.

Donahue, Charles Jr. "The Canon Law on the Formation of Marriage and Social Practice in the Later Middle Ages." *Journal of Family History* (summer 1983) 144–58.

———. " 'Clandestine' Marriage in the Later Middle Ages: A Reply." *Law and History Review* 10 (1992) 315–22.

"Ex officio cases at Paris" *Mélanges Anne Lefebvre* ed. Bernard d'Alteroche et al. (Paris: Éditions Panthéon Assas, 2010) 393–412

———. "The Dating of Alexander the Third's Marriage Decretals: Dauvillier Revisited After Fifty Years," *Zeitschrift für Rechtsgeschichte* (Kanonistische Abteilung 68) 99 (1982) 70–124.

———. "English and French Marriage Cases in the Later Middle Ages: Might the Differences Be Explained by Differences in the Property Systems?" In *Marriage, Property, and Succession*, ed. Lloyd Bonfield, 339–66. Comparative Studies in Continental and Anglo-American Legal History, 10 (Berlin: Duncker & Humbelt, 1992).

———. "Female Plaintiffs in Marriage Cases in the Court of York in the Later Middle Ages: What Can We Learn from the Numbers?" In *Wife and Widow in Medieval England,* ed. Sue Sheridan Walker, Ann Arbor: University of Michigan Press, 1993. 183–213.

———. *Law, Marriage, and Society in the Later Middle Ages: Arguments About Marriage in Five Courts.* Cambridge: Cambridge University Press, 2007.

———. "Law, Marriage, and Society in the Later Middle Ages: A Look at the English and 'Franco-Belgian' Regions." In *Proceedings of the Thirteenth International Congress of Medieval Canon Law*, Esztergom-Budapest, 3–9 August 2008. Ed. Anzelm Szuromi and Peter Landau. Monumenta Iuris Canonici, ser. C, subsidia 14. Vatican City: Biblioteca Apostolica Vaticana, 2010.

———. "The Monastic Judge: Social Practice, Formal Rule, and the Medieval Canon Law of Incest." In *De Iure Canonico Medii Aevi: Festschrift für Rudolf Weigand*, ed. Peter Laundau and Martin Petzolt, 49–69. Studia Gratiana 27. Rome: Libreria Ateneo Salesiano, 1996.

———. "The Policy of Alexander the Third's Consent Theory of Marriage." In *Proceedings of the Fourth International Congress of Medieval Canon Law*, ed. Stephan Kuttner, 251–81. Monumenta Iuris Canonici, C:5. Vatican City: Biblioteca Apostolica Vaticana, 1976.

———. "Was There a Change in Marriage Law in the late Middle Ages?" *Revista Internazionale di Diritto Commune* 6 (1995) 49–80.

———. "What Causes Fundamental Legal Ideas? Marital Property in England and France in the Thirteenth Century." *Michigan Law Review* 78 (1979) 59–88.

Duby, Georges. *Le chevalier, la femme, et le prêtre: Le mariage dans la France féodale.* 1981. Trans. Barbara Bray, *The Knight, the Lady, and the Priest: The Making of Modern Marriage in Medieval France.* New York: Pantheon Books, 1984.

———. *Medieval Marriage: Two Models from Twelfth-Century France.* Trans. E. Forster. Johns Hopkins Symposia in Comparative History 11. Baltimore: Johns Hopkins University Press, 1978.

Eisenach, Emlyn. *Husbands, Wives, and Concubines: Marriage, Family, and Social Order in Sixteenth-Century Verona.* Kirksville, Mo.: Truman State University Press, 2004.

———.Sistemi informali didivorzio e seguenti matrimoni: a Verona nella prima metà del Ciquecento" Trans. Alison A. Smith, *Le Donne a Verona; Riconsiderare la Storia Della Citta,* ed. Paola Lanaro and Alison A. Smith (Verona: Cierre, 2012).

Esmein, Adhémar. *Le mariage en droit canonique.* 2d ed. 2 vols., rev. Ed. Robert Génestal and Jean Dauvillier. Paris: Sirey, 1929–35.

Evergates, Theodore. *The Aristocracy in the County of Champagne, 1000–1300.* Philadelphia: University of Pennsylvania Press, 2006.

———. *Feudal Society in the Bailliage of Troyes Under the Counts of Champagne, 1152–1284.* Baltimore: Johns Hopkins University Press, 1975.

Falzone, Emmanuël. " 'Ad secunda vota rite convolare posse': Le remariage des personnes veuves à la fin du moyen âge dans les registres de sentences de l'officialité de Cambrai (1438–1453)." *Revue d'histoire ecclesiastique* 102 (2007): 815–36.

Farmer, Sharon. "Persuasive Voices: Clerical Images of Medieval Wives." *Speculum* 61:3 (1986) 517–43.

Faulkner, John Alfred. "Luther and the Bigamous Marriage of Philip of Hesse." *American Journal of Theology* 17:2 (April 1913) 206–31.

Fernández, Enrique Gacto. "El delito de bigamia y la Inquisición española." *Anuario de historia del derecho español* 57 (1987) 465–92.

Flandrin, Jean-Louis. *Le sexe et l'Occident.* Paris: Seuil, 1981.

Fortier-Beaulieu, P. "Le charivari dans le Roman de Fauvel." *Revue de folklore français et de folklore colonial* 11 (1940): 1–16.

Fossier, Robert. "Rémarques sur les movements de population en Champagne méridionale au XVe siècle." *Bibliothèque de l'École des Chartes* 112 (1965): 186–89.

Fournier, Edouard. "L'enseignement des Décrétales à l'université de Paris au Moyen Âge." *Revue d'histoire de l'Église de France* 26:110 (1940) 58–62.

Fournier, Paul. *Les officialités au moyen âge.* Paris: E. Plon et cie, 1880.

Fraher, Richard M. "The Theoretical Justification for the New Criminal Law of the High Middle Ages: 'Rei Publicae Interest, Ne Crimina Remaneant Impunita.' " *University of Illinois Law Review* (1984): 577–99.

Friedman, Lawrence M. "Crimes of Mobility." *Stanford Law Review* 43:3 (February 1991): 637–58.

Galpern, A. N. *Religions of the People in Sixteenth-Century Champagne.* Cambridge, Mass.: Harvard University Press, 1976.

Gaudemet, Jean. *Le mariage en Occident: Les moeurs et le droit.* Paris: *Cerf,* 1987.

———. *Sociétés et mariage.* Strasbourg: Cerdic-Publications, 1980.

Gauvard, Claude. "Droit et pratiques judiciaires dans les villes du nord du royaume de France à la fin du Moyen Âge: L'enseignement des sources." In *Pratiques sociales et politiques judiciaires dans les villes de l'Occident à la fin du Moyen Âge: Actes du colloque d'Avignon,* ed. Jacques Chiffoleau, Claude Gauvard, and Andrea Zorzi, 33–79. Rome: École française de Rome, Collection de l'École française de Rome 385, 2007.

———. *De grace especial: Crime, État et société en France à la fin du Moyen Âge.* 2 vols. Paris: Publications de la Sorbonne, 1991.

"Honneur de femme et femme d'honneur en France à la fin du Moyen Âge" *Francia* 28 (2001) 159–191.

———. "La peine de mort en France à la fin du moyen âge: Esquisse d'un bilan." In *Le pouvoir au Moyen Âge,* ed. Claude Carozzi and Huguette Taviani-Carossi, 71–84. Aix-en-Provence: Publications de l'Université de Provence, 2005.

———. *Violence et ordre public au moyen âge.* Paris: Picard, 2005.

Geltner, Guy. *The Medieval Prison: A Social History.* Princeton N.J.: Princeton University Press, 2008.

Gemerek, Bronislaw. *The Margins of Society in Late Medieval Paris.* Trans. Jean Birrell. Cambridge: Cambridge University Press, 1987.

Gil, Federico R. Aznar. "Penas y sanciones contra los matrimonios clandestinos en la península Ibérica durante la baja edad media." *Revista de estudios históricos-jurídicos* 25 (2003) 189–214.

Goldberg, P. J. P. "Marriage, Migration, Servanthood and Life-Cycle in Yorkshire Towns of the Later Middle Ages: Some York Cause Paper Evidence." *Continuity and Change* 1 (1986) 141–69.

———. *Women, Work, and Life Cycle in a Medieval Economy: Women in York and Yorkshire c. 1300–1520.* Oxford: Oxford University Press, 1992.

Gonthier, Nicole. *Le châtiment du crime au moyen âge.* Rennes: Presses Universitaires de Rennes, 1998.

———. "Prison et prisonniers à Lyon." *Mémoires de la Société pour l'histoire du droit et des institutions des anciens pays Bourguignons, Comtois, et Romands* 39 (1982): 15–30.

———. "Les rapports du couple d'après les documents judiciaries a la fin du moyen âge." In *Mariage et sexualité au moyen âge: Accord ou crises?* ed. Michel Rouche. Cultures et Civilisations Médiévales 21. Paris: Presses de l'Université de Paris-Sorbonne, 2000.

Goody, Jack. *The Development of the Family and Marriage in Europe.* Cambridge: Cambridge University Press, 1983.

Gordon, Sarah. *The Mormon Question: Polygamy and Constitutional Conflict in Nineteenth-Century America.* Philadelphia: University of Pennsylvania Press, 2001.

Gorochov, Nathalie. *Le Collège de Navarre de sa foundation (1305) au début du XVe siècle (1418): Histoire de l'institution, de sa vie intellectuelle, et de son recrutement.* Paris: Honoré Champion, 1997.

Gottlieb, Beatrice. "Getting Married in Pre-Reformation Europe: The Doctrine of Clandestine Marriage and Court Cases in Fifteenth-Century Champagne." Ph.D. diss., Columbia University, 1974.

———. "The Meaning of Clandestine Marriage." In *Family and Sexuality in French History*, ed. Robert Wheaton and Tamara K. Hareven, 49–83. Philadelphia: University of Pennsylvania Press, 1980.

Grand, Roger. "La prison et la notion d'emprisonnement dans l'ancien droit." *Revue historique de droit français et étranger*. 4th ser., 19–20 (1940–41):58–87.

Grossman, Avraham. *Pious and Rebellious: Jewish Women in Medieval Europe.* Trans. Jonathan Chapman. Hanover, N.H.: Brandeis University Press, 2004.

Guilbert, Sylvette. "A Châlons-en-Champagne en 1423, gens de ville et gens des champs." In *Compter les Champenois,* ed. Patrick Demouy and Charles Vuilliez. Colloque du Centre d'Etudes Champenoises, Université de Reims, 1996. Reims: Presses Universitaires de Reims, 1997.

———. "À Châlons-sur-Marne au XV siècle: Un conseil municipal face aux épidémies." *Annales ESC* 23:6 (1968): 1283–1300.

———. " 'La fête entre soi': Cours royals en Champagne au XV siècle." In *Fêtes et politique en Champagne,* ed. Sylvette Guilbert, 41–46. Colloque, Centre d'Études Champenoises, Université de Reims, June 1990. Nancy: Presses Universitaires de Nancy, 1992.

———. "Au XVe siècle, les Colbert châlonnais, bourreliers." *Travaux de l'Académie nationale de Reims* 164 (1985): 335–42.

———. "Migrations de tisserands flamands et picards et agitation sociale à Châlons-sur-Marne au début du XIV siècle." In *Population et démographie au moyen âge,* ed. Olivier Guyotjeannin. Actes du 118e congrès national des sociétés historiques et scientifiques, Pau, 25–29 October 1993. Section Histoire médiévale et philologie. Paris: Éditions du CTHS, 1995.

———. "Note sur le clergé rural au diocèse de Troyes au début du XV siècle." In *Le clergé rural dans l'Europe médiévale et moderne* ed. Pierre Bonnassie, 229–36.Toulouse: Presses Universitaires du Mirail, 1995.

———. "Relations entre les administrations des villes champenoises pendant la Guerre de Cent Ans." In *La Champagne et ses administraitions à travers le temps,* ed. Georges Clause, Sylvette Guilbert, and Maurice Vaïsse, 131–41. Actes du colloque d'histoire régionale, Reims-Châlons-sur-Marne, 4–6 June 1987. Paris: La Manufacture, 1990.

Hajnal, John. "European Marriage Patterns in Perspective." In *Population in History: Essays in Historical Demography,* ed. D.V. Glass and D. E. C. Eversley. London: Aldine, 1965, 101–43.

Hardel, A. "Suicide et polygamie." In *Mémoires de l'académie nationale des sciences arts et belles-lettres de Caen.* Académie nationale des sciences, arts et belles lettres de Caen, 12:431–38, 1883.

Hartog, Hendrik. *Man and Wife in America: A History.* Cambridge, Mass.: Harvard University Press, 2002.

Harvey, Howard Graham. *The Theatre of the Basoche: The Contribution of the Law Societies to French Mediaeval Comedy.* Cambridge, Mass.: Harvard University Press, 1941.

Havet, Julien. "L'hérésie et le bras seculier au moyen âge jusqu'au XIII siècle." *Bibliothèque de l'École des Chartres* 41 (1880): 488–517, 570–670.

Hayden, J. Michael, and Malcolm Greenshields. *600 Years of Reform: Bishops and the French Church, 1190–1789.* Montreal: McGill Queen's University Press, 2005.

Helmholz, R. H. *Marriage Litigation in Medieval England.* Cambridge Studies in English Legal History. Cambridge: Cambridge University Press, 1975. Reprint Holmes Beach, 1986.

Herlihy, David. "The Making of the Medieval Family: Symmetry, Structure, and Sentiment." *Journal of Family History* 8 (1983):116–30.

———. "Making Sense of Incest: Women and the Marriage Rules of the Early Middle Ages." In *Women, Family, and Society in Medieval Europe,* ed. David Herlihy and Anthony Molho, 96–112. Providence, R.I.: Berghahn Books, 1995.

———. *Medieval Households.* Cambridge, Mass.: Harvard University Press, 1985.

———. *Women, Family, and Society in Medieval Europe: Historical Essays, 1978–1991.* Providence, R. I.: Berghahn Books, 1994.

Herlihy, David, and Christiane Klapisch-Zuber. *Les Toscans et leurs familles: Une étude du "catasto" florentin de 1427.* Paris: Presses de la Fondation Nationale des Sciences Politiques, 1978.

Herrero, María del Carmen García. "Los matrimonios de Gaspar Eli: Tipología matrimonial en un proceso de 1493." *Aragón en la Edad Media* 7 (1987): 231–44.

Hillman, Eugene. "Polygamy and the Council of Trent." *Jurist* 33 (1973) 358–76

Hsia, Ronald Po-Chia. "Münster and the Anabaptists." In *The German People and the Reformation,* ed. R. Po-Chia Hsia, 51–70 Ithaca, N.Y.: Cornell University Press, 1988.

Hyma, Albert. "Erasmus and the Sacrament of Matrimony." *Archiv für Reformationsgeschichte* 48 (1957) 145–64.

———. *Interpreting Cultural Symbols: Saint Anne in Late Medieval Society.* Ed. Kathleen Ashley and Pamela Sheingorn. Athens: University of Georgia Press, 1986.

Karras, Ruth. "Concubinage in Theory and Practice." In *Law and the Illicit in Medieval Europe*, ed. Ruth Mazo Karras, Joel Kaye, and E. Ann Matter. Philadelphia: University of Pennsylvania Press, 2008.

———. *Sexuality in Medieval Europe: Doing Unto Others.* New York: Routledge, 2005.

Kirshner, Julius. "*Maritus lucretur dotem uxoris sue premortue* in Late Medieval Florence." *Zeitschrift für Rechtsgeschichte* (*Kanonistische Abteilung*), 77 (1991) 111–55.

Klapisch-Zuber, Christiane. "Le complexe de Griselda: Dot et dons de mariage au Quattrocento." *Mélanges de l'école française de Rome* 94 (1982) 7–43.

———. *Women, Family, and Ritual in Renaissance Italy.* Chicago: University of Chicago Press, 1985.

Kleinschmidt, Beda. *Die heilige Anna: Ihre Vereherung in Geschichte, Kunst, und Volkstum.* Düsseldorf: Schwann, 1930.

Knapp, Peggy A. "Alisoun of Bath and the Reappropriation of Tradition." *Chaucer Review* 24:1 (Summer 1989) 45–52.

Korpiola, Mia. *Between Betrothal and Bedding: Marriage Formation in Sweden, 1200–1600.* Leiden: Brill, 2009.

Kuehn, Thomas. *Law, Family, and Women: Toward a Legal Anthropology of Renaissance Italy.* Chicago: University of Chicago Press, 1991.

Kuttner, Stephan. *Die Kanonistische Schuldlehre.* Rome: Vatican, 1935.

———. "Methodological Problems Concerning the History of Canon Law." *Speculum* 30:4 (October 1955) 539–49.

Laiou, Angeliki. "The Evolution of the Status of Women in Marriage and in Family Law." In *Mütter Nonne Diakonin: Frauenbilder im Recht der Ostkirchen*, 71–86, *Kanon* 16 (2000).

Lea, Henry Charles. *A History of the Inquisition of Spain.* 4 vols. New York: Macmillan, 1907. Reprint AMS Press, 1988.

Lefebvre-Teillard, Anne. "Une nouvelle venue dans l'histoire du droit canonique." In *Proceedings of the Sixth International Congress of Medieval Canon Law*, ed. Stephan Kuttner and Kenneth Pennington, 647–57. Monumenta Iuris Canonici, C:7, Vatican City, 1985.

———.*Les officialités à la veille du concile de Trente.* Bibliothèque d'histoire du droit et droit romain, 19. Paris: Sirey, 1973.

———. "Règle et réalité dans le droit matrimonial à la fin du moyen âge." *Revue de droit canonique* 30 (1980) 41–54.

———. "Règle et réalité: Les nullités de mariage à la fin du moyen âge." *Revue de droit canonique* 32 (1982): 145–55.

Lehmann, Prisca. *La répression des délits sexuels dans les États savoyards.* Cahiers Lausannois d'Histoire Médiévale 39. Lausanne: Université de Lausanne, Section d'histoire, Faculté des lettres, 2006.

L'Engle, Susan. "Justice in the Margins: Punishment in Medieval Toulouse." *Viator* 33 (2002) 133–65.

Lévy, Jean-Philippe. *La hiérarchie des preuves dans le droit savant du moyen-âge.* Annales de l'Université de Lyon, ser. 3, law, fasc. 5. Paris: Sirey, 1939.

———. "L'officialité de Paris et les questions familiales à la fin du XIVe siècle." In *Études de droit canonique dédiées à Gabriel le Bras,* 2:1265–94.Paris: Sirey, 1965.

Lindner, Klaus. "Courtship and the Courts: Marriage and Law in Southern Germany, 1350–1550." D. Theol. diss., Harvard University Divinity School, 1988.

Litzenberger, Caroline. *The English Reformation and the Laity: Gloucestershire, 1540–80.* Cambridge: Cambridge University Press, 1997.

Logan, F. Donald. *Runaway Religious in Medieval England, c 1240–1540.* Cambridge: Cambridge University Press, 1996.

Lombardi, Daniela. *Matrimoni di Antico Regime.* Bologna: Il Mulino, 2001.

Longsworth, Robert. "The Wife of Bath and the Samaritan Woman." *Chaucer Review* 34:4 (2000) 372–87.

Maddern, Philippa. "Moving Households: Geographical Mobility and Serial Monogamy in England, 1350–1500." *Parergon* 24:2 (2007) 69–92.

Maes, L. Th. "Les délits de moeurs dans le droit pénal coutumier de Malines." *Revue du Nord* 30 (1948) 5–25.

Makowski, Elizabeth. "The Conjugal Debt and Medieval Canon Law." In *Equally in God's*

Image: Women in the Middle Ages, ed. Julia Bolton Holloway, Constance S. Wright, and John Bechtold. New York: Peter Lang, 1990.

Marriage in Italy, 1300–1650. Ed. Trevor Dean and K. J. P. Lowe. Cambridge: Cambridge University Press, 1997.

Martin, Hervé. *Le métier de predicateur en France septentrionale à la fin du moyen âge, 1350–1520.* Paris: Cerf, 1988.

Matzke, John E. "The Lay of Eliduc and the Legend of the Husband with Two Wives." *Modern Philiology* 5: 2 (October 1907): 211–39.

Mayali, Laurent. " 'Duo erunt in carne una' and the Medieval Canonists." In *Iuris Historia: Liber amicorum Gero Dolezalek,* ed. Vincenzo Colli and Emmanuele Conte, 161–76. Berkeley: Robbins Collection, 2008.

———. "Note on the Legitimization by Subsequent Marriage from Alexander III to Innocent III." In *The Two Laws: Studies in Medieval Legal History Dedicated to Stephan Kuttner,* ed. Laurent Mayali and Stephanie A. J. Tibbetts, 56–72. Washington, D.C.: Catholic University Press, 1990.

Mazour-Matusevich, Yelena. "La position de Jean Gerson (1363–1429) envers les femmes." *Le Moyen Âge* 2 (2006) 337–53.

McCarthy, Connor. *Marriage in Medieval England: Law, Literature, and Practice.* Suffolk: Boydell Press, 2004.

McDougall, Sara. "Bigamy: A Male Crime in Medieval Europe?" *Gender and History* 22:2 (August 2010) 430–46.

———. "The Punishment of Bigamy in Late-Medieval Troyes." *Imago Temporis: Medium Aevum* 3 (2009):189–204.

———. "The Prosecution of Sex in Late-Medieval Troyes." In *Sexuality in the Middle Ages and Early Modern Times,* ed. Albrecht Classen, 691–714. Berlin and New York: De Gruyter, 2008.

McGuire, Brian Patrick. *Jean Gerson and the Last Medieval Reformation.* University Park, Pa.: Pennsylvania State University Press, 2005.

McSheffrey, Shannon. "Detective Fiction in the Archives: Court Records and the Uses of Law in Late Medieval England." *History Workshop Journal* 65 (spring 2008): 65–78.

———. *Marriage, Sex, and Civic Culture in Late Medieval London.* Philadelphia: University of Pennsylvania Press, 2006.

———. "Men and Masculinity in Late Medieval London Civic Culture: Governance, Patriarchy, and Reputation." In *Conflicting Identities: Men in the Middle Ages,* ed. Jacqueline Murray, 243–78. New York: Garland Press, 1999.

———. "Place, Space, and Situation: Public and Private in the Making of Marriage in Late-Medieval London." *Speculum* 79 (2004): 960–90.

———. "Women, the Church, and the Law: Matrimonial Litigation in Lucca Under Bishop Nicolao Guinigi (1394–1435)." In *Chattel, Servant, or Citizen: Women's Status in Church, State, and Society,* ed. Mary O'Dowd and Sabine Wichert, 82–90. Institute of Irish Studies, Queen's University, Belfast, Historical Studies, 19. Belfast, 1995.

Meiss, Millard. *Painting in Florence and Siena After the Black Death: The Arts, Religion, and Society in the Mid-Fourteenth Century.* Princeton, N.J.: Princeton University Press, 1951.

Méthot, Mélanie. 'Bigamists Meet Polygamists: Confronting the Popular Image of Bigamists in Canadian Society." *History of the Family* 12 (2007): 169–77.

Metz, René. *La femme et l'enfant dans le droit canonique médiéval.* London: Variorum Reprints, 1985.

Meyendorff, John. "Christian Marriage in Byzantium: The Canonical and Liturgical Tradition." *Dumbarton Oaks Papers* 44 (1990) 105–6.

Minnis, Alistair. *Fallible Authors: Chaucer's Pardoner and the Wife of Bath.* Philadelphia: University of Pennsylvania Press, 2007.

Molin, Jean-Baptiste, and Protais Mutembe. *Le rituel du mariage en France du XIIème au XVIème siècle.* Theologie historique 26. Paris: Éditions Beauchesne, 1974.

Mollat, G. "La benediction des secondes noces." *Études d'histoire de droit canonique dédiées à Gabriel Le Bras.* 2 vols. Paris: Sirey, 1965.

Morel, Barbara. *Une iconographie de la répression judiciaire.* Paris: Éditions du Comité des travaux historiques et scientifiques, 2007.

Nixon, Virginia. *Mary's Mother: Saint Anne in Late Medieval Europe.* Philadelphia: University of Pennsylvania Press, 2004.

Noonan, John. "Power to Choose" *Viator* 4 (1973) 419–34.

Otis-Cour, Leah. "De jure novo: Dealing with Adultery in the Fifteenth-Century Toulousain." *Speculum* 84:2 (April 2009) 347–92.

———."Lo pecat de la carn: la répression des délits sexuels à Pamiers à la fin du Moyen Âge." *Studi di Storia del diritto* 1 (1996) 335–36.

Ourliac, Paul, and Jehan de Malafosse. *Histoire du droit privé.* 3 vols. Paris: Albin Michel, 1961–68.

Ozment, Steven. *When Fathers Ruled: Family Life in Reformation Europe.* Cambridge, Mass.: Harvard University Press, 1983.

Päpste, Pilger, Pönitentiariae: Festschrift für Ludwig Schmugge zum 65. Geburtstag. Ed. Andreas Meyer, Constanze Rendtel, and Maria Wittmer-Butsch. Tübingen: Niemeyer, 2004.

Payan, Paul. "Pour retrouver un père . . . La promotion du culte de saint Joseph au temps de Gerson." *Cahiers de recherches médiévales et humanistes* 4 (1997): n.p. http://crm.revues.org//index959.html.

Pollock, Frederick, Rev. S. F. C. Milson. and F. W. Maitland. *The History of English Law Before the Time of Edward I.* 2nd ed. Vol. 2. Cambridge: Cambridge University Press, 1968.

Pommeray, Léon. "L'officialité archidiaconale de Paris aux xve–xvie siècles." LL.D. diss., Université de Paris. Paris: Sirey, 1933.

Poos, L. R. "The Heavy-Handed Marriage Counsellor: Regulating Marriage in Some Later Medieval English Local Ecclesiastical-Court Jurisdictions." *American Journal of Legal History* 39 (1995) 291–309.

Poska, Allyson S. "When Bigamy Is the Charge: Gallegan Women and the Holy Office." In *Women in the Inquisition: Spain and the New World*, ed. Mary Giles, 189–205. Baltimore: Johns Hopkins University Press, 1998.

Powicke, F. M., and C. R. Cheney, eds. *Councils and Synods with Other Documents Relating to the English Church.* Vol. 2. Oxford: Clarendon Press, 1964.

Prevost, Arthur. *Le Diocèse de Troyes.* Vol. 2. Dijon: Domois, 1924.

Pugh, Ralph B. *Imprisonment in Medieval England.* Cambridge: Cambridge University Press, 1968.

Raftis, J. Ambrose. *Tenure and Mobility: Studies in the Social History of the Mediaeval English Village.* Pontifical Institute of Mediaeval Studies, Studies and Texts, 8. Toronto: Pontifical Institute of Mediaeval Studies, 1964.

Ravel, Jeffrey. *The Would-Be Commoner: A Tale of Deception, Murder, and Justice in Seventeenth-Century France.* Boston: Houghton Mifflin: 2008.

Reid, Charles J. Jr. *Power over the Body, Equality in the Family: Rights and Domestic Relations in Medieval Canon Law.* Grand Rapids, Mich.: Eerdmans, 2004.

Reider, Paula. *On the Purification of Women: Churching in Northern France.* New York: Palgrave, 2006.

Reynolds, Philip. *Marriage in the Western Church: The Christianization of Marriage During the Patristic and Early Medieval Periods.* Leiden: Brill, 1994.

Ribordy, Geneviève. *Faire les nopces: Le mariage de la noblesse française, 1375–1475.* Studies and Texts, 146. Toronto: University of TorontoPress, 2004.

Rider, Catherine. *Magic and Impotence in the Middle Ages.* Oxford: Oxford University Press, 2006.

Rolker, Christof. "Ecclesiastical Marriage Jurisdiction Around 1100." *Studies in Church History* 43, *Discipline and Diversity*, 159–68. Ecclesiastical History Society. Woodbridge Boydell Press, 2007,

Rosambert, André. *La veuve en droit canonique jusqu'au XIVe siècle.* Paris, 1923.

Rouquet, Chantal, André Boisseua, and Emmanuel Saint-Mars. *Histoire de Troyes.* Troyes: Les Éditions de la Maison du Boulanger, 1997.

Russell, John. *The Sanatio in Radice Before the Council of Trent.* Analecta Gregoriana 138. Rome: Gregorian University Press, 1964.

Sandirocco, Luigi. "Binae nuptiae et bina sponsalia." *Studia et Documenta historiae et iuris* 70, 165–216. 2004.

Schmitt, Émile. *Le mariage chrétien dans l'oeuvre de Saint Augustin: Une théologie baptismale de la vie conjugale.* Paris: Études Augustiniennes, 1983.

Schmugge, Ludwig. *Ehen vor Gericht: Paare der Renaissance vor dem Papst.* Berlin: Berlin University Press, 2008.

Schwab, Christian. "Female Petitioners in the Papal Peneteniary" *Gender and History* 12:3 (November 2000) 685–703.

———. *Augsburger Offizialatsregister (1348–1352): Ein Dokument geistlicher Diözesangerichtsbarkeit, Edition und Untersuchung.* Forschungen zur kirchlichen Rechtsgeschichte und zum Kirchenrecht, 25. Cologne: Böhlau Verlag, 2001.

Schwartzberg, Beverly. "Lots of Them Did That": Desertion, Bigamy, and Marital Fluidity in Late-Nineteenth-Century America." *Journal of Social History* 37:3 (spring 2004): 573–600.

Seidel Menchi, Silvana, and Diego Quaglioni, eds. *Coniugi nemici: La separazione in Italia dal XII al XVIII secolo.* I processi matrimoniali degli archivi ecclesiastici italiani, 1. Annali dell'Istituto storico italo-germanico in Trento, Quaderni, 53. Bologna: Il Mulino, 2000.

———. *Matrimoni in Dubbio: Unioni controverse e nozze clandestine in Italia dal XIV al XVIII*, idem, 2; idem, 57. Bologna: Il Mulino, 2001.

———. *Trasgressioni: Seduzione, concubinato, adulterio, bigamia (XIV–XVIII secolo)*, idem, 3; idem, 64. Bologna: Il Mulino, 2004.

———. *I tribunali del matrimonio (secoli XV–XVIII)*, idem, 4; idem, 68. Bologna: Il Mulino, 2006.

Seoane, Yolanda Serrano. "El sistema penal del Tribunal Eclesiástico de la Diócesis de Barcelona en la Baja Edad Media." *Clio & Crimen* 3 (2006): 334–429; 430–508.

Sheehan, Michael M. *Marriage, Family, and Law in Medieval Europe: Collected Studies*. Ed. James K. Farge. Toronto: University of Toronto Press, 1996.

———. "Marriage Theory and Practice in the Conciliar Legislation and Diocesan Statutes of Medieval England." *Mediaeval Studies* 40 (1978): 408–60; in idem, *Marriage, Family, and Law*, 118–76.

Skinner, Patricia. "The Widow's Options in Medieval Southern Italy," In *Widowhood in Medieval and Early Modern Europe*, ed. S. Cavallo and L. Warner. London: Longman, 1999.

Small, Carola M. "Prisoners at the Castellany of Artois in the Early Fourteenth Century. " *Histoire Social-Social History* 26 (1993): 345–72.

Smail, Daniel Lord. *The Consumption of Justice*. Ithaca, N.Y.: Cornell University Press, 2003.

Smith, Charles E. *Papal Enforcement of Some Medieval Marriage Laws.* Baton Rouge: Louisiana State University Press, 1940.

Smith, Warren S. "The Wife of Bath Debates Jerome." *Chaucer Review* 32:2 (1997) 129–45.

Solonen, Kirsi. *The Pentitentiary as a Well of Grace, 1448–1527*. Helsinki: Suomalainen Tiedeakatemia, 2001.

Soman, Alfred. "Les procès de sorcellerie au Parlement de Paris (1565–1640)." *Annales: Économies, sociétiés, civilisations* 32:4 (1977) 794–98.

Stone, Lawrence. *The Family, Sex, and Marriage in England, 1500–1800.* New York: Harper and Row, 1977.

Stuard, Susan Mosher. "Burdens of Matrimony: Husbanding and Gender in Medieval Italy." In *Medieval Masculinities: Regarding Men in the Middle Ages*, ed. Clare Lees, Thelma Fenster, and Jo Ann McNamara. Minneapolis: University of Minnesota Press, 1994.

Tabbagh, Vincent. "Rouen 1438: De l'extension du champ de la répression judiciare en situation de crise." In *De la déviance à la délinquance, XVe–XXe siècle,* ed. Benoît Garnot, 13–39. Dijon: Éditions Universitaires de Dijon, 1999.

Tanon, Louis. *Histoire des justices des anciennes églises et communautés monastiques de Paris.* Paris: Larose et Forcel, 1883.

Taylor, Larissa. "French Preaching, 1215–1535." In Beverly Kienzle, ed., *The Sermon*. Typologie des sources du moyen âge occidental. Brepols: Turnhout-Belgium, 2000; 711–58.

———. *Soldiers of Christ: Preaching in Late Medieval and Reformation France.* New York: Oxford University Press, 1992.

Turlan, Juliette. "Recherches sur le mariage dans la pratique coutumière (XIIe–XVIe s.)." *Revue historique de droit français et étranger* 35 (1957) 477–528.

Valazza, Marie-Ange Tricarico. "L'officialité de Genève et quelques cas de bigamie à la fin du moyen âge: L'empêchement de lien." *Zeitschrift für schweizerische Kirchengeschichte* 89 (1995): 99–118.

Vaultier, Roger. *Le folklore pendant la Guerre de Cent Ans d'après les lettres de rémission du Trésor des Chartes.* Paris: Librarie Giénégaud, 1965.

Vecchio, Silvana. "La Bonne Épouse." In *Histoire des femmes en Occident* 3 vols. Vol. 2, *Le Moyen Âge*, dir. Christiane Klapisch-Zuber, ed. Georges Duby and Michelle Perrot, 143–180. Paris: Perrin, 2002.

Veuves et veuvage dans le haut moyen âge. Ed. M. Parisse. Paris: Picard, 1993.

Vincent-Cassy, Mireille. "Prison et châtiments à la fin du moyen âge." In *Les marginaux et les exclus dans l'histoire,* 262–74. Cahiers Jussieu no. 5. Paris: Inédit, 1979

Vleeschouwers Van Melkebeek, Monique. "Aspects du lien matrimonial dans le Liber senteciarum de Bruxelles." *Tijdschrift voor Rechtsgeschiedenis* 53 (1985): 43–97.

———. "Bina matrimonia: Matrimonium praesumptum vs. matrimonium manifestum. Hoe passen de officialiteiten van Kamerijk en Brussel in de Vijftiende eeuw canoniek recht en doctrine terzake toe?" *Juris Scripta Historica* 13 (1997): 245–55.

———. "Conflits de juridiction au niveau diocésain dans les pays bourguignons de par deçà." *Centre européen d'Études Bourguignonnes*, 40–40 (2000), 33–47.

———. "Incestuous Marriages: Formal Rules and Social Practice in the Southern Burgundian Netherlands." In *Love, Marriage, and Family Ties in the Later Middle Ages, ed.* Isabel Davis, Miriam Müller, and Sarah Rees Jones, 77–95. International Medieval Research, 11. Turnhout: Brepols, 2003.

———. "Marital Breakdown Before the Consistory Courts of Brussels, Cambrai, and Tournai: Judicial Separation a mensa et thoro." *Tijdschrift voor Rechtsgeschiedenis* 72 (2004): 81–89.

———. "Self-Divorce in Fifteenth-Century Flanders: The Consistory Court Accounts of the Diocese of Tournai." *Tijdschrift voor Rechtsgeschiedenis* 68 (2000): 83–98.

Volterra, Eduardo. "Per la storia del reato di bigamia in diritto romano." In *Studi di Umberto Ratti,* 425–29. Liman: A. Guiffrè, 1934.

Walker, Sue Sheridan, ed. *Wife and Widow in Medieval England.* Ann Arbor: University of Michigan Press, 1993.

Walravens, Christelle. "Insultes, blasphèmes ou hérésie? Un procès à l'officialité épiscopale de Troyes en 1445." *Bibliothèque de l'École des Chartes* 154 (1996): 485–507.

———. "L'Officialité épiscopale de Troyes à la fin du Moyen Âge." PhD diss., École des Chartes, 1995.

Weigand, Rudolf. *Die bedingte Eheschliessung im kanonischen Recht.* 2 vols. Münchener theologische Studien, Kanonistische Abteilung 16, 39. Munich: M. Hueber, 1969, 1980.

———. *Liebe und Ehe im Mittelalter.* Bibliotheca eruditorum 7. Goldbach: Keip, 1993.

Wemple, Suzanne Fonay. *Women in Frankish Society: Marriage and the Cloister, 500 to 900.* Philadelphia: University of Pennsylvania Press, 1981.

Wieben, Corinne. " 'As Men Do with Their Wives': Domestic Violence in Fourteenth-Century Lucca." Presented at CICIS, University of California at Santa Cruz, 2008.

———. "A Kind of Marriage: Marriage in Dispute in Medieval Lucca (1341–1361)." (Ph.D. diss., University of California at Santa Barbara, 2010.

Winroth, Anders. *The Making of Gratian's Decretum.* Cambridge: Cambridge University Press, 2000.

Witte, John. *From Sacrament to Contract: Marriage, Religion, and Law in the Western Tradition.* Louisville, Ky.: Westminster John Knox Press, 1997.

Witte, John, and Robert Kingdon, eds. *Sex, Marriage, and Family in John Calvin's Geneva: Courtship, Engagement, and Marriage.* Grand Rapids, Mich.: Eerdmans, 2005.

Wunderli, Richard. *London Church Courts and Society on the Eve of the Reformation.* Cambridge, Mass.: Medieval Academy of America, 1981.

Yver, Jean. *Égalité entre héritiers et exclusion des enfants dotés.* Paris: Sirey, 1966.

Zuchuat, Valérie Lamon. "Mariages clandestins dans le diocèse de Sion à la fin du Moyen Âge." *Annales valaisannes: Bulletin trimestriel de la Société d'histoire du Valais romand.* 2004.

INDEX

Abraham, patriarch, 68, 90; as model husband and father, 68
absence. *See* bigamy and the marital debt
Adam and Eve. *See* marriage, Adam and Eve
adultery, 17, 23, 37–41, 48, 57, 65–69, 80–81, 90–94, 101–105, 115–116, 128–129, 137, 139, 167, 172, 179 (*see also* bigamy, motivation by adultery); as grounds for divorce, 92; punishment in England, 37–41, 65; punishment in France, 44, 66; Roman law and Byzantine law, 92, 102
Alexander III, Pope, 1, 13, 27, 161, 179
Anne, Saint, 91
Avignon, Carole, 16, 31, 41, 156–158, 163–164, 166, 182

banns, 4, 13–15, 18, 31, 39, 56, 76, 79, 103, 106–107, 136, 139, 163
baptism, 124, 131–132, 135, 139
basoche, 125
bigamy: bribery, 63–63, 87, 106, 136, 190 n. 61; fines, 14–15, 19, 25–26, 30–49, 72, 76, 82–86, 97–98, 119, 122–123, 133, 137; fraud, 5, 49–50, 60–64; as heresy, 138; jurisdiction, 35–36, 42–43, 121–122; motivations for, 98, 101–106, 119–126; motivation by abandonment, 98; motivation by adultery, 101–102; motivation by childlessness, 103–104; pre-contract, 97–98; punishment for, 37–41, 97–100, 113–115, 119–131, 133, 137; punishment in Dijon, 33; punishment in England, 37–41; punishment, sixteenth century, 4, 33, 140, 166 nn. 116–118, 153 n. 5, 154 n.8; sentencing, 33, 38–39, 46–51, 123–134; serial monogamy, 98–99, 141; sermons, 118–119, 127–128; stories about, 31–32, 107–111; successive, 21–22; theology, 19, 23–27; three-party suits (*see* bigamy, pre-contract)
Bishops of Troyes, 42–43, 117–119
blasphemy, 32, 73, 117, 124, 131–132
Boccaccio, 108–109
Bonnart, Antoine, 62, 171 n. 31
Bourrouche, Bertrand, 64, 171 n. 34.
Bouvier, Barthélémy, 62–63, 129, 148–149
Braque, Jean, bishop of Troyes, 42
bribery. *See* bigamy, bribery
brigandage, 33, 47, 73, 113, 124–125
Brown-Grant, Rosalind, 67
Butler, Sara, 40, 82, 88, 99–104, 112

Caesarius of Heisterbach, 108–109
Casini "le Noble," 60, 128, 151–152
Cent nouvelles nouvelles, 110–111
Charageat, Martine, 35, 41
charivari, 25–27
Chenalier, Pierre, 54–56, 169–170
Chenilloy, Hugh, 100, 127–128
children, legitimacy, 28, 48–50, 103–104
Christian identity, 5, 12, 19, 59–60, 111, 135–138
clandestine marriage, 1–4, 13–18, 40–41, 45–46, 106, 115, 136, 138–141; and the Council of Trent, 4, 14–15, 17, 132, 138–141; and the Fourth Lateran Council, 13–14
Clark, Katherine, 24
Cleree, Jean, 127–128
Colette, wife/widow of Jean de Feuges, 77–81, 143–144
competence. *See* bigamy, jurisdiction
Council of Trent, Tametsi. *See* clandestine marriage; Council of Trent
creantare, 15, 175 nn. 30 and 31
Cristellon, Cecilia, 102

d'Arras, Gautier, 31
D'Avray, David, 19, 23, 100, 129, 136
Davis, Natalie Zemon, 5, 135
de Giverny, Étienne, Bishop, 118
de Louay, Pierre, 52, 61–63, 168 n. 8

denunciation, 51, 65, 119–120
des Maraulx, Renaud, 53–55, 62, 168–169
desertion. *See* bigamy, motivation for abandonment
devil, 128–131
Donahue, Charles Jr., 32, 36–37, 39, 96, 125–126
Duby, Georges, 10–12, 99

education, clergy of Troyes, 67, 117–118
Eisenach, Emlyn, 31
Ephesians, 20–21
Etienne "Languedoc," 46–47, 61–62, 126–127, 144–145

Falzone, Emmanuël, 31
Ferrand, Jean, 128, 184 n. 56
Freppier, Jean, 54–56, 169–170, nn. 17–18

"Gast of Gy," 24
Gauvard, Claude, 25, 66, 114
gender, and bigamy, 6, 51, 71, 73, 136
Gerson, Jean, 67–68, 89–90, 93
Gillion de Trasignes, 109–110
Goody, Jack, 10
Gottlieb, Beatrice, 18, 45–46
Grands Jours de Troyes, 42–43
Gratian, 27–28

Hartog, Hendrik, 141
Helmholz, R.H, 155, 168, 177–178
heresy, 45, 73, 114–116, 129, 131–132, 138
Herlihy, David, 108
honor, 5, 27, 70, 78, 89–91, 93–94, 135–136. *See also* husbands, honor; wives, honor
Hostiensis, 22, 29–30, 32
Hundred Years' War, 7, 11, 52, 68, 86, 104, 113–114, 117, 119, 122, 132–134
husbands, 59, 65–67, 70; honor, 70

identity. *See* Christian identity
incest, 10–13, 16, 96–97, 115
informal separation. *See* self-divorce
Innocent III, Pope, 13, 21, 23, 91, 123, 139
inquisitor of heretical depravity, 131–132
insult, 45, 65, 92, 116

Jehan, Jean, 57, 105, 147–148
Jerome, Saint, 20, 111
Joseph, Saint, 67–70

Karras, Ruth, 32

ladder. *See* scala
Le Jon, Manchin. *See* Vautier, Isabelle
le Nieps, Jean, 60–61, 150–151
legal separation, 44, 101–102
Leguise, Jean, Bishop, 118–119
Lugnet, Simon, 56, 102, 152–153
Luther, Martin, 13, 16, 45, 141

Maddern, Philippa, 98–99
Maitland, F.W., 12, 97
marital debt, 69, 90–91, 127, 130
marriage: Adam and Eve, 21–27, 47–48; age at marriage, 58–59; banns, 4, 13–18, 31, 39, 56, 76–79, 103, 106–107, 128, 138–139; crisis, 1–4, 10–18, 43, 114, 122, 137–138; *de futuro*, 13, 15, 106; *de presenti,* 13, 15, 106; duration of first and second marriage, 58–59; *in facie ecclesie*, 15, 60, 57–76, 80–83, 88, 102, 106–107, 124, 143–145, 147–151; publicity, 1–2, 4, 13–18, 25, 50, 56, 76–78, 83, 88, 106–107, 111, 139; rights and obligations, 19, 47, 68, 70, 74, 89, 91, 94; solomnized, 40, 62, 106–108; symbolism, 10, 19, 23, 25, 47. *See also* clandestine marriage; weddings
Mary, Virgin, 67–68, 90
McSheffrey, Shannon, 37, 65, 96
midwife, 131
Morel, Barbara, 32, 124
murder, 115–116, 124, 129–131

nuptial blessing, 25–27, 79

officialities: Burgundian (including modern Belgium), 15, 17, 31, 33–34, 44, 47–48, 121–122; England, 14–15, 24, 31, 34–44, 65–69, 82, 96–102; Germany, 30–31, 36; Paris, 3, 7, 13–14, 30–33, 50, 51, 121, 124, 133; Rouen, 3, 14, 30–33, 39, 42, 77, 114, 121–122, 132; Spain, 35. *See also* Troyes, officiality
order of matrimony, 1, 70, 125, 129, 133, 136–137
Ozment, Steven, 1–2

Panormitanus, 30
papal penitentiary, 34, 43
perjury, 39, 45, 47, 61, 73, 107, 115, 124, 127–131
Perrette, wife of Jean Jehan, 71–72, 88, 105, 147–148
Pietrequin, Jean, 128, 146–147
plague, 7, 64, 114, 137

polygamy, 20–21, 118, 141; Anabaptist, 141; Jewish, 20–21, 118; Mormon, 141; Muslim, 118; patriarchs, 20–21
Pomier, Guillaume, 102, 179 n.21
Pommeray, Léon, 32, 98
preaching. *See* bigamy, sermons
priest, parish, 27, 31, 36, 56, 59–62
prison, 35–36, 43, 121–122
promotor, 44, 80, 118–119
proof, 60–61, 85–86; oral testimony, 61, 85–86; sworn oath, 60; written evidence, 60–61
proof of death, 28, 30, 60; in canon law, 28–30; in de Beaumanoir, 29; in the *Siete Partidas*, 29
prose romance, 109–110

Raymond of Peñafort, 22–23, 28–29
reform, role of in prosecuting bigamy, 113–134
remarriage, 2–4, 9, 13, 16, 17, 20–25, 31–34, 99, 105–107, 141. *See also* proof of death; Wife of Bath
Rucin, Mathieu, 102–103, 146–147

Sara, wife of Abraham, 90
Sara, wife of Tobit, 90
scala (ladder of the scaffold) 32–33, 42, 46–47, 51, 64–65, 71–75, 87–88, 95, 100, 121–124
self-divorce (separation), 99
sentencing, language of, 126–132
separation. *See* legal separation
sermons. *See* bigamy, sermons
Sheehan, Michael, 37, 99
sorcery, 38, 114, 124, 129, 132
statutes, synodal, 14–15, 25, 30, 32–33, 42, 46, 52, 56, 60, 78, 119

Ten Commandments, 131
testimony, false, 29, 32, 45, 61–62, 75, 84, 86–88, 124, 131, 137
theft, 85, 121
Troyes officiality, 34, 42–43, 118–122; complaints against by royal officials, 34, 42–43, 121–122; jurisdiction (*see* bigamy, jurisdiction); officials, 118–119. *See also* bigamy, punishment; prison; promotor

Vautier, Isabelle, 84–88
violence, 42, 45, 92, 104, 116
Voltaire, 5

weddings: as celebrated in Italy, Spain, England, France, and Sweden, 14; as celebrated in northern France, 14, 106
whipping. *See* adultery, punishment; bigamy, punishment
widows, 3, 7, 22–28, 31, 43, 60–63, 76–78
Wife of Bath, 111–112, 137
witchcraft. *See* sorcery
wives, 3, 20, 25, 66, 71–94, 101, 103, 108, 114, 140; abandoned, 71–94, 101, 103, 108; honor, 90–91

ACKNOWLEDGMENTS

It gives me great pleasure to take this opportunity to thank all who helped me with the research and writing of this book. My heartfelt thanks are due first and foremost to Ruth Karras, for her essential criticism, her generous support, and her inspiring scholarship.

Thanks also to editor Jerry Singerman, to Caroline Winschel, to Noreen O'Connor-Abel, and to everyone at the University of Pennsylvania Press.

Natalie Zemon Davis is the obvious inspiration for this book, and I am so grateful for her encouragement. I am also especially grateful for the help of Shannon McSheffrey and Charlie Donahue, whose patience and generosity I hope to continue to take advantage of. Marcia Colish and David d'Avray deserve special thanks for their willingness to read and comment on this work at many stages, as do Paul Freedman and Anders Winroth for their continuing support.

It is an honor and pleasure to thank additionally Carole Avignon, Sara Beam, Veronique Beaulande, Peggy Brown, Martine Charageat, Jacques Chiffoleau, Cecilia Cristellon, Fabian Drixler, Emlyn Eisenach, Emmanuël Falzone, Ted Evergates, Claude Gauvard, Beatrice Gottlieb, Alexandra Guerson, Marie Kelleher, Anne Lefebvre-Teillard, Anne Lester, Dana Wessell Lightfoot, Laurent Mayali, Nicole Lemaître, Jeff Rider, Jamie Smith, Dan Smail, Christelle Walravens-Creff, and Corinne Weiben. Thanks to Jim Whitman, without whom this book would not have been possible.

It is a thrill to thank my wonderful colleagues and students at John Jay College.

Thanks also to Bill Nelson and Dan Hulsebosch, and to all the participants in the Legal History Colloquium at New York University Law School, where I was privileged to be a Samuel Golieb Fellow in 2009–2010.

A Bourse Chateaubriand, YCIAS grant, and the École Normale Supérieure gave me the opportunity to conduct extensive research in France. Additionally, the Beinecke Rare Book and Manuscript Library provided a research fellowship that allowed for dedicated study of late-medieval sermon collections. I was also able to take advantage of the remarkable holdings of the Rare Book Collection at the Yale Law Library, and I thank Mike Widener for his assistance with the collection. The hardworking interlibrary loan staff at John Jay College also provided excellent research support. The archivist and staff of the Archives Départementales de l'Aube and of the Médiathèque de Troyes generously shared their collections with me, as did the staff of the Archives Nationales, the Bibliothèque Nationale, and the Bibliothèque St. Geneviève in Paris.

I also thank my family for their support and understanding over the years.

This book is dedicated to Barbara Diefendorf.